Baroque Counterpoint

Baroque Counterpoint

Revised and Expanded Edition

Christoph Neidhöfer and Peter Schubert

Published by State University of New York Press, Albany

For information, contact State University of New York Press, Albany, NY
www.sunypress.edu

Library of Congress Cataloging-in-Publication Data

Names: Neidhöfer, Christoph, author | Schubert, Peter, author
Title: Baroque counterpoint : revised and expanded edition
Description: Albany : State University of New York Press, [2023] |
    Includes bibliographical references and index.
Identifiers: ISBN 9781438493251 (paperback) |
    ISBN 9781438493244 (ebook)
Further information is available at the Library of Congress.

10   9   8   7   6   5   4   3   2   1

We affectionately dedicate this book to Roe-Min and Lori

CONTENTS

ACKNOWLEDGMENTS

ACKNOWLEDGMENTS TO THE REVISED AND EXPANDED EDITION

We are immensely grateful to the many colleagues who have been using the original edition of this book and who encouraged us to publish a new edition when the first went out of print. We owe a big thank you to Richard Carlin, who made the reissue of a revised and expanded edition a reality by offering a new home for the book at State University of New York Press and who participated at every stage in the production process. We are especially grateful to Joshua Nichols and Aaron J. Kirschner, who took on the huge task of resetting the entire text and all the musical examples (using music font by Abraham Lee called MTF-Scorlatti). We thank William Benjamin, David Cohen, and Derek Remeš for their detailed comments, especially concerning chapter 10, which made us rethink a number of things. We are grateful to Houman Behzadi and Cathy Martin from the Marvin Duchow Music Library, McGill University; to Greg Houston, Michael Miller, and Jennifer Innes from McGill Libraries for their assistance with scanning materials; and to our McGill colleagues Nicole Biamonte, Sean Ferguson, Brenda Ravenscroft, and Jonathan Wild for their input and support. We thank Alexandrea Jonker for assisting us in various editing tasks and for preparing the new index and Jenn Bennett-Genthner, Carly Miller, Aimee Harrison, and the production team at SUNY Press for their valuable contributions. We also wish to thank Robert O. Gjerdingen for his permission to use his transcriptions of Fenaroli's Partimenti from *Monuments of Partimenti* and William Renwick for his permission to use his Partimento transcriptions from *The Langloz Manuscript*.

ACKNOWLEDGMENTS TO THE FIRST EDITION (2006)

We owe the greatest debt to Bruno Gingras, a doctoral student in music theory here at McGill, who taught the first twelve chapters of this book in the first of a two-semester tonal counterpoint sequence. He made many excellent suggestions for presenting and ordering the material, fleshed out instructions, and provided several of his own exercises, which we included. Other teachers who used the materials in draft form and provided helpful suggestions were Per Broman, Timothy Newton, and Frauke Jürgensen. We are grateful also to harpsichordists Ewald Demeyere, who turned us on to Kirnberger's own fugues, and Hank Knox, who pointed us toward Pasquini. Our lively discussions with colleague

William Caplin helped us define the role of cadences, although he is in no way responsible for the results. We were greatly encouraged by the interest shown by Mark Janello, Jim MacKay, Elizabeth Hellmuth Margulis, Panayotis Mavromatis, Anton Vishio, and Stephen Slottow. Special thanks go to Cynthia Leive and the staff of the Marvin Duchow Music Library, who were always there when we needed them (which was often). Of course it is the people who suffered most who deserve our thanks the most: the four years of students who waited patiently while we decided whether we should generate chord progressions by throwing dice, and what exactly we meant by strict style.

The heart of this book is the musical examples, of which an unusually large number are by George Friderich Handel. We found that his clear, concise, emphatic style and richness of ideas made him an excellent model for students. Therefore we are especially grateful for a generous grant from the David Edelberg/Handel Collection Endowment (Marvin Duchow Music Library, McGill University), whose mission it is to support Handel performances, scholarship, recording, and education. This assistance helped to defray the cost of printing the numerous and lengthy examples by Handel. (For a complete list, refer to "Handel" in the index.)

We wish to thank some of our teachers, who contributed in shaping whatever thought process led up to this book: Chris Hatch, who quipped, "greatness is of necessity eccentric," which encouraged us to look outside of J. S. Bach; Patricia Carpenter, who said that each of the melodies in a harmonic progression is one of its various "surfaces," as if the progression were a kind of "object" that you could turn this way and that; and David Lewin, who recommended (and would regularly do so himself) playing one voice of a two-part contrapuntal combination and singing the other in order to experience the independence of the parts. We are also grateful for the generous feedback from the reviewers commissioned by Prentice Hall: Anthony K. Brandt, Rice University; Per Broman, Bowling Green University; Harry Bulow, University of North Carolina—Charlotte; Ewald Demeyere-Baudhuin, Koninklijk Vlaams Muziekconservatorium of Antwerp; Brian T. Kilp, Indiana State University; Richard Perkins, Anoka Ramsey Community College; Mark Richardson, East Carolina University; and Joseph Rivers, University of Tulsa, many of whose suggestions found their way into this book. Finally, we thank Prentice Hall's Chris Johnson, who "acquired" us, and Sarah Touborg and Joe Scordato, and at Stratford Publishing Services Ginny Somma, Hilly van Loon, and Dennis Dieterich for their careful and timely contributions.

Part I

STRICT STYLE

Part 1

भाग शिल्प

1

INTRODUCTION

Why Study Counterpoint?; Learning by Modeling; Tasting the Food; Different Road Maps through the Book

WHY STUDY COUNTERPOINT?

You have no doubt heard many works of Handel, Vivaldi, and Bach. Their music is played all across the world in concert halls, movie theaters, living rooms, and fast-food chains. These works have given many people the most profound musical experiences of their lives, and they remain cultural landmarks. Baroque fugues especially amaze and fascinate us. As Alfred Mann puts it, "The term fugue . . . suggests . . . the most intricate expression of the complex language of Western music."[1] As musicians, we are fortunate to be able to play and study this music—and once we have studied it, we not only admire it but we begin to understand why it is so powerful.

Counterpoint is a well-defined discipline with a long tradition that is central to the study of all music. By studying it, we reenact the activities not only of Baroque musicians (especially church organists, who had to be able to improvise chorale preludes and fugues) but also of later composers. The works of Haydn, Mozart, Beethoven, Hensel, Mendelssohn, Clara and Robert Schumann, Brahms, Schoenberg, Webern, and Hindemith would not be what they are without a solid grounding in Baroque counterpoint. It is important even to movie composers, like Jerry Goldsmith, who wrote the score for the movie *Patton*. For that score, he said he composed three themes, each representing a facet of General Patton's character (warrior, religious man, intellectual), and added, "It was designed contrapuntally so that all three could be played simultaneously, or individually, or two at a time, whatever."[2]

His remark shows how counterpoint stresses independence of melodic parts, which is quite different from the concept of "melody and accompaniment." The distinguished eighteenth-century German theorist Johann Mattheson (who helped us write this book) gives a good illustration of the difference. For each of the two phrases of a little gigue, Mattheson provides two different basses. The basses in examples 1.1a and 1.1b supply harmonic accompaniment; those in examples 1.1c and 1.1d provide

Example 1.1a. (Mattheson)

Example 1.1b. (Mattheson)

Example 1.1c. (Mattheson)

Example 1.1d. (Mattheson)

harmonic support too but, in addition, imitate. "It is the imitation," says Mattheson, "without which everything would sound wooden."[3] The two versions have almost the same chord progression, but solutions c and d are more contrapuntal.

Studying counterpoint is broadly useful because it teaches us to "think in music." The activity of writing counterpoint starts from a given problem to which one is to find an appropriate solution. Eventually, you develop an instinct for spotting the musical potential of an idea because of your experience with a wide range of musical situations.[4] Knowing how to write or improvise counterpoint (even if you do not plan to be a composer or improviser yourself) means understanding how music works. Such knowledge is invaluable to performers in an ensemble or orchestra, who need a good understanding of their role in the texture; to conductors, who need to understand how to bring out this or that melodic part; to musicologists, who need to get into the composer's mind when studying sketches or analyzing pieces; and to theorists, for whom the rigorous mental exercise is fun in its own right.

The reader of this book will run across examples from trio sonatas, dances, concertos, and choruses and arias from cantatas, oratorios, and operas. But our focus is fugue because it's theoretically richer, with more technical constraints than other genres. If you can write a fugue, you can probably write a ritornello, but it doesn't work the other way around.

You will need to know basic harmony: scales, intervals, triads, keys, figured bass, voice-leading rules, and nonharmonic tones. Musical examples involving continuo are presented without any keyboard realization, so a familiarity with figured bass is important and some keyboard skills are necessary. Note: You will need to obtain a copy of Bach's *Well-Tempered Clavier* (*WTC*), books I and II, as we refer to its fugues often throughout this book.

LEARNING BY MODELING

This book teaches Baroque compositional technique through writing and improvisation exercises and analysis of repertoire examples. Because compositional technique is fundamental to style, the book teaches appreciation of Baroque style from the inside out. We focus largely on principles taught in the period from 1680 to 1780 as documented in treatises, and thus provide the student with a historical outlook. The most important difference between this book and all the other ones we have looked at is its emphasis on the harmonic progression as the basis for contrapuntal study. Other books begin with two-part writing, which we have always found to be too difficult for the beginner.

Many of the exercises we propose consist of material taken from treatises or repertoire, and the student is to add complementary material. Mattheson believes that the best way to learn to compose is to model on good composers. He says:

> One cannot advise a beginner better than to say that he first do an exercise by trying to compose a bass to an upper voice already made by someone else. . . . It goes without saying that whoever wants to take pleasure and profit from this exercise must hide from his eyes the basses of the master and not see a note of it until he has tried his luck himself. . . . The comparison of the new bass with the old will soon show where it is wrong, where it is good, and also where it could have been better.[5]

He also suggests taking a bass and composing a new upper line: "One hereby proceeds as before, namely, by means of choosing one or another piece already written by a competent master and keeping the upper voice secret until one can compare the melody invented over the bass alone with the original. The best opportunity can be found in extended sections of church pieces."[6] Of three-part pieces, he suggests leaving out one or two voices and composing the remainder. Here he says that if the student is given the first upper part and the words, "one can even invent the second voice and the bass. The teacher has to give a *little* assistance and help. The *less* such takes place, the sharper the student's reflection becomes."[7]

Now who are his "competent masters?" When it comes to three-part music, Mattheson lists, among others, Marcello, Corelli, Fux, Handel, and Krieger. We quote them and many others. Just as Bach tinkered with fugues by Reincken and Fischer, we will use contemporaneous materials as the basis for our exercises. We have included a wide range of composers in part I to give a picture of mainstream Baroque music in Bach's time. We all want to study the *Well-Tempered Clavier*, but the models it provides are too complex for the beginner. Art critic Peter Schjeldahl put it nicely. Reviewing an exhibit at the Guggenheim that recreated the Salon Exhibition of 1900 in which several Impressionist masters were shown for the first time, along with lesser contemporaries, he wrote, "Gems by Cezanne, Degas, Munch, Klimt, and other heroes of modernity [at first] seemed . . . tormented by the context, like aristocrats at a tractor pull." But such contrast is valuable, he says, because "a cultivated appreciation of the pretty good sets us up to register the surprise of the great, which baffles our understanding and teaches us little except how to praise."[8] By studying the often easier-to-understand music of Bach's contemporaries, you may better appreciate the features that make his music stand out.

TASTING THE FOOD

If music is like food, composing is like cooking. You must always taste what you are doing. We encourage you to sing and play as much as you can—everything you write or analyze—and not to use the computer to write something and then find out how it sounds by having it played back through MIDI (Musical Instrument Digital Interface). It's better to struggle through slowly. Later on you can be like the Italian tailors, who measure so carefully they never need to have the customer try on the clothes—you'll know how your music sounds! Playing and singing all your compositions and exercises helps range, crossing voices, skippiness, and rhythm stay under control. Mattheson says that vocal music is the most basic type and a good training for writing instrumental music.[9] He says writing vocal music helps the beginner learn where to place cadences and to emphasize melody over harmony. He says that instrumental melody has more "fire and freedom," more leaps, a wider range, a more "impulsive, punctuated nature," and more regular phrase structure than vocal melody[10] but that it's dangerous for beginners: "Through the great freedom in writing for instruments one is led to all kinds of shapeless melody."[11]

DIFFERENT ROAD MAPS THROUGH THE BOOK

There are more exercises and topics in this book than any class can cover, so depending on your purpose, you can skip some chapters. If the focus of the class is imitative pieces, it will be OK to skip chapter 5 on variation techniques. If your goal is to write fugues on given subjects, it will not be necessary to read chapter 17, "Writing an Original Subject." You may not have time to master invertible counterpoint at the tenth and twelfth and so may skip chapter 16. We strongly recommend skipping chapter 14, "Advanced Embellishment—Free Style," since many sophisticated techniques can be accomplished in strict style and students have trouble managing the use of dissonance in free style.

We also recommend working in three parts, trading the fourth part for more sophisticated techniques like tonal answer and stretto. Here are some scenarios for teachers of a one-semester course:

(1) "Take it slow": Do chapters 1–6 and 12 with beginners. The first six chapters are highly detailed, putting together harmony and counterpoint. Chapter 6 shows pieces with imitative openings and sequential continuations; if sequences (chapter 12) and invertible counterpoint at the octave (chapter 9) are consulted early, students will be able to write successful chorale preludes, trio sonatas, or two-part inventions. If things go well, imitation at the fifth can be undertaken (chapters 7–8).

(2) "Get fancy in three parts": If your students are comfortable with harmony and embellishing tones, skip chapters 1–5 (except for the definition of "strict style" in chapter 4) and do chapters 6–13. Final projects can be three-part double fugues with tonal answer, invertible counterpoint, intermediate cadences, and sequential episodes. If things go well, the class can leap ahead to writing original subjects, stretto, or pedal (chapters 17–19).

(3) "Hands on": This revised, expanded edition includes many new partimento and rule of the octave exercises. Carried out at the keyboard or written, these exercises can account for most of the work in the course. They have been carefully chosen to reflect the content of the chapters they appear in. Thus partimento exercises at the end of chapter 8 contain remodulations and retransitions and no partimento before chapter 10 uses tonal answer. If students have prepared a partimento fugue at the keyboard, they can rely on one line as a guide but are playing the rest of the music out of their head! Whether written or partially memorized and played, partimento affords a deeper knowledge of a single piece and a tangible realization of the concepts introduced in the particular chapter. With such restraints, partimento assures stylistic and technical success.

In two semesters, the most sophisticated techniques in the book (multiple splices, hybrid themes, time-shifted countersubjects, augmentation and diminution, multiple counterpoint, and mirror inversion) can be attempted. We believe it may still be a good idea to work in three parts while mastering these techniques.

NOTES

1. Mann, *The Study of Fugue*, p. ix.
2. Composer Jerry Goldsmith, interview by Terry Gross, *Fresh Air*, WHYY-FM, January 7, 2002.
3. Mattheson, *Der vollkommene Capellmeister*, III, 16, §§5–6.
4. See the little story about J. S. Bach in "A Bach Story" in chapter 16.
5. Mattheson, *Der vollkommene Capellmeister*, III, 16, §3, §7, and §8.
6. Mattheson, 16, §15.
7. Mattheson, 17, §38.
8. Peter Schjeldahl, review of "1900: Art at the Crossroads," *New Yorker*, August 7, 2000, pp. 79–80.

9. "The former, so to speak, is the mother, but the latter is the daughter. . . . For as a mother must necessarily be older than her natural daughter, vocal melody doubtlessly existed in this lower world before instrumental music. The former thus not only has the rank and priority but also requires the daughter to adjust to her motherly direction to make everything beautifully singable and fluent so that one may hear whose child she is" (Mattheson, *Der vollkommene Capellmeister*, II, 12, §4). Mattheson asks, "Does not everybody first reach for all kinds of instrumental pieces, sonatas, overtures etc. before he knows how to sing and notate a single chorale correctly, let alone artistically?" (§6).

10. Mattheson, II, 12, §20.

11. Mattheson, §9.

2

MELODY OR HARMONY?

Canon—The Melody as Surface of the Progression; Chord Factors; Composing a Canon—Unpacking the Box; Composing a Canon—The Melodic Approach; Puzzle Canon; Fugue and Other Imitative Genres

An important debate in the eighteenth century focused on the question, Which is more basic, melody or harmony? It may be just a chicken-and-egg question, but it is as important to us now as it was then. Do you start with a nice melody and then worry about harmonizing it, adding other lines, or do you start with a completely conceived progression? One of the reasons Baroque counterpoint is so challenging is the way the roles of melody and harmony are in constant struggle. In so-called homophony (e.g., in a minuet or a hymn), a single melody predominates, and other lines can be "just accompaniment," providing a harmonic background. In polyphony (inventions, fugues, trio sonatas, chorale preludes), by contrast, several interesting melodies must interact; each of them must have shape and character; each must maintain a high degree of independence, and yet they all must contribute to a reasonable harmonic progression.

On the side of melody, Johann Mattheson argues, "I thus still insist, in the first instance, upon a single refined melody as the most beautiful and natural in the world. . . . Everybody immediately jumps into part-writing, and the most experienced composers often lack nothing more than melody: because in their efforts they always put the horse behind the cart. . . . We, however, consider melody to be the basis of everything in composition." He argues that melody stands well without accompaniment and "that the proper beginning for composing would necessarily have to be made with melody only" and "often even the most beautiful harmony is tasteless without melody."[1]

Johann Philipp Kirnberger takes the opposite stand when he says: "Each piece always has as its basis a series of chords following one another according to certain rules; from these the melodies of single voices are in part determined."[2] Johann Sebastian Bach seems to fall into this camp. Carl Philipp Emanuel Bach says: "[My father's] pupils had to begin their studies by learning pure four-part thorough bass. . . . He particularly insisted on the writing out of the thorough bass in [four real] parts. . . . The realization of a thorough bass and the introduction to chorales are without doubt the best method of studying composition."[3]

Friedrich Wilhelm Marpurg and Jean-Philippe Rameau take a middle position. Marpurg says:

The surest meaning appears to be this, according to my opinion, that both parts, the harmony and melody, arise at the same time, (a) since in the natural course of things, along with any succession of single sounds, a succession of as many others can be conceived at the same time, with which to make harmony; (b) because one cannot imagine harmony without imagining simultaneously as many melodies as the harmony contains notes, set on top of one another.[4]

Rameau, writing of all multivoiced music, admits that although the melody *may* seem to come first,

the capable man rarely composes one part without feeling at the same time the effect of the other parts which are to accompany it. . . . Although we ordinarily start with one part, which we try to infuse with all the melodic beauty we can imagine (called "the subject"), if the other parts are proportionately robbed of beauty, then this diminishes the beauty of the subject. . . . The melodies of two or three parts should be almost equal; thus it is said, quite appropriately, that a melodic bass promises us beautiful music.[5]

In general, when one melody is somehow more important, we can call it a "theme," and the other melodies can be called "countermelodies."

We believe that Marpurg's and Rameau's position is ultimately the best. For beginners we start as Rameau, Kirnberger, and Bach did, by emphasizing the role of the harmonic progression, insisting in part I (chapters 1–13) that the student be able to identify a harmonic progression at all times. In most cases, every time a subject is heard in a piece it will be part of the same harmonic progression (although we will allow occasional substitute chords). This is the most economical approach as well as the safest. In part II, this rule is abandoned altogether.

CANON—THE MELODY AS SURFACE OF THE PROGRESSION

Rameau illustrates the relationship between melody and harmony very nicely in his description of how to compose a canon, or "perpetual fugue":

The most common types occur at the unison or at the octave, according to the range of the voices or instruments. All you need to do to accomplish this is to compose a pleasing melody to which you add as many parts as you want. Then from all these parts you compose a single *Air*, in such a way that the melody of one part can make a pleasing succession with that of the others. After that you make the *Air* start with one of the parts, following it immediately by another when it has finished the first melody that was composed. Thus each part follows consecutively, and when the first gets to the end, it begins again. . . . Once you have imagined one of the melodies contained in each of these five parts, you can easily add the others; then you make a succession out of them, creating an *Air* that is as flowing as good taste can prescribe. This is the hardest part of making the canon whose *Air* is shown here [example 2.1c]. You can easily see the melodies of each of the five parts of this canon, to which we have added some little notes for the tastefulness of the melody, each of the parts starting the *Air* one after the other when the preceding one is at the note or beat marked thus: 𝄋 .[6]

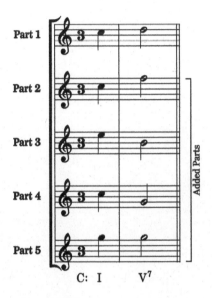

Example 2.1a. (Jean-Philippe Rameau)

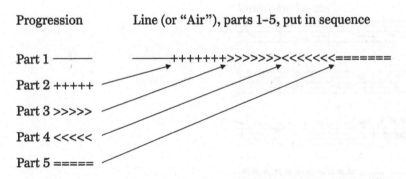

Example 2.1b. (Jean-Philippe Rameau)

Example 2.1c. (Jean-Philippe Rameau)

Example 2.1d. (Jean-Philippe Rameau)

Example 2.1e. (Jean-Philippe Rameau)

Example 2.1f. (Jean-Philippe Rameau)

We learn some important things from this:

1. The "pleasing melody" in this case is only two notes long! It is the topmost line in example 2.1a. All the other melodies can be considered countermelodies.

2. Adding "as many parts as you want" means harmonizing the melody by adding other lines that are parts of a chord progression (in this case I–V⁷). Four added parts appear beneath the top line in example 2.1a. Note that the parts are very close together in register (this is a canon for equal voices), and part 4 has the "bass line."

3. To produce the *Air* we need to dismantle the five parts in example 2.1a as schematized in example 2.1b. The *Air* is the sequence of all five lines, as shown in example 2.1c.

4. "Some little notes for the tastefulness of the melody" include one nonharmonic tone (an échappée, parenthesized in example 2.1d) and many rearticulations within a long note.

A performance of this canon is shown in score form in example 2.1d. The first voice begins alone, the second comes in when the first has reached the 𝄋, and so on. Notice that once all the voices are in, the listener hears the same progression every three beats (bracketed beneath the score). Measure 5 has the same content as m. 6, m. 7, and so on ad infinitum! The beginning of the performance is the most interesting because we can hear how each new voice imitates the previous ones.

CHORD FACTORS

The relation of harmony to melody can be expressed in terms of chord factors. Simple triads consist of three members, or factors: the root, the third, and the fifth, which we abbreviate with R, T, and F. Seventh chords have an additional chord factor, the seventh, abbreviated with S. In the little canon above, each of the five melodic parts consists of two chord factors. We can label them as shown in example 2.1e. The first part consists of the root of the I chord going to the fifth of the V chord; the second consists of the root of the I chord going to the seventh of the V chord, etc. The melodic parts will *always* be members of the I chord on the third beat, then the V chord for the first two beats of the next measure. The complete melody (example 2.1c) is just a succession of members of two chords. We can go back and label the factors in the original chord progression that was made by harmonizing a "pleasing melody" (example 2.1f).

COMPOSING A CANON—UNPACKING THE BOX

Marpurg suggests first writing a "harmony" (i.e., a chord progression) and then sounding each voice in turn in a single line, to be performed imitatively. The total range of all voices in the progression shown in example 2.2 is only a twelfth, making for very close spacing but also making it easy to sing. The canon is to be performed by reading each line in succession from the top line down, each singer beginning with the top line when the preceding singer begins the second line. The lowest voice is the third line down (bass). Note that the canon contains a sequential 5–6 progression (see chapter 12). Label all the factors in each chord (disregard embellishing eighth notes). Sing the melody alone, then in canon.

Nadia Boulanger taught the same thing. To help her students memorize all the voices in a standard cadential progression (example 2.3a), she had them sing each voice one at a time in canon (example 2.3b). The resulting "melody," with its two-octave range, is absurd, but it not only helped her students to memorize all the voices, it also helped them *hear* them. Label the chord factors in example 2.3b. When you come to compose a canon, you may want to change the register of some of the melodic parts, and you may want to question the order in which the parts appear. For instance, singing Boulanger's progression as shown in example 2.3c makes a much better melody. Note the continuity that comes from all the little falling thirds (shown with slurs). Who knew such a plain progression contained such a cute little melody? Do not bother about 6/4 chords at this point (we will put restrictions on their use later).

Example 2.2. (Friedrich Wilhelm Marpurg) *This and other examples in this chapter contain dissonances that are discussed in chapters 4 and 14.*

Example 2.3a. (Nadia Boulanger)

Example 2.3b. (Nadia Boulanger)

Example 2.3c. (Nadia Boulanger)

Any harmonic progression can be pulled apart to yield rudimentary imitation, presented in a variety of thinner and successively thicker textures. The harmonic progression may not be perfectly clear when we hear the first melody alone, but it gradually becomes clearer. The progression represented in Roman numerals is a kind of abstraction, which is "tasteless without melody"—obviously, harmony cannot be expressed without *some* melodies!

In an imitative texture, one voice starts first, then other voices enter one at a time, with the same tune. In that context, we realize that a melody alone can "stand for" a whole progression. Two voices are a richer and clearer expression of the same progression, and so forth. Arnold Schoenberg said, "Imitations are primarily repetitions."[7] In each of the above canons, we "hear" the whole chord progression repeated with every passing *period*. The length of the period is the length of the *time interval of imitation*.

If you follow the suggestions of Marpurg and Boulanger, you can think of the harmonic progression as a "box" of lines that you "unpack" to make a long melody that can be sounded in an imitative texture by several parts. The concept of unpacking a harmonic progression is extremely useful, and you will see it again in chapters 6, 7, 11, 16, and 17. It does require that you be able to compose a reasonable progression, which is something you need to have learned already.

COMPOSING A CANON—THE MELODIC APPROACH

The opposite of unpacking the box is packing it up, the traditional way to compose a canon, as shown in example 2.4. You start with a melodic fragment (circled in step 1), copy it into the next part a little later (circled in step 2), and add a continuation to the first line (circled in step 3). This continuation is the new melodic fragment that must be copied into the second voice (circled in step 4), and so on. The problem with this method is that you may not get a very interesting progression.

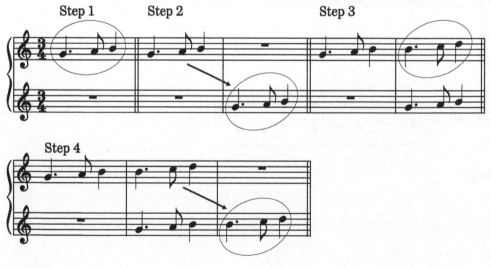

Example 2.4

PUZZLE CANON

A popular pastime in the eighteenth century was making and solving puzzle canons. The puzzle is presented as a single melody, and the solver has to determine the time and pitch interval of imitation. A sample is shown in example 2.5a. By sliding the melody around on an imaginary piece of clear plastic, we could eventually come up with the solution shown in example 2.5b.

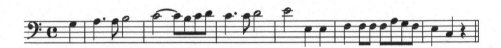

Example 2.5a.

Example 2.5b.

EXERCISE 2-A

1. *Writing (short):* Compose a canon at the unison (for equal voices) using one of the given bits of melody in example 2.6; you may add a text. Proceed as in example 2.1a, harmonizing the given melody in four parts and putting the four parts in sequence (as in example 2.1b—unpacking the box). All voices must begin in the same metric position, after the given fragment. You will notice that the chord factor of the fifth may occur as the lowest note, producing a 6/4 chord. Don't worry about this for now.

Example 2.6.

2. *Composing from scratch:* Compose a harmonic progression (a "box") à la Nadia Boulanger, starting with a succession of chords, then stringing the voices out in a canon at the unison (example 2.3). Remember that each voice has to begin on the same beat of the measure and that it must connect smoothly. Play or play and sing every pair of voices. Again, you may move voices into better octave registers so that they can be sung comfortably.

3. *Composing from scratch:* Compose a canon using the melodic approach described above and illustrated in example 2.4. Start with a melodic fragment in the leading voice. This will determine the time interval of imitation and the length of the period. Copy this fragment into the second voice to make the second period and compose some counterpoint in the first voice. Copy this counterpoint

Example 2.7a.

Example 2.7b.

Example 2.7c.

into the second voice following the first fragment. Repeat as needed. How do you like your harmonic progression?

    4. *Writing (short):* Solve the puzzle canons in example 2.7.

FUGUE AND OTHER IMITATIVE GENRES

Most imitative contrapuntal textures are neither strict canon nor free imitation (see example 1.1) but lie somewhere in between these two possibilities. In fugue, for example, substantial stretches of music are imitated, but adjustments may occur, as we shall see later. Generally, a piece in imitative texture teaches us its thematic material by presenting it first as a single line, then gradually adding new voices that enter with the same material. The original melody may almost be lost later in a thick contrapuntal fabric (as in the crossed voices of the *WTC I* C-sharp major fugue or *WTC II* B minor fugue), but we can follow it because we first learned the unaccompanied version. We can accept some harmonic mystery in the opening melody because we eventually hear the whole progression, with the harmonies represented by all chord factors in the countermelodies.

    Imitative polyphony makes two demands: that the music be of good quality in the melodic dimension (i.e., that each melody have a good sense of direction, good rhythmic shape, etc.), and that all the combined melodies make chords that are full and that move forward convincingly. As Marpurg said, "In a fugue, all parts compete and none has precedence, as is the case in other genres of musical pieces."[8]

NOTES

    1. Mattheson, *Der vollkommene Capellmeister*, II, 5, §19, §21.

    2. Lester, *Compositional Theory in the Eighteenth Century*, p. 241.

    3. David et al., *The New Bach Reader*, p. 399.

    4. Marpurg, *Handbuch bey dem Generalbasse und der Composition*, p. 23. For the beginning of the quote, see Lester, *Compositional Theory in the Eighteenth Century*, p. 235.

    5. Rameau, *Traité de l'harmonie réduite à ses principes naturels*, p. 346.

    6. Rameau, pp. 369–70.

    7. Schoenberg, *Theory of Harmony*, p. 155.

    8. Marpurg, *Abhandlung von der Fuge*, V, §4, p. 149.

3

HARMONIZING A SUBJECT IN SIMPLE COUNTERPOINT

Simple Counterpoint or Chorale Style; Harmonic Rhythm, or "Steps"; Fundamental Bass or Root Progression; Chord Factors; The Principal Triads; Rules for Using Only Principal Triads in Simple Counterpoint; Inverted Chords; Other Triads and Substitute Chords; Rules for Exercises in Harmonizing Given Subjects Using All Available Triads and Inverted Chords; Tips for Writing Good Bass Lines

In this chapter we will harmonize melodies that will be used in later chapters. We believe that thinking harmonically is the most efficient way to approach the problem of adding contrapuntal lines to a given melody. It is by no means the only approach, however. One also thinks of melodic direction and energy, rhythmic activity and independence, and even the mere succession of vertical intervals. We have decided to put these considerations off until later chapters, focusing for now on the color and sense of forward motion that harmony alone imparts.

SIMPLE COUNTERPOINT OR CHORALE STYLE

Simple counterpoint consists of plain note-against-note voice-leading, like first species counterpoint in the Renaissance. Such unembellished counterpoint is sometimes referred to as *chorale style*. Kirnberger says: "If one only looks at the pure harmony and good voice-leading as they are written down, one calls this simple counterpoint."[1] He believes that simple counterpoint underlies all ornamented music: "Whoever wants to make the effort to strip the embellishments from the most beautiful arias will see that the remaining tones have the shape of a well-constructed and correctly declaimed chorale."[2]

Simple counterpoint is easier to handle for beginners than embellished. Rameau says: "You should not ornament the upper part at all when you want to stick to the fundamental bass, for ornamented melody can only embarrass beginners. Thus each note of the upper part should last at least one beat."[3] Each contrapuntal part in simple counterpoint contains only pitches that are chord factors of the underlying harmonies (see chapter 2). We limit simple counterpoint to vertical sonorities that are simple triads; that is, we exclude seventh chords. In other words, the contrapuntal parts in simple counterpoint contain only roots, thirds, and fifths of triads.

HARMONIC RHYTHM, OR "STEPS"

Kirnberger likens harmonic rhythm to the motions involved in walking or dancing: "Simple, plain melody, which is called chorale, is similar to the common walk which progresses in equal steps. . . . Here each note . . . presents a step to further progress."[4] According to Kirnberger, each note in a plain or unembellished melody thus occupies one "step," which corresponds to "one of the principal time units of the measure," as expressed in the time signature.[5] This is usually the denominator in a time signature, but it can also be half that value (e.g., the quarter in cut time) or a multiple of it (e.g., the dotted quarter in 6/8). In other words, the step is the shortest note value on which the harmony can change, but harmonies may last for more than one step.

Harmonies are to change with the regular melody notes, primarily on the principal steps of the meter. However, the downbeat is to be treated specially, always receiving changes of harmony. Rameau says we should not have the same harmony on a strong beat and the weak beat preceding it.[6] Example 3.1 shows Rameau's illustration of good and bad harmonic rhythm.[7] In Rameau's notation, the pitches in bass clef do not form an actual bass line but represent what he calls the *fundamental bass*. The fundamental bass shows the roots of the harmonies. Rameau did not expect us to play the fundamental bass. The parallel fifths between the soprano and fundamental bass in the second measure of example 3.1b are thus never heard as such—an actual bass line for this progression would make use of chordal inversion to avoid illegal parallels. Rameau's fundamental bass essentially serves the same purpose as present-day Roman numerals. Example 3.2 recasts Rameau's example using Roman numerals instead of fundamental bass notes.

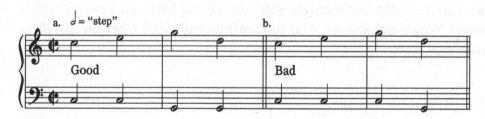

Example 3.1. (Rameau)

Example 3.2. (With Roman numerals)

Kirnberger explains Rameau's rule: "One must never, except at the beginning of a piece, put the same chord on a strong beat that had occurred on the previous weak beat because the progression to a different chord, which the ear expects, is hampered, causing an erroneous monotony."[8] Kirnberger's examples (example 3.3) show actual bass lines, not the fundamental bass. Disregard inverted chords for now to focus on harmonic rhythm. We have added Roman numerals to illustrate harmonic rhythm. Note that Kirnberger allows the use of the same harmony on a weak beat and the following strong beat *at the very beginning* of a phrase (examples 3.3c and e).

Example 3.3. (Kirnberger)

EXERCISE 3-A

1. *Analysis:* Here are some examples following Rameau. Just considering harmonic rhythm, which examples do you think are better? Which are worse? Add Roman numerals and label the parallels between the soprano and fundamental bass.

Example 3.4. (After Rameau)

FUNDAMENTAL BASS OR ROOT PROGRESSION

When harmonizing a melody, it is necessary to have a clear idea of its harmonic implications. Rameau says: "Any melody always has a natural [fundamental] bass [i.e., harmonic progression] which is more appropriate to it than any other, and which occurs to us first."[9] In this chapter, we will analyze some given subjects, first finding the best root progression, then later writing good bass lines. The fundamental bass, or root progression, is the same regardless of how the voices are disposed. Chordal inversion does not affect the harmonic progression. Rameau says: "You can equally well put the third, the fifth, or the octave in any part at all."[10]

CHORD FACTORS

As you know, the essential members ("factors") of triads are the root, the third, and the fifth (abbreviated R, T, and F). The process of harmonization consists of deciding, for each note in the melody, what chord factor it is. Beginners often laboriously try all possibilities, but you soon develop a sense for what sounds right. For instance, if you have a melody in C major that starts on a G, you would be very unlikely to make it the third of a iii chord! You should always be aware of the role a note plays in a chord because we will refer to chord factors often throughout this book.

Kirnberger believes that when the fifth or the root appear in the soprano over root position chords, the music has a static quality because the chords sound so stable that they demand no continuation (example 3.5a). He proposes two realizations of the same bass in example 3.5; he prefers example 3.5b, of which he says, "The harmony is more continuous because the upper voice has mostly the thirds above the roots which are not sufficiently restful, and hence make us expect further progression."[11] Label the chord factors in the soprano in both examples.

Example 3.5a. (Kirnberger)

Example 3.5b. (Kirnberger)

THE PRINCIPAL TRIADS

Kirnberger says that it is possible to harmonize any melody using only the three principal triads of the key: I, IV, and V in major and i, iv (IV), and v (V) in minor. He says, "If one considers this ascending scale as a melody, then one can add a strict bass which consists only of the triads of the tonic, dominant, and subdominant."[12] See example 3.6a. In the harmonization of the octave scale in the minor, the seventh degree is to be raised, and if the sixth degree leads to the seventh, it too must be raised (making the IV chord major—example 3.6b).

Example 3.6a. (Kirnberger)

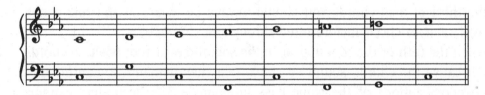

Example 3.6b. (Kirnberger)

RULES FOR USING ONLY PRINCIPAL TRIADS IN SIMPLE COUNTERPOINT

In example 3.7, you are given some melodies, and you are to decide what harmonies should underlie each of the notes they contain. At first we will only use the principal triads of the key, and every melodic note is to be a chord factor.

There are two ways of doing the exercises:

Method 1: Below each note of the melody you are to write a bass note which is the root of the harmony (chord) that you think the melody implies. There may be more than one reasonably good progression. You are finding the fundamental bass, not writing a nice bass line, and you need not worry about bad voice-leading. Go ahead, have parallel fifths! Right now all you have to do is *label them*; later we'll fix these mistakes by changing chord inversions.

Method 2: Instead of representing the harmonic progression by means of the fundamental bass, write down the Roman numerals of the chords you think the melody implies.

We recommend that you play your examples. For the present purpose, the best instrument for this would be the accordion, where you push one button to get an entire diatonic triad. You simply sing the given melody and with each note of the melody you press that button on the accordion that produces the harmony of your choice. You do not have to bother about the actual voice-leading because the instrument does not allow you to do so!

If you and your teacher can bear the thought of not being bothered by illegal voice-leading for a moment, you may also play your examples on the piano or guitar by adding triads in root position, that is, by paying no attention to inversion, good bass line, and so on. If you cannot stand playing illegal parallels, use method 2 above and hold off your performance until we reach the section on inverted chords below. Here is how you do exercise 3-B, using either method 1 or method 2:

1. Specify the key of each example and find a harmonic progression that works with the given melody. No melody note may be dissonant with the harmony assigned to the "step." Harmony may change only at the beginning of each step, never during it. The beat unit that defines the basic pulse, or step, is indicated at the beginning of each subject. Repeated notes may have the same harmony or change harmonies. Notes longer than the basic pulse may be treated as repeated notes. It may be good to change harmony during long or repeated notes.

2. Do not use the same harmony on a weak beat and the following strong beat *except at the very beginning* of a phrase.

3. You may begin with a dominant harmony.

4. Melodic skips may be treated as members of the same harmony (arpeggiations) or as members of two different chords. If two or more melody notes are treated as parts of the same harmony, you can tie all the roots into a single long value.

5. If the subject begins with a rest on a downbeat, the initial rest must be "harmonized" as if the first melody note sounded on the downbeat.

6. Be careful to note points of harmonic arrival. Some of these melodies end with half cadences, and some modulate to the dominant at the end (in the latter cases, you will use V of the dominant key).

7. If you use method 1, label bad voice-leading.

Compare your solutions with those of other class members. Which solutions do you like best? As Nadia Boulanger used to say, "You must always have an opinion!"

EXERCISE 3-B

1. *Writing:* In these exercises you are to use only the principal triads in simple counterpoint. The first four subjects in example 3.7 are chorale melodies (as you will see in chapter 17, Mattheson

suggests using chorale melodies as the basis for fugue subjects, illustrating how chorale harmonization was a basic prerequisite for fugue writing in the eighteenth century). The next six are from vocal fugues and the last three are from instrumental fugues. Sing each one. Harmonize each one; write and hand in a fundamental bass (à la Rameau example 3.1) or Roman numeral analysis, or write out the full chords. You may play your solution, as suggested earlier.

Example 3.8 shows two sample solutions to the "problem" posed by subject example 3.7k. Solution A assigns two harmonies to the first note (this is OK since the "basic step" is indicated as the quarter note). The "plagal" cadence at the end of the subject is uncharacteristic for a subject ending. Solution B has a much more interesting start, but the harmonic rhythm in the second bar is awful! The half cadence at the end is a big improvement, though. See if you can come up with a better solution than either of these.

Example 3.7a. (Subjects for exercises)

Example 3.7b. (Subjects for exercises)

Example 3.7c. (Subjects for exercises)

Example 3.7d. (Subjects for exercises)

F minor   Es   ist   der   al – te   Bund

Example 3.7e. (Subjects for exercises)

A Minor Cru – ci – fi – xus

Example 3.7f. (Subjects for exercises)

G minor   The   ways   of   Zion   do   mourn_____

Example 3.7g. (Subjects for exercises)

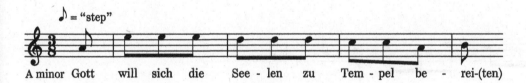

A minor Gott   will   sich   die   See - len   zu   Tem - pel   be – rei-(ten)

Example 3.7h. (Subjects for exercises)

G major Their re - ward al - so

Example 3.7i. (Subjects for exercises)

Example 3.7j. (Subjects for exercises)

Example 3.7k. (Subjects for exercises)

Example 3.7l. (Subjects for exercises)

Example 3.7m. (Subjects for exercises)

Example 3.8. (Two sample solutions for Subject 3.7k)

INVERTED CHORDS

Kirnberger explains the function of different chord inversions: "There hardly needs to be a reminder that a bass consisting of only three chords would slip into an annoying monotony; hence this first way to set the bass would be almost completely unusable if one did not help it through inversions of the triads. A bass that basically consists of only three chords can still acquire diversity and variety by means of proper inversion."[13] In example 3.9, he shows the seven notes of the scale harmonized with the three principal triads and their first inversions (the exception is under the B, where he has a 6/4 chord so as not to double the leading tone).

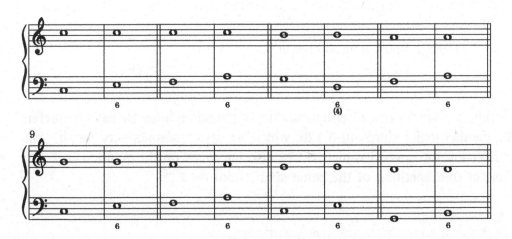

Example 3.9.

If all the chords are in root position, the effect is of a lot of equally weighted clunks. Kirnberger believes that progressions of root position chords (especially those in which the soprano has a perfect consonance above the bass) cause a lack of continuity "because one can stop on each chord."[14] He says that such progressions "have the imperfection that one can stand still on every step because the ear is so satisfied that it has no reason to expect further progression." He recommends using inverted chords, which "make the ear expect even more consonant chords to follow." This is because "the most beautiful coherence of the harmony exists when the ear is kept in constant expectation of a more perfect harmony which does not occur before the end of the entire phrase" (as in example 3.10).[15] (In the following examples, Kirnberger uses not only I, IV, and V chords but also iii, vi, and ii.)

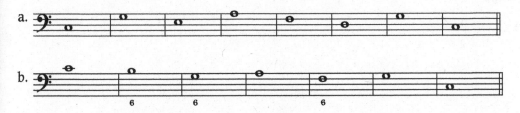

Example 3.10. (Kirnberger) *Examples a and b are essentially two versions of the same harmonic progression.*

Kirnberger considers what to do with a long note (or many repeated notes) in a melody: "Not that there needs to be a new harmony on every beat: often the chords of the tonic and dominant are sufficient; but one has to alternate between them not in a single manner [as in example 3.11a], but use their different inversions in various ways," such as in Example 3.11b.[16]

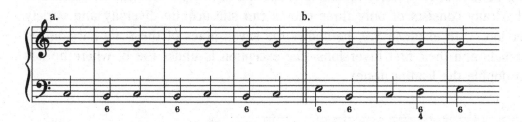

Example 3.11. Alternating I and V chords, adapted from Kirnberger.

In the next example, Kirnberger shows three harmonizations of the same tune. He says he prefers 3.12a because it avoids the parallel major thirds in 3.12b, which he says, "sounds very harsh" (but we will not use chromatic inflection for now). Example 3.12a also improves on the solution in 3.12c, which is "very weak because of the repetition of the same sixth chord on F."[17]

Example 3.12. (Kirnberger)

Inversions are particularly useful to us because they can produce a more interesting line in the bass as well as the imperfect consonances between the bass and the soprano that, according to Kirnberger, keep things going. Nadia Boulanger used to suggest that chord factors of the third and root were best to use in the outer voices, often *exchanging,* as in example 3.13, where chord factors have been labeled (R = root, T = third). Smooth melodic motions in the bass often lead to skips in the upper parts, and vice versa.

Example 3.13.

OTHER TRIADS AND SUBSTITUTE CHORDS

Now you may use the supertonic, submediant, mediant, and subtonic or leading-tone chords. In some cases you may think of these as *substitute chords*. That is, the submediant often substitutes for the tonic, the leading-tone chord for the dominant, the mediant for the tonic, and the supertonic for the subdominant.

RULES FOR EXERCISES IN HARMONIZING GIVEN SUBJECTS USING ALL AVAILABLE TRIADS AND INVERTED CHORDS

1. Start in root position, but you can end the subject on a first-inversion chord to show that the piece goes on after the subject has been stated.

2. Use only correct voice-leading.

3. While any note can be the root, third, or fifth of a harmony, there are certain standard implications for many melodic motions. A long second scale degree may be harmonized with ii–V instead of just V. Descending scales may be harmonized with the circle of fifths (two chords to a note) or with parallel 6/3 chords.

4. Repeated melodic patterns should be harmonized sequentially (see chapter 12). Note that scales are a type of melodic sequence!

TIPS FOR WRITING GOOD BASS LINES

1. Avoid tonal closure (doubling the tonic note in outer voices) before the end of the subject.

2. In Baroque style, the bass is likely to skip more than the melody, but if the melody skips, it is good to let the bass move by step.

3. Use octave skips instead of sustained notes to keep activity going in the bass.

EXERCISE 3-C

In these exercises you are to use all available triads and inverted chords. The first four melodies are chorale tunes, the next five are from vocal fugues, and the last four are from various instrumental pieces. If you and your teacher recognize the sources of any of these subjects, you can go check that composer's harmonization and compare it to yours.

1. *Writing or improvisation:* To the melodies in example 3.14, add basses that use all available triads and inverted chords, still expressing one chord to a step. You may improvise your solutions, hand in just the melody and a figured bass, or hand in full four-part realizations, depending on your teacher's instructions. Always do a Roman numeral analysis.

Example 3.14a. (Subjects for Exercises)

Example 3.14b. (Subjects for Exercises)

Example 3.14c. (Subjects for Exercises)

Example 3.14d. (Subjects for Exercises)

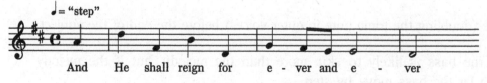

Example 3.14e. (Subjects for Exercises)

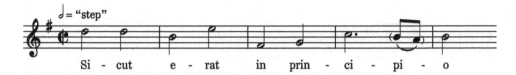

Si - cut   e - rat   in   prin - ci - pi - o

Example 3.14f. (Subjects for Exercises)

denn er wird mei - nen Fuss aus dem Net - ze zie - - hen

Example 3.14g. (Subjects for Exercises)

muss täg - lich von neu - em dich Jo - seph er - freu - (en)

Example 3.14h. (Subjects for Exercises)

und   al - le Welt für - chte ihn

Example 3.14i. (Subjects for Exercises)

Example 3.14j. (Subjects for Exercises)

Example 3.14k. (Subjects for Exercises)

Example 3.14l. (Subjects for Exercises)

Example 3.14m. (Subjects for Exercises)

Example 3.15.

2. *Writing or improvisation:* Use the melodies in exercise 3-B (example 3.7) as the basis for exercises as above. While in exercise 3-B you were permitted to use just the principal triads, you now have a much larger vocabulary of chords available and you will get much better results.

3. *Writing:* Write *four* different harmonizations of the subject given in example 3.15, each having at least *two* chords that are different from the other versions. You must use a new chord for every quarter note (moving to a different inversion counts as a new chord). At least one version must be harmonized in a different key from the others. One version must be modulating (begins in one key and ends in a different key). Overall, use at least *three* non-principal triads (supertonic, mediant, submediant, leading-tone chord, and subtonic in the minor).

NOTES

1. Kirnberger, *Die Kunst des reinen Satzes in der Musik*, I, 10, p. 141.
2. Kirnberger, 11, p. 224.
3. Rameau, *Traité de l'harmonie réduite à ses principes naturels*, III, 40, p. 315. In the same vein, Kirnberger says: "We advise prospective composers not to occupy themselves with the composition of embellished or so-called galant pieces before they have acquired experience with this counterpoint so that its voice-leading is completely strict. . . . Hence this counterpoint is to be considered as a succession of complete chords" (Kirnberger, *Die Kunst*, I, 10, p. 142).
4. Kirnberger, I, 11, pp. 189–90.
5. Kirnberger, p. 191.
6. Rameau, *Traité de l'harmonie*, III, 40, p. 317: "You should always regard the first beat of each measure as the principal beat. Thus if you notice that the note in the bass . . . is appropriate to the first [nearest] beat that precedes or follows, then it is better to advance or delay this note, so it can be heard on the first beat."
7. We have replaced the original time signature of 2/1 in Rameau's example III, 121, with 2/2.
8. Kirnberger, *Die Kunst*, II–1, p. 32.
9. Rameau, *Traité de l'harmonie*, III, 40, p. 313.
10. Rameau, p. 186.
11. Kirnberger, *Die Kunst*, I, 10, p. 146.
12. Kirnberger, example 3.6a, II–1, 1, p. 4.

13. Kirnberger, II–1, 1, p. 5.
14. Kirnberger, p. 162.
15. Kirnberger, I, 6, pp. 92–93.
16. Kirnberger, II–1, 1, p. 32.
17. Kirnberger, p. 20.

4

MELODIC EMBELLISHMENT IN STRICT STYLE

Strict Style; Dance Steps and Dissonance; Rules for Embellishment in Strict Style; The Types of Embellishment; Compound Melody; Reduction; Brief Summary of Rules for Strict Style

Baroque music is considered to be analogous to Baroque art, rich in complicated, small-scale decoration. In music, the decoration consists of chordal skips and nonharmonic melodic embellishments. Embellishments allow the composer more flexibility in creating melodic shapes than would be possible with the use of chord tones only. The introduction of skips and faster motion animates the music, adding movement in a way that is not possible with the slow, predominantly stepwise motion in simple counterpoint shown in the previous chapter. Embellishments are used to dramatize the independence between voices by allowing them to move at different speeds. Without dissonance, a faster moving line would be forced to arpeggiate constantly over a slower moving bass line. In part I of this book, we use these embellishments in a fairly restricted way, which is called *strict style*, in order to keep the harmonic progression clear and to ensure that lines are singable.

STRICT STYLE

As we saw in the previous chapter, an unembellished melody consists exclusively of chord factors occurring on the basic beat units ("steps") of the meter. Strict style is different from that simple counterpoint in that it features some dissonant embellishments. Strict style is related to sixteenth-century polyphonic style, which is vocally conceived and moves fairly slowly in mostly stepwise motion. It is sometimes characterized by longer "old-fashioned" (*stile antico*) note values where the half note is the basic unit. Kirnberger says: "In strict style, each chord and almost every note in the vocal parts is emphasized; there are only few embellishments, or few non-harmonic passing tones. . . . Strict style gives a grave quality to the melody. . . . Strict style is used primarily in church music."[1]

DANCE STEPS AND DISSONANCE

The placement of dissonance is always evaluated in terms of its relation to metric position and to harmony. In an embellished melody, the time occupied by a beat is filled in (or "divided") with notes of shorter values. In Kirnberger's words,

> The steps are embellished just as one would make a little side motion with the lifted foot instead of progressing straight forward. . . . Just as one can make several small decorative motions with every step before the foot comes down again, the steps of the melody can also be ornamented with several notes. After the note that marks the downbeat or the beginning of the step has been indicated, one can add many kinds of embellishing notes, stepwise or leaping, in the time in which the simple melody would stand still; but all [the notes] that sound together with the note on the downbeat must not take more than one principal time unit [step].[2]

RULES FOR EMBELLISHMENT IN STRICT STYLE

You are to follow these two rules for dissonant embellishments between onsets of the basic pulse, or step. Remember the definition of the step in chapter 3: it is the shortest note value at which harmonies can change.

1. Except for suspensions, the legal accented passing tone (or "legal ap," see p. 51), and passing sevenths in dominant chords, dissonance can only occur on the weak subdivisions of the step.

2. When writing embellishments, we will generally not use subdivisions smaller than one quarter of the step.

If you are writing in 2/2, you can have nonharmonic tones (NHTs) on the weak quarter note or any of the three weak eighths within the half note. If you are writing in 3/4, you can have NHTs on any weak eighth note or any of the three weak sixteenths. However, sometimes in 3/4 the eighth note is the step, and harmonies change faster than at the quarter-note level; in that case you can only have dissonance on the weak sixteenth. As in chapter 3, we usually let you know what the step is in a given exercise.

THE TYPES OF EMBELLISHMENT

The types of embellishment we will look at in this chapter are suspension (sus), arpeggiation (arp), passing tone (p), neighbor (n), double neighbor (dn), échappée (ech), anticipation (ant), and descending accented passing tone (legal ap). Only in chapter 14 will we treat other types of dissonance, including other types of accented passing tone (ap).

SUSPENSION (SUS)

We know Kirnberger liked inverted chords for creating a sense of continuity and for the sense of direction that stepwise motion brings. "However," he says, "there is an even better way to weave the succession of chords together so that each [chord] almost necessarily leads the ear to the next. This method entails connecting a few notes, i.e. tying them over from one chord to the next."[3] The sense of inevitability results in part from tied common tones and in part from the obligatory treatment of dissonance.

There are two kinds of dissonant suspensions: those that resolve over the same harmony, and those that are chordal sevenths and move to a different harmony. The former kind includes 4–3, 7–6, and 9–8 suspensions. These are prepared by consonance on a weak beat, tied to a dissonance on a strong beat, and resolved down by melodic step to a consonance. The dissonance may last a part of a step or a full step, and resolution may occur on the next step or the weak part of the principal step. Do not go beyond these two possibilities. Note that the tie between the preparation and the suspension can be eliminated so that the same note is repeated from the weak to the strong beat.

Example 4.1 shows five cases of an F suspended over a C in the bass, approached in different ways; five cases of a D suspended over a C, each approached differently; and finally one example of a 7–6 suspension. In all these examples the step is the half note, the dissonance lasts half a step, and the resolution occurs on the weak half of the step, except for the last example where the dissonance lasts a full step and the resolution occurs on the next step.

Example 4.1. (After Kirnberger)

The other kind of dissonant suspension creates chordal sevenths. The resolution of the seventh must be either the third of the next chord (if the roots move down a fifth) or the fifth of the next chord (if the roots rise a step). Example 4.2a shows seventh chords with roots moving up a step; example 4.2b shows seventh chords resolving as roots move down by fifths. Note that in both examples the sevenths last a full step, are prepared, and resolve down by melodic stepwise motion, as required.

Example 4.2a. (Kirnberger)

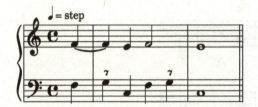

Example 4.2b. (Kirnberger)

Always remember that dissonances can occur in the bass as well. Once we use different chord inversions and suspensions in the bass, many different bass lines become available. Here is a nice example by Rameau of many different bass lines that express the same harmonic progression (it is a descending circle-of-fifths sequence, discussed in chapter 12), several of them involving suspended sevenths. In terms of the fundamental bass, or harmonic progression, shown on the bottom staff (example 4.3g), all of the bass lines in examples 4.3a–f are "equivalent," but of course they all sound different because of chordal inversions. Sing each bass, naming chord factors, while a colleague plays the realization.

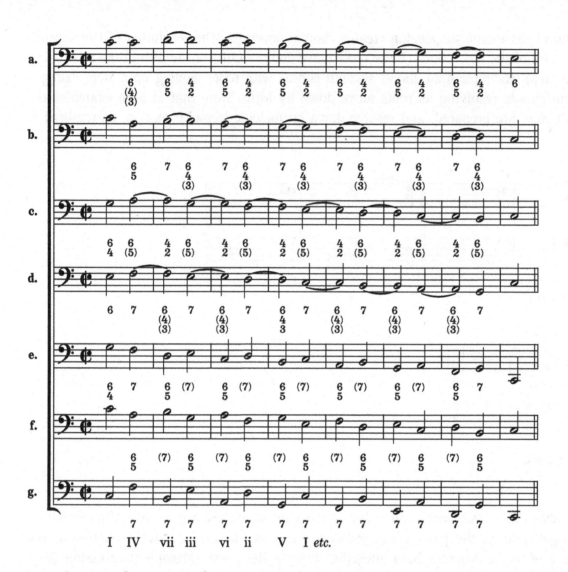

Example 4.3. (After Rameau, figures in parentheses are based on the harmonies indicated on line g, the fundamental bass.) *We do not use 6/4 chords at the beginning of a piece as in examples c and e—Rameau does this to make a theoretical point. For a special treat, play or sing all four basses a–d simultaneously; play all four basses b–e simultaneously. These combinations work together because they are alternative voices of a good realization. Why don't basses a and e work together? Why don't basses c and f work together?*

SUSPENSIONS IN ONLY TWO VOICES.

A suspension is clearest if the tied note and the new note in the other voice on the strong beat actually make a dissonance, but in two parts, where the harmonies are incomplete, the implications may not be clear. In example 4.4, the F-sharp on the downbeat of m. 5 is not the root of an F-sharp major chord, which would be awkward after the V$^{4/2}$ immediately preceding; the correct interpretation is that the root of the downbeat chord is C-sharp, and the F-sharp is a dissonant suspension, correctly prepared and resolved. The same thing happens on the next downbeat. That this is so is proven by the corresponding place on the downbeat of m. 9.

Example 4.4. (Bach, WTC II, F-sharp major fugue, mm. 1–10) *Although the suspensions in this passage are acceptable in strict style, the unprepared sevenths in mm. 4 and 8 and the descending chromaticism are deviations from strict style.*

THE FAKE SUSPENSION (F. SUS).

The fake suspension (sometimes called the "consonant fourth") is commonly used over a relatively long dominant note and is preceded by a root-position dominant chord on the downbeat. In example 4.5, the preparation phase in the suspension figure is not consonant as it normally should be; it is the fourth of a 6/4 chord, so we call the figure *fake suspension*.

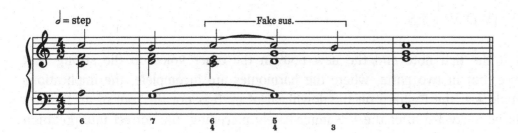

Example 4.5. (Kirnberger)

THE CADENTIAL 6/4 CHORD.

The cadential 6/4 chord is often prepared as a suspension. It embellishes a dominant harmony with a (dissonant) 4–3 suspension and a (consonant) 6–5 suspension. The fourth must be prepared but the sixth need not be. Both suspensions, however, are treated as NHTs and must resolve above the same bass note. In example 4.6c the passing seventh lasts a full step (see example 4.12).

Example 4.6. (After Kirnberger) *In a, both the fourth and sixth are prepared. In b, only the fourth is prepared.*

THE PASSING 6/4 CHORD.

Kirnberger insists that the passing 6/4 chord function as the dominant of the following chord and that the upper note of the fourth be sustained. Example 4.7b is wrong because the G in the upper voice is not prepared; examples 4.7c and 4.7d are wrong because the G is not sustained across the bar line. Note that these uses of the 6/4 chord are best when the seventh of the chord is present (i.e., a 6/4/3), but this option is not available in strict style because the seventh cannot be prepared, nor can it be a passing seventh, in these cases.

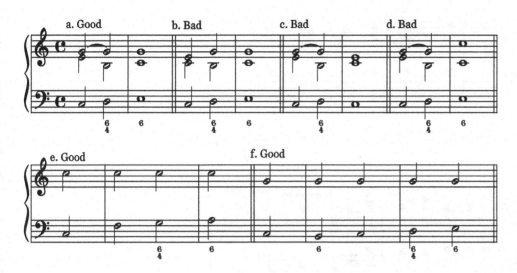

Example 4.7. (Kirnberger)

ARPEGGIATION (ARP)

Here the embellishment leaps about between chord factors of the underlying harmony *during the basic pulse*. In strict style, all leaps from strong to weak beats within a step must be arpeggiations so that both notes are consonant.

Example 4.8. (Kirnberger) *Do a harmonic analysis and label chord factors.*

Arpeggiation is more frequently used in instrumental style than in vocal style. Since we are writing primarily in vocal style at the basic level, we will use arpeggiation with restraint: it should occur at a slow speed and be easy to sing, and there should not be too much of it. *Skips to and from dissonances are not permitted. All chord sevenths must be either passing on weak parts of steps (except for dominant sevenths, which may enter in descending stepwise motion on the strong part of the step and last a whole step) or be prepared and resolved.*

With arpeggiation a single part is essentially transformed into several implied voices. The voice-leading of these implied voices must follow the usual voice-leading rules for strict style. Here is an incorrect example and its corrected version (from Kirnberger; see also examples 4.24 and 4.25 under Compound Melody):

Example 4.9a. (Kirnberger) *Implied voice-leading is incorrect: parallel octaves between alto and bass are revealed in reduction.*

Example 4.9b. (Kirnberger's corrected version and some others)

THE ARPEGGIATED 6/4 CHORD.

We have to beware of skipping to or from the fifth chord factor in the bass. We can only skip *to* the fifth of the chord if it is on a weak part of the basic step and it is either continued with another member of the same triad (i.e., it is buried in an arpeggiation; examples 4.10a and c) or it moves by stepwise motion to a member of the next triad (examples 4.10b and d). We can skip *from* the fifth of a chord if it occurs on a weak part of the step and if it is followed by another member of the same triad (examples 4.10a and c).

We can skip from the fifth of a chord occurring on the *strong* part of the beat if it is preceded by a melodic step and if it skips immediately to another factor of the same chord (see example 11.13 by J. C. F. Bach, in the motet "Wachet auf," m. 183).

Example 4.10a. (Kirnberger)

Example 4.10b. (Bach, Cantata 4, v. 5, mm. 21–24)

Example 4.10c. (Bach, Cantata 4, v. 5, mm. 21–22)

Example 4.10d. (Bach, Christmas Oratorio, 64, mm. 18–19)

The above applies primarily to three- and four-part writing. In two-part writing, however, "implied" 6/4 chords can occur on strong beats if they are incomplete, containing only the sixth, not the fourth (see example 4.19, m. 2; example 6.16, m. 5).

PASSING TONE (P)

Passing tones connect two chord factors via stepwise motion *in the same direction*.

Example 4.11. (Kirnberger) The step is the quarter note.

When the dominant seventh chord or other applied dominant seventh chords are used, the sevenths may be introduced as accented passing tones lasting a full step.

Example 4.12. (Kirnberger) *LTMRU means "leading tone must resolve up"; SMRD means "seventh must resolve down."*

NEIGHBOR NOTE (N)

A neighbor note moves stepwise above or below the main note and returns to it. The passages in example 4.13 have both passing and neighbor motions.

Example 4.13. (Kirnberger) *Sing, analyze harmonies, and label neighbor and passing tones.*

DOUBLE NEIGHBOR (DN)

A double neighbor can be considered as an upper and a lower neighbor with a missing chord tone in between. When using a double neighbor, you can have two dissonances in a row with respect to the main triad and a skip between dissonances.

Example 4.14. (Kirnberger)

ÉCHAPPÉE (ECH)

An échappée must last half a step or less and must be used only to decorate structural notes that descend by step. A common form might be called the *consonant échappée* because it interrupts the motion from the seventh to the sixth in a 7–6 suspension with a move up to the octave above the bass (example 4.15b).

Example 4.15a. (Arcangelo Corelli, *Sarabanda*, op. 2, no. 10, mm. 1–4)

Example 4.15b. (Handel, "Consonant échappée")

ANTICIPATION (ANT)

The anticipation falls on a weak beat, is usually very short (half a step or less), and sounds the consonant note that is to come on the strong part of the next step. It is best approached by step, but may be leapt to, very rarely, as in the Corelli example (4.16a at the asterisk). Use leaps into anticipations sparingly. The anticipation occurs often at cadences, but if it is used in the course of a line, it is best used as a recurring motive, as in Example 4.16b, where Kirnberger first shows the unembellished version.

Example 4.16a. (Corelli)

Example 4.16b. (Kirnberger)

DESCENDING ACCENTED PASSING TONE ("LEGAL D3Q")

This very narrow exception to the rule prohibiting accented passing dissonance is inherited from the Renaissance. In music where the half note is the "step," the first of two quarters following a half note may be dissonant *if it is preceded and followed by descending motion* (i.e., both intervals are descending). In example 4.17 the first d3q between tenor and bass in m. 2 does not appear dissonant—it's only when we hear the same thing in m. 3 between soprano and alto that we realize that the harmony is a vii[6] chord. The "legal d3q" can also occur in diminution, for example when the step is the quarter note rather than the half note, in which case we define the dissonant first of two eighths following a quarter simply as "legal accented passing tone" ("legal ap"; see example 8.6a, mm. 2, 4, 6, 8, 10).

Example 4.17. (Bach, "Dona nobis" from B minor Mass, Gloria)

TWO DISSONANCES IN A ROW

If there is an accented dissonance in one voice, resulting from a suspension, and its resolution coincides with an unaccented dissonance on the weak part of the same beat in another voice, we might get two vertical dissonances in a row, as shown in example 4.18.

Example 4.18.

HEMIOLA

In triple meter, a hemiola rearranges the metric accents of two measures so that they form a large triple meter whose beats are twice as long. Two successive 3/4 measures are heard as a large 3/2 measure; two successive 3/8 measures are perceived as a 3/4 measure, and so forth.

Each larger beat of a hemiola is considered a strong beat. All rules for the use of embellishments apply to the three beats of the hemiola, not those of the notated meter. Hemiolas usually appear at the ends of phrases. The second and third measures of the following example form a hemiola at the conclusion of the first phrase of the piece. Hence, the dissonance on the downbeat of m. 3 falls on a weak metric position (the C in the soprano is a passing tone). Hemiola provides an *apparent* exception to the rule that the same harmony should not be repeated from a weak beat to the next downbeat. In example 4.19 the iv harmony is heard on both sides of the bar line, but that's OK because both eighths are part of the second quarter-note beat of an imaginary 3/4 bar.

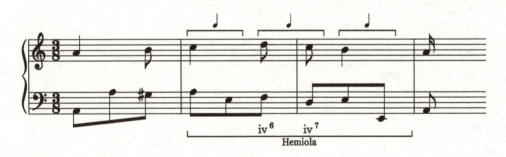

Example 4.19. (Bach, Sinfonia 13, mm. 1–4)

EXERCISE 4-A

1. *Analysis:* Beginning in m. 5, circle the embellishments in example 4.20 and label each with its initials.

Example 4.20. (Corelli)

2. *Writing:* Go back to the melodies in example 3.14 and write new bass lines using suspensions in the melody and/or the bass; in the bass you may also add other embellishments discussed in this chapter.

3. *Writing and improvisation:* Realize each of Rameau's basses in example 4.3.

4. *Analysis*: In examples 4.21 and 4.22, circle and label all embellishments. Identify the key(s) and add figured-bass figures. There are a few deviations from strict style in example 4.22. Mark them.

Example 4.21. (Elizabeth Turner, Gigue from Lesson III for the Harpsichord)

Example 4.22. (Handel, Xerxes, "Ombra mai fu")

5. *Analysis, improvisation, and writing*: Circle and label all embellishments in example 4.23 and add figured-bass figures where needed. Then improvise and/or write out a figured-bass realization in three or four parts. Do a Roman numeral analysis (if you write out your realization).

Example 4.23. (Barbara Strozzi, Ritornello from Arie, op. 8)

COMPOUND MELODY

In compound melody, two or more voices in a progression are transformed into a single melodic part, with that part leaping between the factors in the chord progression. *Compound melody differs from arpeggiation in that the leap can take place across a harmonic boundary, whereas arpeggiation always takes place within a step (arpeggiation across steps is only possible if the harmony is sustained).* In example 4.24, Mattheson shows how a counterpoint in two parts (a) can be presented in a single line in instrumental style (b, c). In leaping from a chord factor in one chord to one in a different chord, we may leap difficult intervals, particularly sevenths, as in example 4.24b.

Example 4.24a. (Two-part counterpoint)

Example 4.24b. (Compound melody)

Example 4.24c. (Compound melody)

In a compound melody situation, when the seventh is correctly prepared and resolved, we have what appear to be skips to and from dissonances. In the last measure of Example 4.25a, the seventh (G) is prepared at the end of the penultimate measure; the melody leaps into an inner voice and then back to the "continuation" of the tied note. Example 4.25b shows the upper voices in two-part counterpoint.

Example 4.25a. (Kirnberger)

Example 4.25b. (Kirnberger)

A common use of compound melody, inherited from the early seventeenth century, involves skipping away from the suspension into another voice. This is OK in strict style *as long as the correct resolution appears immediately afterward* (example 4.26).

Example 4.26.

REDUCTION

The opposite of embellishment is reduction. When we *reduce* a melody, we simplify it, eliminating from the melody all the embellishing notes that are not chord factors and even some that are. We reduce the melody to tones that represent the basic harmonic and linear structure.

Mattheson explains how Kuhnau enlivened a simple melody (example 4.27a):

> In order for it not to sound too simple, he uses diminution, and by continuing to repeat the same note for all three notes . . . makes eight or nine. This produces quite some liveliness. . . . The notes of the subject are of one value; but the beginning with the little rests nicely breaks the uniformity.[4]

The "three" notes are C, D, and E. We would reduce Kuhnau's theme like this (example 4.27b):

Example 4.27a. (Kuhnau)

Example 4.27b.

BRIEF SUMMARY OF RULES FOR STRICT STYLE

Accented dissonant passing tones are prohibited. (Exceptions to this are the "legal ap" and sevenths in dominant chords.) Suspensions must be prepared and resolved. Suspended dissonance is never longer than the consonance by which it was prepared. Dissonance must progress immediately to a consonance.

(An exception to this is discussed under Compound Melody.) Melodic motions of augmented and diminished intervals are avoided (but diminished fourths, diminished sevenths, and tritones are OK in compound melody). The resolution of a seventh is never transferred to another voice or omitted. Applied dominants may be used, but applied leading tones must immediately resolve (see example 4.12). Descending chromaticism is forbidden. Incomplete neighbors are not permitted.

EXERCISE 4-B

1. *Analysis:* Label all embellishing tones in the given examples (examples 4.28a–b), using the abbreviations given above. You must, of course, first do a harmonic analysis.

2. *Writing (short):* Add a bass to example 4.24a; play it with example 4.24b; play it with example 4.24c.

3. *Analysis:* Reduce the (compound) melodies in examples 4.29a–d to their simple steps.

4. *Writing:* Embellish the skeletal tunes in examples 4.30a–g using the given rhythms. First provide a simple harmonic framework in which the melody tones are consonant, then place embellishments in between using the rhythms given. If you want more practice, ask your teacher to reduce some other melodies from the literature, then embellish them and compare yours with the original.

Example 4.28a.

Example 4.28b.

Example 4.29a.

Example 4.29b.

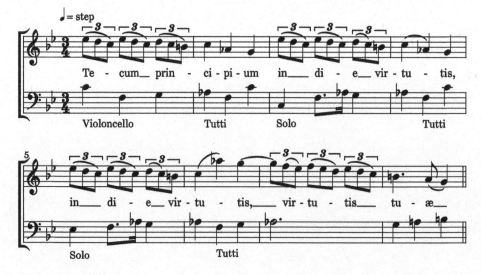

Example 4.29c.

Example 4.29d.

Example 4.30a.

Example 4.30b.

Example 4.30c.

Example 4.30d.

Example 4.30e.

Example 4.30f.

Example 4.30g.

5. *Writing:* Expand these chord progressions into compound melodies (examples 4.31a–d). Try to use every note in the upper parts at least once. For any given solution, see if the richness of the original progression is maintained in the compound melody version.

Example 4.31a.

Example 4.31b.

Example 4.31c.

Example 4.31d.

NOTES

1. Kirnberger, *Die Kunst des reinen Satzes in der Musik*, I, 5, p. 80.
2. Kirnberger, I, 11, pp. 191–92.
3. Kirnberger, p. 93.
4. Mattheson, *Der vollkommene Capellmeister*, III, 23, §18.

5

VARIATION TECHNIQUES

WHY VARIATION?

Variation technique is fundamental to Western music. Generally, people like to hear music they have heard before because it gives them a sense of familiarity and emotional security. But hearing the exact same music over and over can be boring, and hence the more attractive listening experience is one in which we recognize something familiar that nevertheless changes. ("Hey, I know this music, but look, it sounds different each time it is repeated. I know the music, but it keeps surprising me.")

Friederich Erhardt Niedt explains that "there is nothing more delightful and more necessary in human life than the variation of all artful and natural things. If there were no summer and winter, planting and harvesting, freezing cold and heat, day and night etc., which creature could stand this life? . . . No skill gives more delightful pleasure to the understanding ear than the artful and unforced variation of musical sounds. . . . The greatest pleasure consists in variation."[1]

Mattheson agrees about the importance of the unexpected. In Baroque music, the kinds of variety these theorists are talking about could affect speed, register, texture, dynamics, direction of melodic motion, number of voices, and so forth. Beyond basic kinds of contrasts in these areas, however, there is a specific, much narrower notion of variation that has to do with thematic or melodic variation to be discussed in this chapter. We will not talk about changes in texture and register until later in this book.

Many Baroque forms employ variation techniques. You find them in concertos, dances, and arias, as well as in the music we are about to study in this chapter. You will learn to write different melodies over the same harmonic progression, add shorter notes to a simple melody in strict style, add interesting lines to a simple chorale tune, and vary simple motives by transposing them, inverting them, and/or retrograding them.

CHACONNE, PASSACAGLIA, GROUND, VARIATION

In these types of pieces, a bass line (or the same harmonic progression with different bass lines) repeats over and over, but different melodic "surfaces" are added above, strung together into meaningful shapes. The harmonic progression is repeated in phrases or segments of the same length called periods. One of the games composers play is to have the added melody elide across the period boundary, causing the listener to lose track of the regular periods.

Although the progression stays basically the same, the bass line may be altered from one period to the next to produce different chordal inversions within the same harmonic progression, and it is also common to find substitute chords. Here are examples by Handel and Campra in which small alterations of this sort have been labeled, as well as a few deviations from strict style (shown with arrows). Note that Handel occasionally uses a substitute chord in the sixth measure—IV–ii rather than just ii in m. 6 of variations 5 and 51. In each example, label NHTs in the melody.

Example 5.1. (Handel, Chaconne, Var. 8, 5, 13, 51) *We have presented what is really variation 8 as the "theme" because it, not the first one, is the simplest. This piece contains sixty-two variations, or periods, many of which are not in strict style.*

Example 5.1. *(concluded)*

Example 5.2. (Campra, Aria)

Example 5.2. *(Concluded)*

EXERCISE 5-A

1. *Analysis:* How long are the periods in example 5.2? Indicate the beginning and end of each period.

2. *Analysis:* Do a harmonic analysis of the first period, and note substitute chords when they occur in later variations.

3. *Analysis:* In example 5.2, there is a hemiola in mm. 11–12; find other hemiolas. Do the beginnings and ends of the vocal line coincide with the boundaries of the periods? How does Campra make it seem like not every cadence is an authentic cadence?

4. *Keyboard harmony and improvisation:* The teacher or a student plays a bass line from example 5.3 and other students take turns improvising/playing different soprano lines one after another. You can warm up for this by asking your teacher to improvise a line over one period, then having the class sing back the improvised line in the next period. You may compose your own bass lines, use the ones in the examples above, or choose from the ones below.

Example 5.3a. (Henry Purcell, Chacony)

Example 5.3b. (Pachelbel, Canon)

Example 5.3c. (Buxtehude, Ciacona)

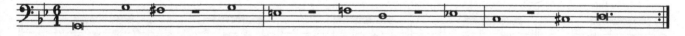

Example 5.3d. (Strozzi, Ritornello)

MOTIVES

Motives are melodic patterns that repeat. In the Handel Chaconne (example 5.1) you probably noticed that each variation has a distinct character, in spite of the fact that each period contains the same harmonic progression. This comes about because of the consistent use of rhythmic and melodic patterns in each variation. In example 5.1c, for instance, every measure contains, exclusively, the rhythm ♪♫, except on the very first beat and the very last beat. This pattern is a rhythmic motive. If the note patterns also repeat, we refer to the whole pattern as a *melodic motive*. If we define a melodic motive as what comes within a beat, we can say there are only five different melodic motives in the variation (labeled a–e in example 5.1c). The small number of motives and the variety of ways they are connected is a fundamental feature of Baroque music.

Campra's aria has much more variety within each period, but on the other hand, some motives repeat from one period to the next. Two have been labeled (a and b in example 5.2). Find recurrences of motive a. Does it repeat at the same moment in the period? With the same harmonies? What is the effect of its repetition? When motive b is repeated, it retains its rhythm and contour, but the intervals are not repeated exactly. How does it function with respect to the periods?

INVENTORY OF TYPICAL MOTIVES

Two of the most basic characteristics of Baroque music are a regular rhythmic surface and motivic consistency. This gives a strong sense of momentum, which has been negatively characterized with the epithet "sewing machine music." Vivaldi's many concertos are considered the worst offenders, but that is only because many lack variety in other domains. If used carefully, motivic repetition can be as powerful a tool for creating unity and forward motion as harmony is.

Some motives are so ubiquitous that they are found in the work of most mainstream composers. Here are ten typical motives that we have gathered from repertoire (example 5.4). You should memorize them and use them to begin your commonplace book. Note that there are no clefs in the example. This means that the motives can appear anywhere in the diatonic arrangement (i.e., with various tone/semitone arrangements) and in a variety of harmonic contexts. For the moment we will insist on preserving the diatonic intervals (seconds, thirds, etc.) rigorously. The last x-shaped note indicates that it may be of any rhythmic value.

Example 5.4. (Inventory of commonplace motives)

MOTIVE AS EMBELLISHMENT

Each of the above motives lasts a quarter note and the following downbeat attack (i.e., at least five sixteenth notes), and thus connects two harmonies each lasting a quarter-note "step." Motive c can be considered as the embellishment of a simple motion down a third from quarter to quarter, and so it can connect two chord factors a third apart on successive beats. It could thus connect the fifth to the third or the third to the root if both quarters had the same harmony (examples 5.5a and b). Or it could connect the various factors of different chords. Any time the consonant factors of two successive chords are a third apart, you should be able to fit this motive in. The only time you must beware of such voice-leading opportunities is when illegal motions result from the embellishment, as shown in examples 5.6i and j.

Example 5.5. (Motive c spanning a single harmony)

HARMONIZING MOTIVES

Example 5.6 shows different harmonizations for each of motives c and f, respectively. We have labeled the principal chord factors represented in the motives. Skips in motives occur only between chord factors—one never skips to a dissonance (except as described in chapter 4).

Example 5.6. (Sample harmonizations of motive c from example 5.4, a–d; sample harmonizations of motive f from example 5.4, e–h; illegal voice-leading resulting from embellishment, i–j)

Motive f can be considered a variant of motive c, spanning a descending step instead of a descending third. The similarity lies in the continuous string of three descending steps. As we will see later, these motives are often used together in a piece, particularly in a fugue, because of their similarity.

EXERCISE 5-B

1. *Writing:* Using the same ground basses you improvised on, compose *compound* melodies that clearly express the harmonies. You will find it easier if you get into a "groove," that is, a rhythmically regular, repeating pattern. If possible, make use of specific motives, and also think about rests and elision. Show the Roman numeral analysis in the first period and whenever the harmonic progression is altered in other periods. You may want to set a text.

2. *Writing (short):* Harmonize each of the remaining motives from example 5.4 four different ways, using the format of example 5.6: determine a suitable key and harmonize each quarter (it is OK to repeat the same harmony on two successive quarters). Notate the roots of the chords as bass notes below the motive (or, if the motive moves from one *root* to another you can put the motive in the bass so as to avoid parallels, as shown in examples 5.6d and h). Label the chord factors in the motive. Play or sing each example. Which harmonization do you like best?

3. *Writing (long):* Connect any *two* motives from example 5.4 so that the last note of the first motive becomes the first note of the next. The second motive may need to be transposed accordingly. (In this elision the duration of the last note of the first motive is replaced by the duration of the first note of the second motive.) Harmonize the result in at least two different ways. A sample for this exercise is shown in example 5.7. Example 5.7a shows motives a and g, whose pitch level is as yet

undetermined. Example 5.7b determines the pitch level of motive a and transposes motive g to start on the last note, F, of motive a. Example 5.7c elides the two motives. Examples 5.7d and e provide two different harmonizations of example 5.7c.

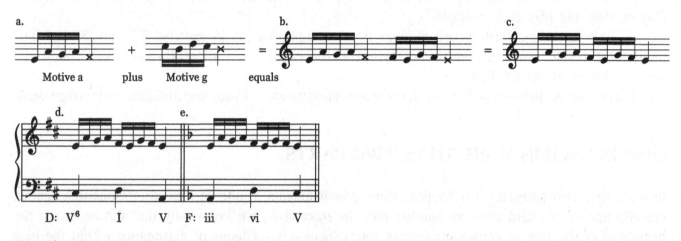

Example 5.7.

4. *Keyboard harmony and improvisation or writing:* Once you have strung two motives together, you may have begun to develop a sense of direction in the resulting line. Imagine a further continuation for the results of exercise 5-B, no. 3. You have an obligation not only to the general shape of the line but to the next harmony. What should that be? Adding on this way, you gradually accumulate both linear and harmonic energy, and you need to make sure one does not dominate at the expense of the other.

FASTER HARMONIC RHYTHM

The motives can also be harmonized in a faster harmonic rhythm. Example 5.8 shows three different possibilities for motive b from example 5.4. Example 5.8a harmonizes each quarter. Example 5.8b harmonizes each of the first two eighths. Example 5.8c harmonizes all four sixteenths of the first beat. Note that the bass lines of examples 5.8b and c alternate between the roots and thirds of the chords (i.e., they also use first-inversion chords).

Example 5.8.

EXERCISE 5-C

1. *Writing (short):* Harmonize the remaining motives (a, and c through j) of example 5.4 at the eighth- and/or sixteenth-note level. You should avoid harmonic rhythm of ♪♪♪. Identify the harmonies. Play or sing and play each example.

2. *Writing:* String together two motives from example 5.4 (as in exercise 5-B, no. 3) and harmonize the result, combining harmonic rhythm at the eighth- and sixteenth-note level. Follow the presentation of exercise 5-B, no. 3.

3. *Writing:* As in exercise 5-B, no. 4, compose continuations of your line and harmonic progression.

DISSONANCE IN MORE THAN TWO PARTS

In more than two parts, it often happens that embellishments in one part create dissonances against embellishments or chord tones in another part. In strict style, we insist only that the attack on the beginning of the step be consonant (except for suspensions)—pileups of dissonance within the beat are acceptable. You have to decide what level of crunchiness you can tolerate. In Bach's early cantatas we often find a lot of dissonance between the beats. In this example from Cantata 21, the harmony at the beginning of each quarter-note "step" is perfectly clear, but in between the lines bump against each other and create dissonances. Generally, if the sense of direction of each line is convincing, we can tolerate these crunches, but we think it is best to avoid parallel seconds, which are hard to sing.

Example 5.9. (Bach, Cantata 21, first chorus, mm. 39–44)

Sometimes the passing tones accidentally add up to a new consonant chord on a weak beat, like the A minor 6/4 in example 5.12 on the last eighth of the first measure.

EXERCISE 5-D

1. *Writing (short):* Using one or more different motives from example 5.4, add another line to the combinations you made in exercise 5-B, no. 2. Clashes are encouraged as long as all other voice-leading rules are obeyed (i.e., parts should not move in parallel fifths, etc.).

2. *Writing (long):* Take a four-part framework (e.g., a chorale tune harmonized in simple counterpoint), and embellish the three upper parts, sprinkling them with motives from example 5.4.

MELODIC INVERSION

Most of the motives from example 5.4 can be used in melodic inversion as well. We invert a motive by turning its melodic intervals upside down. Example 5.10a illustrates the procedure for motive c from examples 5.4. Note again that we have not provided a clef here. The motive and its inversion can appear on any scale degrees. Example 5.10b shows the melodic inversion of motive f from example 5.4. Like their original forms, the inverted forms of motives c and f can be considered variants of each other, and we can expect to find them both in the same piece.

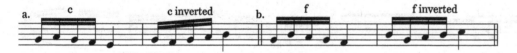

Example 5.10.

EXERCISE 5-E

1. *Keyboard harmony and improvisation:* Invert motives b, d, e, and g from example 5.4. (The inverted forms of examples 5.4a, h, i, and j occur much less frequently in repertoire.)

2. *Writing (or improvisation):* Harmonize each of the inversions of motives b, d, e, and g in three different ways. Use the format of example 5.6 or 5.8. Determine a suitable key. Play or sing each example.

3. *Writing:* Connect any two of the inverted motives as in exercise 5-B, no. 3 above. Harmonize the result in at least two different ways.

4. *Writing:* Connect any motive from example 5.4 with its inversion. Harmonize the result.

5. *Writing:* Connect any motive from example 5.4 with the inversion of another motive and harmonize the result.

6. *Writing:* Continue the lines you made in questions 3, 4, and 5 above, feeling out their sense of direction and possible harmonic continuations.

7. *Writing:* Realize the following ground bass adapted from the Handel Chaconne (example 5.1) in three parts (two upper parts plus the given bass), using mostly sixteenth notes. Try to saturate one of the upper parts with one or two of the motives shown in example 5.4. Inversions of the motives can be used as well.

Example 5.11. (After Handel)

CHORALE PRELUDES

The technique of using one or several commonplace motives against a given harmonic progression is frequently employed in chorale preludes, with the harmonic progression taken from the chorale harmonization. We think that in a chorale prelude the composer starts with the chorale tune, conceives a harmonization, and then fills in the other parts, scattering a handful of motives about as often as possible.

In example 5.12 the chorale tune appears in the soprano. An unusual feature of this setting is that the first two notes of the tune, B and G (circled in the example), are embellished with the motives that are used later throughout the setting. The bass line makes use of a number of the motives we have discussed earlier in combination with some new ones. We have labeled all the motives in the example. Note that the harmony on the last eighth of m. 1 is *not* a ii^6/4 chord. Rather, the E in the

Example 5.12. (Johann Gottfried Walther, "Liebster Jesu, wir sind hier" [Dearest Jesus, we are here], mm. 1–5) *The arrow in m. 4 signals a deviation from strict style. "I (f)" stands for "the inversion of motive f."*

bass is an ascending passing tone against the seventh of the V chord in the soprano. Also note that the last note of motive a in m. 4 is changed. Alterations of this sort are quite common, as we shall discuss next.

MOTIVIC VARIATION

Walther's saturation of the phrase above with just four unaltered motives is unusual; more often we find composers varying the motives in specific ways. While the core of each commonplace motive generally remains unaltered, the boundary notes may be varied. This makes the motive more flexible and appropriate in more harmonic contexts than the motives in example 5.4. In addition, the first note may be replaced by a sixteenth-note rest (however, in strict style, remember that the first note after a rest must be consonant).

Example 5.13 shows how Bach uses motive a from example 5.4. He uses four different final notes, as shown in example 5.14, and he often eliminates the first note altogether. (We have indicated adjustments of this sort in example 5.14 with a vertical dotted line between the adjusted note and the rest of the motive.) In example 5.13, the first note of the motive (the second sixteenth note) can be the same as the downbeat note or it can be the resolution of a dissonance on the downbeat (m. 4). Provide a harmonic analysis of example 5.13, label all instances of motive a, and label all NHTs on every step in the alto, tenor, and bass.

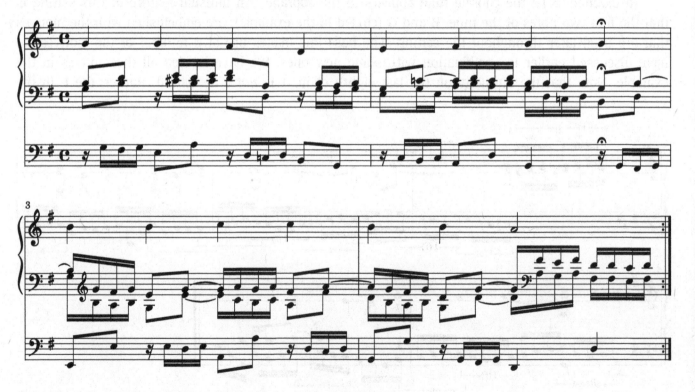

Example 5.13. (Bach, "Alle Menschen müssen sterben," mm. 1–4)

Example 5.14. (Bach) *Alterations of the last melodic interval of motive a.*

EXERCISE 5-F

1. *Analysis:* Do a harmonic analysis of example 5.12.

2. *Analysis:* Do a harmonic analysis of example 5.15 like the one you did for example 5.12. Identify the motives from example 5.4 (and their inversion, if applicable) that are used in example 5.15. Label all motives and NHTs in the example. Note one deviation from strict style. Then list each motive separately, using the format of example 5.14 above, and show the various alterations of the last and/or first melodic intervals.

3. *Writing/improvisation:* The bass lines in example 5.16 are chorale tunes. Compose a single

Example 5.15. (Friedrich Wilhelm Zachau, "Jesu meine Freude," mm. 1–6)

line above each, using motives from example 5.4 exclusively. We recommend that you write a simple four-part realization as a first step, and then add motives and embellishments. Do not alter any of the motives except for the last note, and then only if you are making elisions between motives. If you are writing, label the motives, provide a harmonic analysis, and label all NHTs. Try to put a motive on every beat and try to use as few different motives as possible.

Example 5.16a. ("Ein' feste Burg ist unser Gott")

Example 5.16b. ("Der Herr ist mein getreuer Hirt")

Example 5.16c. ("Nun komm, der Heiden Heiland")

4. *Writing:* Show all the possibilities in which the three motives given in example 5.17 can be placed in the given chorale harmonization of "Herr Christ, der ein'ge Gottes-Sohn" in example 5.18. The motives have to be used in strict style only. Each motive may be preceded by a note or sixteenth rest, but the first note after the sixteenth rest must be consonant. The sixteenth rest must always be on the onset of the quarter. The beginning has been done for you as a sample. Notate each possibility on a page of empty staves and in one register only (with the understanding that it could be used in other registers as well). Indicate if a motive cannot be used in the bass and indicate which motives take the place of the bass. Show the Roman numerals for the chorale harmonization and label the chord factors and NHTs. Measures 8–10 are identical with mm. 2–4 and need not be filled in.

Example 5.17.

Example 5.18. ("Herr Christ, der ein'ge Gottes-Sohn")

5. *Writing:* Using a chorale melody from those given in chapter 3, model on Walther's example 5.12. First decide on a harmonization (or use the one you made in chapter 3); then add a bass line consisting as much as possible of two or three motives; finally, add an alto voice to fill out the harmonies. You may find that as you add motives, you experience a desire to change the harmonization you had originally planned. This is a normal part of composing, and you should feel free to respond to these urges; sometimes the lines have a life of their own.

6. *Writing:* Using the harmonization of the first six measures of "Ach, was soll ich Sünder machen?" ("What am I, a sinner, to do?") given in example 5.19 and the suggested sixteenth-note motives in example 5.20, write a four-part organ chorale prelude. The chorale melody must be in the soprano. Do not change the chorale melody or the given harmonization. Choose two from the five motives listed in example 5.20 and use them as accompanimental motives throughout, except on the last chord of m. 6. ("Throughout" means that there has to be at least one of the two motives on *every* quarter, except in situations where neither of them *can* be used. Indicate if this is the case.) You and

your teacher may wish to limit the choice of motives to d and e that are easier to work with. Motives should be used in the pedal part as well. When it is not using a motive, the pedal part should move in eighth notes or in longer note values. Write your prelude as an organ score (see example 5.13) and make sure it is playable.

Example 5.19. (Chorale harmonization)

Example 5.20. (Motives)

7. *Composing from scratch:* Compose a three-part chorale prelude modeled on Walther's example 5.12, where the motives occur in the bass and the alto is filler. Your chorale prelude has to be playable!

CHORALE CANTUS FIRMUS IN LONGER NOTE VALUES

In many chorale preludes the chorale tune is augmented to sound in longer note values (most commonly half notes, but other longer note values are possible too). As a result, more than one motive can appear against each note of the cantus firmus. In the following example, the chorale tune "Ich ruf' zu dir, Herr Jesu Christ" ("I call to you, Lord Jesus Christ") moves in half notes in the soprano. The middle and bass voice use motives from our list, some of which are inverted and/or altered at either end. Note that motive j contains the dissonance and the resolution of a suspension. One deviation from strict style has been indicated with an arrow. Do a harmonic analysis and label all motives.

Example 5.21. (Johann Pachelbel, "Ich ruf' zu dir, Herr Jesu Christ," mm. 4–8)

Example 5.22. (Pachelbel, "Durch Adams Fall," mm. 4–8)

The chorale tune in the soprano of example 5.22 is also augmented, moving in half notes. The two added parts again use motives we have discussed earlier. Note that in m. 6 Pachelbel uses an augmented version of the altered motive h in the bass, and the harmony changes in the course of the motive. Do a harmonic analysis and label all motives.

In the following example (5.23) the chorale tune in the soprano moves again in half notes. You will recognize most of the motives used against this tune, but now they all move in eighth rather than sixteenth notes. In other words, both the note values of the tune and the motives set against it are augmented. Do a harmonic analysis, label all the motives, and mark deviations from strict style.

Example 5.23. (Pachelbel, "Der Tag, der ist so freudenreich")

RETROGRADE AND RETROGRADE INVERSION

You can generate even more motives from the list in example 5.4 by retrograding and retrograde-inverting them. Because in some cases not all five notes are easy to work with, we will focus on the four sixteenths that are the core of the motive. Not all of the motives derived this way are equally well suited for practical use, as you will see. Example 5.24a takes the four sixteenth notes of a motive and shows its inversion, retrograde, and retrograde inversion (note that the original here is the inversion of motive c in example 5.4). In example 5.24b, Zachau uses all four forms of the motive. Find and label them P = prime, I = inversion, R = retrograde, and RI = retrograde inversion; provide a harmonic analysis; and note a few deviations from strict style.

Example 5.24a.

Example 5.24b. (Zachau, "Herzlich tut mich verlangen") *The chorale tune proper (in the top voice) does not enter until the third measure, but during the first measure and a half, the first note of the middle voice on each beat spells out the chorale tune with embellishments, and the bass sounds a transposition of the tune.*

OTHER MOTIVES

So far we have only worked with motives that subdivide the quarter-note beat into four sixteenth notes. There are many other possible patterns, and we will only consider two more examples here. In example 5.25, Walther employs a motive of an eighth followed by two sixteenth notes marked "K" in m. 1. The motive appears inverted in m. 2 as indicated. The chorale tune in the soprano moves in half notes. Do a harmonic analysis and label all motives. Keep in mind that the first note of the motive and the first note on the next beat may be changed. Indicate with a dotted line if this is the case.

Example 5.25. (Walther, "Ach was soll ich Sünder machen?" var. e, mm. 1–5)

The next excerpt (example 5.26) is in compound triple meter. The chorale tune is the same as in example 5.12 above, but this time the "step" is the dotted quarter. Do a harmonic analysis and identify the motives that recur. Label them m, n, o, and so on. Remember that motives that are related under I, R, and RI must be assigned the same letter name. Note that since three-note motives are often paired together repeatedly, you could identify new six-note motives that last for two steps. This is much more efficient.

Example 5.26. (Walther, "Liebster Jesu, wir sind hier," var. b, mm. 1–10)

EXERCISE 5-G

1. *Analysis:* Do a harmonic analysis of the following excerpt, label all motives, and mark deviation(s) from strict style.

Example 5.27. (Bach, Cantata 4, v. 1, mm. 30–35, vocal parts and continuo only)

2. *Writing (short):* Produce the retrograde and retrograde inversion of the core of motives b, c, d, e, g, and i from example 5.4. (The retrograde and retrograde-inverted forms of examples 5.4a, h, and j occur much less frequently in repertoire.) You will notice that the retrograde of motive e is the same as its inversion, and the retrograde inversion is the same as the original. Because you have already used these forms in exercises, you need not use motive e here.

3. *Writing (short):* Harmonize the motives obtained in no. 2 as follows: Find a suitable bass note below each motive. Determine a suitable key. Choose a harmony that may follow, and find an appropriate bass and soprano note for the onset of that second harmony. Which motives do you like best?

4. *Writing (short):* Repeat the previous exercise and come up with a second solution for each motive.

5. *Writing (short):* String together two motives chosen from no. 2 above, example 5.4, or exercise 5-E, no. 1 and harmonize the result. Provide the bass notes and the harmonic analysis.

6. Continue as in exercise 5-E, no. 6, continuing the lines you made in no. 5 above, feeling out their sense of direction and possible harmonic continuations.

THE RULE OF THE OCTAVE

A popular tool, used from around 1700 on for the harmonization of a given bass line, is the "rule of the octave." This device consists of a model harmonization of an ascending and descending scale in the bass, to be memorized and then applied, in whole or in part, whenever the occasion arises.[2] Examples 5.28 and 5.29 show different versions in major and minor. There are further alternatives found in the repertoire. Note how some authors show the ascending and descending scale in the bass running between the tonic and its upper octave (François Campion and Fedele Fenaroli in examples 5.28a and 5.29a–b)—hence the term *rule of the octave*—while others show different segments from the scale (Johann David Heinichen and Francesco Gasparini in examples 5.28b–c and 5.29c–d). Also take note that some of the seventh chords are not used in strict style because the sevenths cannot be prepared. Exceptionally, you are allowed to use such unprepared sevenths in the rest of this chapter,

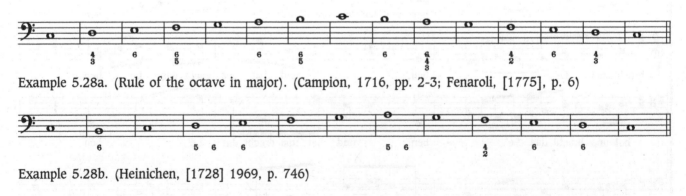

Example 5.28a. (Rule of the octave in major). (Campion, 1716, pp. 2-3; Fenaroli, [1775], p. 6)

Example 5.28b. (Heinichen, [1728] 1969, p. 746)

Example 5.28c. (As reported in Heinichen, [1728] 1969, p. 763)

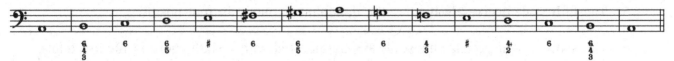

Example 5.29a. (Rule of the octave in minor). (Campion, 1716, pp. 2-3)

Example 5.29b. (Fenaroli, [1775], p. 7)

Example 5.29c. (Heinichen, [1728] 1969, p. 746)

Example 5.29d. (As reported in Heinichen, [1728] 1969, p. 763)

as long as they are part of rule of the octave progressions. Keep in mind, however, that Heinichen's and Gasparini's progressions *are* available in strict style because the seventh of the dominant seventh chord in the descending scale is introduced as a passing tone, on the fourth scale degree in the bass (compare with example 4.12, mm. 2 and 4).

François Campion explains how we are to use the rule: "For the accompaniment, one has to consider in which octave [i.e., key] one is, and on which note above the first scale degree, [and whether one is] ascending or descending in the harmonic progression; it's the safest and easiest way to find the necessary chord, and I don't believe that until now anything more general and simpler has been proposed."[3] The basic principle behind the rule of the octave is that the first and fifth scale degrees carry the tonic and dominant harmony, respectively, in root position, while the remaining scale degrees have various versions of triads and seventh chords. When you memorize these progressions, keep in mind the following:

1. The first scale degree in the bass always carries the tonic triad in root position.

2. Ascending or descending, the second scale degree always has a dominant-functioning harmony (vii°⁶ or V⁴/³).

3. The third scale degree always has the tonic triad in first inversion.

4. In the ascending bass, the fourth scale degree has a predominant chord (ii⁶, ii⁶/⁵, or IV in major; ii°⁶, ii°⁶/⁵, or iv in minor) because it is followed by the dominant harmony, while in the descending bass the fourth scale degree is always harmonized as V⁴/². It follows the dominant harmony on the fifth scale degree and continues to the tonic harmony in first inversion.

5. The fifth scale degree always has the dominant harmony in root position.

6. The sixth scale degree is almost always harmonized with a sixth chord in the ascending scale (IV⁶, Gasparini has vii°⁶/V in major). In the descending scale, the sixth scale degree has a predominant sixth chord (IV⁶ or iv⁶ in major or minor, respectively), a secondary dominant (V⁴/³/V or vii°⁶/V in major, or French augmented sixth chord in minor), or, in minor, a predominant ii°⁴/³ chord.

7. When ascending, the seventh scale degree has V⁶ or V⁶/⁵, resolving to the tonic. When descending, the seventh scale degree carries a first inversion dominant harmony without the seventh (V⁶ in major, v⁶ in minor), because the following chord is not a tonic harmony.

Most of the time, composers use only fragments of the rule of the octave.[4] The opening from the Courante by Élisabeth Jacquet de la Guerre shown in example 5.30, for instance, employs two segments from the progression, one moving up from the fourth to the sixth scale degree in the bass and the other descending from the sixth scale degree down to the seventh scale degree, as shown by the brackets. The model for this is Heinichen's version (example 5.29c) and, to some extent, Gasparini's (example 5.29d). Note that the A in the bass toward the end of m. 2 is used as a passing tone, rather than the root of the tonic triad.

Example 5.30. (Élisabeth Jacquet de la Guerre, Courante from Suite in A minor, the shortest step is the quarter)

Have you ever wondered how Christoph Willibald Gluck came up with the amazing melody in Orfeo's famous aria from *Orfeo ed Euridice* shown in example 5.31? As it turns out, the passage is largely based on segments from the rule of the octave, as we have bracketed in the example. Measures 7–9 move through the first five scale degrees of the rule (see circled C–D–E–F–G in the cello/ double bass part). Measures 12–13 present the same harmonic progression at a faster speed, as do mm. 14–15, now in *forte* (see circled bass notes). And as we can see in mm. 10–12, even two notes in the bass can be taken as a rule of the octave segment (I⁶–V⁴/³ over E–D). All this accounts for the smooth harmonic progression underlying the melody. Note how Gluck inserts the root of the V⁷ on the second beat of m. 8 but otherwise uses a complete segment from the rule of the octave between the first and fifth scale degree in the bass of the first three measures. The root of the V⁷ is also inserted on the second beat of mm. 11 and 12. Note that the F in the first violin and voice at the end of m.

Example 5.31. (Christoph Willibald Gluck, "Che farò senza Euridice?" from Orfeo ed Euridice, mm. 7–16, "What will I do without Euridice? Where will I go without my love?")

13 deviates from strict style (unprepared seventh), as does the G in the first violin and voice on the downbeat of m. 9 (suspension that resolves upward). Circle and label all other embellishments.

If a movement modulates, the rule of the octave may occur in different keys. This is the case in the following figured bass by Fenaroli. Mm. 1–4 are in G minor, with the notes we have bracketed harmonized according to the rule of the octave. Mm. 5–7 are in the relative major (B flat major) and use the rule of the octave as marked. After a stretch in C minor in mm. 8–9, the movement returns to G minor. Identify rule of the octave segments in mm. 8–16 and bracket the corresponding bass notes.

Example 5.32. (Fenaroli, Partimenti, Book I, No. 2, Gj 1302)

EXERCISE 5-H

1. *Improvisation and writing:* Realize the rule of the octave progressions in examples 5.28b–c and 5.29c–d (Heinichen and Gasparini) in three parts, keyboard style (i.e., with the two upper parts in the right hand). Then transpose the progressions into all major and minor keys with up to four sharps or flats in the key signature.

2. *Improvisation and writing:* Realize the rule of the octave progressions in examples 5.28a–c and 5.29a–d in four parts, keyboard style (i.e., with the three upper parts in the right hand). Then transpose the progressions into all major and minor keys with up to four sharps or flats in the key signature.

3. *Improvisation:* Play one of the progressions from the previous exercise and ask the class to identify which version of the rule of the octave you picked.

4. *Writing:* Take your realizations in three parts of the rule of the octave according to Heinichen and Gasparini in no. 1 above and expand the right-hand parts into a compound melody.

5. *Improvisation and writing:* Realize the figured bass shown in example 5.33. Proceed as follows: (1) identify the keys, (2) look out for rule of the octave segments and bracket the corresponding bass notes, (3) identify the scale degrees in the rule of the octave segments, and (4) harmonize the example in three or four parts, keyboard style. Which versions of the rule of the octave does this example use? Note that the figures in the penultimate measure indicate a fake suspension.

Example 5.33. (Fenaroli, Partimenti, Book I, No. 1, Gj 1301)

6. *Improvisation and writing:* Harmonize the excerpt shown in example 5.34 in four parts using the rule of the octave. Improvise your solution or hand in your realization of the continuo part with figures added where necessary (i.e., where the harmony is not in root position).

Example 5.34. (Strozzi, Ritornello from Arie op. 8)

7. *Improvisation and writing:* Harmonize the unfigured bass shown in example 5.35 using the rule of the octave. Proceed as follows: (1) identify the key areas and cadential bass progressions, (2) look out for rule of the octave segments and bracket the corresponding bass notes, (3) identify the scale degrees in the rule of the octave segments, and (4) harmonize the example in three or four parts, keyboard style. You may use any of the rule of the octave versions. Note that in m. 11 the first quarter is divided into two steps.

Example 5.35. (Adapted from de la Guerre, Aria from Sonata for violin and harpsichord in A minor)

8. *Analysis:* Go back to examples 4.21–4.23 and identify rule of the octave segments by circling and bracketing the corresponding bass notes. In example 4.22 (Handel) there are some harmonizations we haven't seen yet in examples of the rule of the octave. What do you think are the reasons for these harmonizations?

9. *Analysis:* Go back to examples 5.1a and 5.2 and bracket segments from the rule of the octave, keeping in mind that some harmonies are embellished.

EXERCISE 5-I

Earlier in this chapter, we studied ways of enlivening a harmonic progression, such as that of a ground bass or a chorale, by placing repeating motives in it. In the following exercises we will now explore this idea with respect to the rule of the octave (harmonization of a scale in the bass) and in harmonizations of an ascending or descending scale in the soprano. We might wonder, for instance, in how many different ways the motive shown in example 5.36a can be placed above the scale in C major, harmonized according to the rule of the octave. Example 5.36b provides the answer, listing all possible placements of this motive against the rule of the octave shown on the bottom staff.

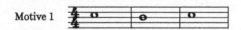

Example 5.36a.

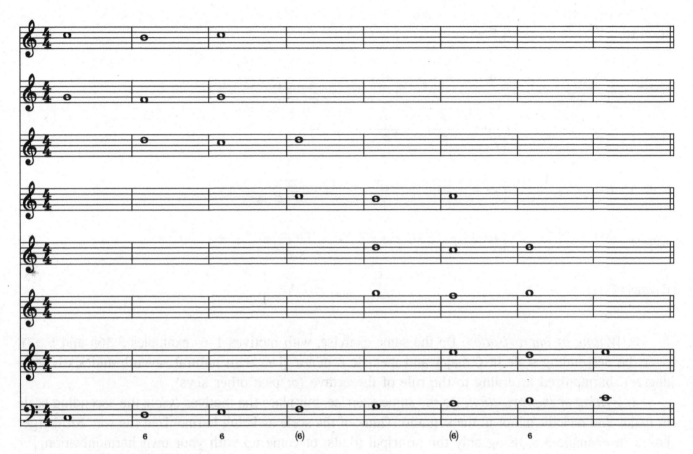

Example 5.36b. (whole note = step)

1. *Writing or improvisation:* Find all the possibilities in which motive 1 from example 5.36a above can be placed in one of the rule of the octave harmonizations of the ascending scale in melodic C minor. If you do this assignment in writing, produce a chart like the one in example 5.36b.

2. *Writing or improvisation:* Find all the possibilities in which motives 2–6 shown in example 5.37 can be placed in one of the rule of the octave harmonizations of the ascending scale in C major and melodic C minor. If you do this assignment in writing, again produce charts like the one in example 5.36b.

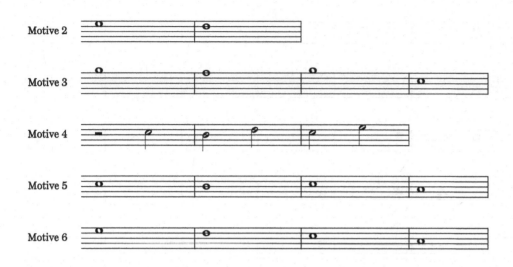

Example 5.37.

3. *Writing or improvisation:* Do the same exercise, with motives 1–6 (examples 5.36a and 5.37), over the descending scale in C major and melodic C minor (i.e., with natural seventh and sixth scale degree), harmonized according to the rule of the octave (or pick other keys).

4. *Writing or improvisation:* Do the same exercise, but place the motives *below* the ascending scale in major and melodic minor in the soprano. Think of the scale as being harmonized the way Kirnberger has it in example 3.6, using only the principal triads, or come up with your own harmonization.

5. *Writing or improvisation:* Do the same exercise as in no. 4, but place the motives below the descending scale in major and melodic minor in the soprano. Before you start, work out a good harmonic progression in major and melodic minor.

6. *Writing or improvisation:* Embellish each motive in examples 5.36a and 5.37 with motives from example 5.4, or their inversions. Augment the rhythms of the motives from example 5.4 so that the sixteenth note is now a quarter, because the step is now a whole note. Then redo exercises no. 1–5 (also for the ascending scale in the bass in major) with these embellished motives. There will be fewer possibilities. Why?

7. *Writing or improvisation:* Take a four-part realization of the rule of the octave from examples 5.28 or 5.29 and embellish the three upper parts, sprinkling them with motives (rhythmically augmented as in the previous exercise) from example 5.4.

NOTES

1. Niedt, *Musicalische Handleitung*, vol. 2, I, pp. 1–3.
2. For more detailed discussions of the rule of the octave, its historical sources, and its applications, see Gjerdingen, *Music in the Galant Style*, pp. 467–70, 472; Holtmeier, "Heinichen, Rameau, and the Italian Thoroughbass Tradition"; Rotem and Curtice, "The Rule of the Octave"; Sánchez-Kisielewska, "The Rule of the Octave in First-Year Undergraduate Theory"; Sanguinetti, *The Art of Partimento*.
3. Campion, *Traité d'accompagnement*. Our translation.
4. For good examples, see Rotem and Curtice, "The Rule of the Octave."

6

IMITATION AT THE UNISON OR OCTAVE

Imitative Trio Sonata Openings; Tips for Good Three-Part Writing; Inverted Chords and Substitute Chords; Total Reharmonization; Openings of Keyboard Dances and Inventions

IMITATIVE TRIO SONATA OPENINGS

One of the most characteristic textures of the Baroque is the trio sonata. A trio sonata is actually played by four people: two melody instruments (or voices) and the continuo group, which consists of a chordal instrument and a bass line instrument. The texture is called a trio because only three parts are written down; the player of the chordal instrument improvises, looking at the bass part, which is usually provided with figures that indicate which chords are to be played (hence the term *figured bass*).

Trio sonatas often begin as follows: a progression, played by the continuo group, supports a single melody (played by an instrument or sung)—then the progression, often with the same bass line, repeats while another voice or instrument enters with the same melody. The second voice or instrument, by repeating what the first played, creates an imitative texture. When the second part enters, the first continues, sounding new material, a countermelody (called "melody 2" in example 6.1). The harmonic progression is repeated *periodically* (in phrases or segments of the same length called *periods*).

The repeating periodic progression reminds us of the ground bass pieces we saw in the last chapter, but there, only a single voice sounds above the continuo group, and it may or may not repeat melodic material, while here, the second period is enriched by the thicker texture and the often surprising entry of the repeating melody. In other ways, this texture is like the canon at the unison that we saw in chapter 2: as each new voice enters, the voices that are already in sound countermelodies, new chord factors of the same progression. However, in a trio sonata, we usually hear the first melody only twice before the composer moves on to other ideas. We can schematize the trio sonata opening as follows. The major compositional challenge here, as in the canon, is how to continue the first melody, tacking on melody 2 with its other set of chord factors, in a convincing way.

1st instrument	Melody 1———————	Melody 2 '''''''''''''''''''''''
2nd instrument	(Rests)	Melody 1———————
Continuo: Keyboard	*****************	*****************
Bass line	*****************	*****************
	Progression	Progression repeated
	........Period 1........	........Period 2.........:

Example 6.1.

In our first three examples, the bass line repeats exactly, as it does in ground bass pieces, and the second voice imitates the first at the octave below. In all three, the bass has a clearly "instrumental" character (that is, it's hard to sing), as opposed to the smooth upper parts. In each example, the harmonic period has been labeled beneath the bass line, as well as the component melodies.

The first example comes from one of the famous psalm paraphrases by Benedetto Marcello that Mattheson admired. The opening resembles a ground bass piece with a two-measure period played by the continuo alone. The majestic, dotted rhythm of the bass in 4/2 meter, the emphasis on perfect vertical intervals, the octave singing in repeated notes, and the slow declamation, all reflect the severity of the Old Testament text ("ormai Signore questi nemici apprendano . . . ["by this time, Lord, these enemies are learning . . ."]). A fourth period begins normally, but in m. 8 the suspended A is now part of an applied dominant to E (a substitute chord). After the half cadence, the "ground bass" will start over in the dominant, not shown here.

Example 6.2. (Benedetto Marcello)

The next example, also from a Marcello psalm paraphrase, likewise begins with a continuo introduction. This introduction, however, differs slightly from the bass that sounds under the imitating upper voices. This introduction ends on the tonic, and makes a slightly clumsy joint with the first period, which begins on the tonic. But it sets the tone, resembling gentle undulations of waves ("He leads me to the banks of quiet and clear water which restore me and sweetly extinguish my thirst"). The imitating upper voices are part of a progression in two-bar periods. Why do you think the bass changes in the third period (m. 9)? This example is continued so you can see more of the context. We'll discuss mm. 13ff later, in chapter 8.

Example 6.3. (Marcello)

The next example ("Is this how you feel sorry for me?") is by Agostino Steffani. A simple tonic-prolongational progression two beats long is sounded in two voices, then repeated in three. The continuation of the second voice (m. 3) is harmonized differently, perhaps to break the monotony of root-position chords: the i chord on "mi" is in first inversion, and the B in the melody, instead of being a dissonant passing tone as it was in the previous period, is supported by a passing chord. Thus a faster progression, in quarter notes, is inserted into one that moves in dotted half notes, suddenly speeding up the harmonic rhythm (mm. 5 and 6 are included to show how the basic idea is repeated in the relative major after a modulatory progression—see chapter 8).

Example 6.4. (Agostino Steffani)

TIPS FOR GOOD THREE-PART WRITING

Before we move on to writing exercises, here are some principles from Mattheson that you can keep in mind when writing in three parts:

1. Try to sound all three chord factors in each chord. (Marcello's example 6.2 is weak in this regard.) Rameau says that "when you compose in three parts, you have to make the chords complete as much as possible . . . the [interval of the] octave being used only seldom, except . . . in perfect cadences, where all the parts normally end on the tonic note."[1] It is best to include the third at the expense of the fifth: Kirnberger says that "the third can never be omitted from the harmony."[2]

2. Don't be punctilious about principle 1. Mattheson says example 6.5a has a poor melody in the middle voice, trying to get complete triads; b is acceptable and c is the best, even though only one chord is complete.

Example 6.5. (Mattheson) *Examples of tips for good three-part writing.*

3. Of example 6.5d, Mattheson says: "Since the bass in some sense competes with the upper voice for predominance, in a trio two tend to work against one. That is to say, usually the two lower voices keep company and provide a counterweight to the upper [voice] because the latter already reigns sufficiently, and would overpower the bass if its forces were to be doubled. Since the rougher [lower] sounds do not enter our ears as noticeably as the finer [higher] ones it is better to reinforce the lower than the upper parts. . . . But, where nothing *concertato* is needed, and where only a steady harmonic progression is required, things are different. In this case the two upper parts can be coordinated in their motions because they are not in a fight with the lowest part."[3] In other words, he says that if the two upper parts move together, the bass will sound like mere harmonic support; he suggests that if the bass is to be heard as an independent (concertato) part, it will need to be in rhythmic unison with the second line.

4. If you have a suspension in one voice, don't also syncopate in both of the other voices; at least one voice needs to be marking the regular metric "steps" at all times. Kirnberger says: "If the embellishments in one voice make the metric movement unclear, then another voice will have to make it clear. If, for example, in 4/4, one voice has half or

whole notes, then another voice must have quarter notes. . . . [example 6.6] can serve as an example. Since in each of the first two measures there is no motion in the bass, it [the meter] is determined by the upper voice; however, in the fourth measure it becomes clear in the bass, and in the third measure in both parts. The metric movement is expressed most easily and most certainly by the bass notes. And the composer needs to treat this aspect with caution because otherwise his part-writing will become confused. Mainly, wherever the movement is obscured through ties in one voice, it must be made clear in another voice, as at the asterisks."[4]

Example 6.6. (Kirnberger)

5. Never have a voice enter (i.e., after a silence) on a note that is dissonant with the harmony prevailing on the step. Another part could be in mid-suspension, however, and this is considered a good thing.

Example 6.7. (Bach, B minor Mass, "Et expecto") *Disregard the free style F-sharp in the bass (circled) at the end of the third measure of this example.*

EXERCISE 6-A

1. *Composing (short):* Mattheson repeatedly recommends that the teacher choose a good piece, copy only one or two voices, and let the student add the missing voice or voices on blank staves. That is what you will do in the following exercises. In some, suggestions for the rhythm of the added part have been offered, which you or your teacher may decide to use or not. You may want to do some in class for practice; they need not take long.

If you are given the bass, you must (1) find the repeating period (note that the basses may be figured or unfigured—you may add figures), (2) compose a line for the first voice over the first period, (3) imitate that melody at the octave or unison in the second voice over the second period, and (4) compose a continuation (countermelody) in the first voice.

If you are given the upper voices, you must compose a bass line that works in both periods. If the continuation of the first voice is not given, compose it as well.

Example 6.8. (Exercises)

Suggested rhythm for upper parts: ♩ ♪ | ♩. ♫ ♩ etc.

Why so full of grief, O my soul?

Why so full of grief, O my soul?

Example 6.8. *(Concluded)*

2. *Improvisation and keyboard harmony:* The teacher might play the bass for one period alone, then have one student improvise a melody over the first period. The rest of the class can memorize that line. Then the first student can sing alone over the first period, and the class can enter singing the same line in the second period while the first student improvises a counterpoint. The first student has to know what will go with the first improvised line!

INVERTED CHORDS AND SUBSTITUTE CHORDS

Kirnberger says: "Whoever is in command of harmony can always use other harmonies or inversions of the original harmonies in places where the same melody is repeated."[5] The following examples, like those above, imitate at the unison or octave, but the bass is varied in some way, either by different inversions of the same harmony or by different harmonies. The following example shows a simple change of chord inversion: the third chord in the first period is in first inversion, but in the second period it is in root position. Presumably, Marcello did this to have parallel thirds and more imperfect consonance at the beginning, features that are given to the continuation of the first tenor.

Example 6.9. (Marcello, "Therefore you deign to guide my steps") *Which rule of Kirnberger's does Marcello break in mm. 4–5? What justification can you offer?*

The next example shows three changes: the root position tonic in the first period is replaced by the submediant at the beginning of the second period, the ii$^{4/2}$ chord in the first period is replaced by ii$^{6/5}$ in the second, and the V^6 in the first is replaced by V in root position. These are very common substitutions. The E-flat–D suspension in the first measure is so interesting that Marcello lets the countermelody have it in the second period—the bass provides harmonic support while the alto gets the good line.

Example 6.10. (Marcello, "I am covered beneath so much misery")

More substitute harmonies are illustrated in the next example, by Steffani. The first period has a modulation to the relative major (B-flat) on "miei lamenti" (hatched area), with the E-flat–D of the soprano providing the seventh of the F chord and the third of the B-flat tonic. But the second time this modulation is replaced by a iv–i prolongational progression, with the corresponding tenor E-flat–D acting as third and fifth. Note that there is a little transition (circled) from the end of the first period back to the tonic at the start of the second; such transitions are common if there has been a move away from the tonic, but we will not model on them for now.

Example 6.11. (Steffani, "My laments don't have the strength")

When the bass line repeats exactly, the first melody note in each period is the same chord factor above the bass, as shown in the following hypothetical example (6.12a), where the note on the first word of the melody ("Deh") is the fifth factor of a tonic chord. What Steffani actually wrote, however, is shown in example 6.12b, where he has made a substitution for the first chord of the second period at the entry of the second voice. If Steffani had wanted the second voice to begin with the same chord factor, he would have had to wait until a tonic arrival on a downbeat, as in example 6.12a. However, he has *telescoped* the second entry with the end of the first. He can do this because the melody begins on the fifth scale degree, which can be *either* the fifth of the tonic chord *or* the root of the dominant chord. Such telescoping prevents the overly obvious stop-and-start effect of a tonic chord at the end of the first period and another at the beginning of the second. Here the end of the first period is *elided* with the beginning of the second.

We have analyzed the periods as overlapping, but we could also have analyzed them in terms of the melodies alone, in which case we would have two shorter periods, as bracketed underneath in example 6.12c. This analysis is better because it permits us to see how the V chord at the beginning of the second period substitutes for the tonic harmony in the first period (shown with a dotted arrow).

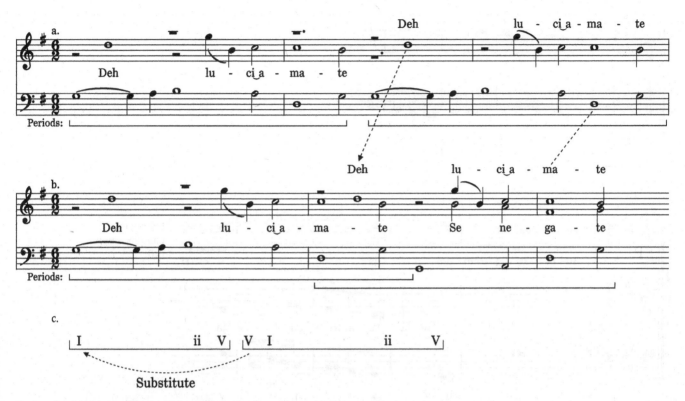

Example 6.12. (Steffani, "Ah, beloved eyes, if you deny . . .")

TOTAL REHARMONIZATION

Finally, here are a couple of substitutions that amount to total reharmonizations. As shown in example 6.13a, Marcello's melodies might have been harmonized with a simple i–V–i progression both times. However, Marcello variously substitutes VI and vii⁷/V for i (example 6.13b), probably to paint "tremendous anger." He can do this because the root and third degree of C minor can also serve as fifth and seventh chord factors of VII⁷/V.

a.

b.

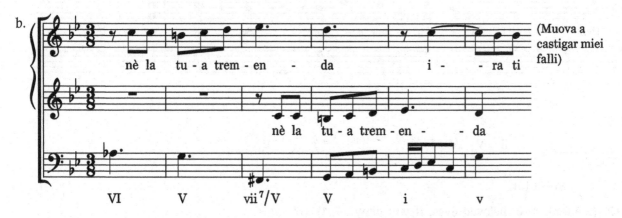

Example 6.13. (Marcello, "In your tremendous anger you are moved to punish my weakness") *This section is not the beginning of a piece, so he can start this phrase on VI.*

EXERCISE 6-B

1. *Composing (short):* The following exercises are like the preceding ones but involve inverted chords, substitute chords, and/or telescoping. When you are given the bass only, it may not be as immediately obvious where the periods are. In some cases the moments of entry are given with arrows to help you out. Remember that some of these basses may be unfigured.

Example 6.14.

2. *Composing from scratch:* Write a trio sonata opening.

3. *Composing from scratch:* Write a trio sonata opening according to the following scheme (model on examples 6.3 and 6.4).

Table 6.1

Inst. 1	Mel. 1	Mel. 2	Free	(Rest)	Mel. 1
Inst. 2	(Rest)	Mel. 1	Free	Mel. 1	Mel. 2
Bass	Progression in I	Progression in I	Modulation to near key (V if major, III if minor)	Progression in V (or III)	Progression in V (or III)

OPENINGS OF KEYBOARD DANCES AND INVENTIONS

These genres feature imitation at the unison or octave and the repetition of a progression, like the ground basses and the trio sonatas we saw in the previous chapter and in the beginning of this chapter. However, they are often in only two parts, and projecting a harmonic progression clearly is more difficult in so thin a texture. Composers compensate for this by using arpeggiation and compound melody a good deal to supply more chord factors, and often the themes are quite short, simply alternating tonic and dominant harmonies. Nevertheless, we still find a fair amount of harmonic ambiguity in these pieces.

One of the most common vehicles for imitation is the gigue movement of a suite. In the following example by Handel, the first two measures alternate tonic and dominant harmony. The first note might be part of a i chord or a V chord—we can only find out by looking ahead; at the end of the second beat of m. 1 we see that it is part of a V chord. If you are unsure how to interpret a note in a one-voice texture, it is helpful to look ahead at a multivoiced setting of the same tune. Here, what we called melody 1 and melody 2 have been labeled a, b, and so on. After the first two periods, Handel continues meandering between the chord factors of tonic and dominant harmonies, loosely using the principle of canon.

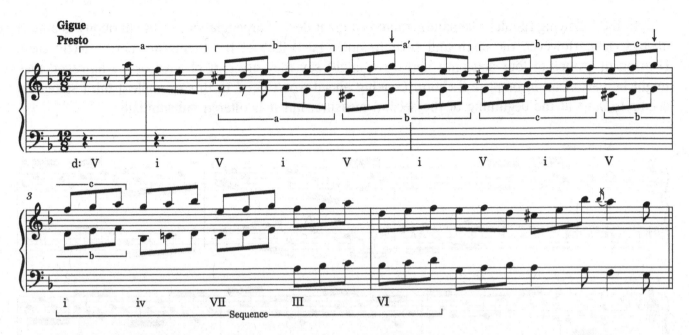

Example 6.15. (Handel) *Measures 3–4 are provided for the discussion of sequences in chapter 12. Note unprepared sevenths at arrows.*

In this well-known Bach invention, the tonic harmony alternates with vii⁷. The first melody is restated after the first two periods, but an octave higher—with the rise of melody b in mm. 3 and 4—giving the opening of the upper voice a strong dynamic progression in register. Note that melody b is first above melody a, then below it (varied, hence our label b').

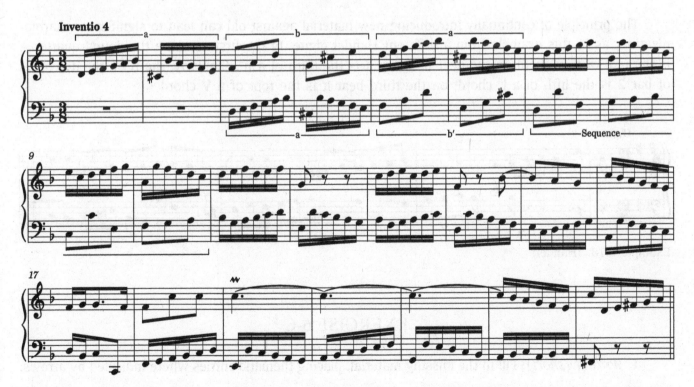

Example 6.16. (Bach, D minor invention) *Mm. 11–14 have been printed here for the discussion of sequences in Chapter 12.*

In the following Handel Allemande, there is a great deal of arpeggiation, so the harmony is almost always clear. However, the sixth and seventh notes (G–B-flat) of the theme are not perfectly clear. Hearing in groups of four sixteenth notes, we might say they are part of a vii or V^7; however, they might be part of an incomplete ii chord. Looking ahead won't help! In this example a third statement seems to start at the beginning of the second measure, but it is altered substantially.

Example 6.17. (Handel) *Note that the apparent move from E to D-flat in the left hand of m. 2 is the result of compound melody. The C goes to the D-flat and the E doesn't resolve. The continuation has been provided for the discussion of sequences in chapter 12. Note deviations from strict style.*

The principle of continually introducing new material against old can lead to significant reharmonization, as in this example from a different Handel gigue. In the first measure the dotted quarter A is the root of a iv chord; in the next measure it is the third of a ii^6. Similarly, the B on the downbeat of bar 2 is the fifth of a i^6 chord; on the third beat it is the root of a V chord.

Example 6.18. (Handel)

EXERCISE 6-C

1. *Writing (short):* Fill in the missing material, placing thematic entries where indicated by arrows.

Example 6.19. *The implied 6/4 on the weak part of the first beat of m. 3 is allowed after a rest as an arpeggiation presuming an implied G on the downbeat and because the fourth above is not actually sounded (see chapter 4).*

2. *Composing:* Using the themes given in example 6.20, compose two-part keyboard invention openings three or four measures long. The melody found in the first measure in the right hand should be imitated an octave below in the left hand in the second measure, while the continuation in the right hand should use a different rhythm to add some variety. Write one measure of free material and a cadence (see chapter 13). Try to vary rhythmic values and avoid rhythmic homophony (i.e., both parts moving together rhythmically). Your composition should show motivic coherence. It should include at least some passages of compound melody and should not use exclusively tonic and dominant chords. Remember that arpeggiated 6/4 chords can be used more freely in two parts.

Example 6.20a.

Example 6.20b.

Example 6.20c.

Example 6.20d.

3. *Composing:* Write a short theme, present it in the right hand, imitate it an octave lower in the left hand, compose a continuation in the right, and imitate that an octave lower in the left, and so forth, progressing as in example 6.15.

4. *Composing:* Write a short theme, present it in the right hand, imitate it an octave lower in the left hand, compose a continuation in the right, and repeat the first theme an octave higher, as in example 6.16.

5. *Composing (short):* Write a short theme, present it in the right hand, imitate it an octave lower in the left hand, compose a continuation in the right, and reharmonize the continuation in the left hand by adding members of different chords above, as in example 6.18.

6. *Composing (long):* Write a trio sonata opening, using the "unpack the box" method discussed in chapter 2. The process is illustrated in example 6.21, using the Boulanger cadential progression in chapter 2.

- *Step 1:* Compose a cadential progression in four parts.

- *Step 2:* Choose one part other than the bass line and present it as a theme in the right hand over the bass line in the left hand. You may add embellishments to make the theme more interesting. This is your first period. Repeat the bass line and the right-hand theme. This is your second entry. Go back to your four-part harmonization and select one of the two hitherto unused melodies or make up a new melody. Add that melody to your second entry in the voice that sounded the first entry.

- *Step 3:* Add a free continuation in three parts following the second entry that leads into a cadence (here, it is a vii^6 cadence).

Example 6.21.

7. *Writing or improvisation:* Go back to chapter 5, example 5.36b, and look for instances where the motive repeats at the unison or octave. Turn each of these instances into a trio sonata opening where the imitation at the unison/octave is harmonized over the rule of the octave. Proceed as follows: (1) Assign the motive to one of the two upper voices and its imitation at the unison or octave to the other upper voice, over the ascending bass line. (2) If the first statement of the motive ends before the imitation enters, extend the motive so that the extension also works in imitation. If this is not possible, fill in free material. (3) Write or play a continuation in the first voice against the imitation

in the second. (4) See if that continuation, or parts of it, could be imitated in the second voice. If not, compose or improvise another continuation in the second voice. (5) Continue each upper voice to the end of the passage. If you improvise this exercise, you need to make sure that you can play both of the upper two parts in your right hand.

8. *Writing or improvisation:* Same exercise as no. 7, using the chart you came up with in Exercise 5-I, no. 1.

9. *Writing or improvisation:* Same exercise as no. 7 with motives 2–4 given in example 5.37, using the charts you came up with in Exercise 5-I, no. 2.

10. *Writing or improvisation:* Embellish the two upper parts in the trio sonata openings you came up with in nos. 7–9. You may use motives from example 5.4 or their inversions, augmented so that the sixteenth note is now a quarter, or any other embellishments in mixed or equal note values that you can think of. You must make sure that the embellishments you add to the opening motive also work in imitation.

NOTES

1. Rameau, *Traité de l'harmonie réduite à ses principes naturels*, III, 43, p. 329.
2. Kirnberger, *Die Kunst des reinen Satzes in der Musik*, p. 148.
3. Mattheson, *Der vollkommene Capellmeister*, III, 17, §§15–16.
4. Kirnberger, *Die Kunst*, I, 11, pp. 196–197.
5. Kirnberger, 10, p. 147.

7

IMITATION AT THE FIFTH

Why Imitate at the Fifth?; Imitation at the Fifth in Trio Sonatas; The Splice; Different Types of Splice; Not a Splice—The Modulation; Imitation at the Fifth in the Minor Mode; Note on Dorian and Mixolydian Key Signatures; Partimento Exercises

WHY IMITATE AT THE FIFTH?

The fifth is a structural interval of long standing. In sixteenth-century modal music, different adjacent voice ranges (e.g., tenor and alto) were a fifth apart. A note in the middle of the alto range is about a fifth away from a midrange note for the tenor. Thus the alto can sing the "same" tune as the tenor a fourth or fifth higher, and it will "sound" the same, at least in terms of degree of vocal comfort. The normal octave ranges of these adjacent voices are about a fifth apart, and so if one sang the range from D to D, the other would sing from A to A or G to G.

Another benefit of imitation at the fifth is that you can imitate exactly for a span of six notes without altering any notes in the diatonic arrangement. The medieval hexachord (ut re mi fa sol la) is the longest span that can be transposed without the use of accidentals. The hexachords on C and G, a fifth apart, have the identical tone and semitone positions, so imitation within those hexachords will be exact. To complete the major scale of the key a fifth above only requires one new note, the seventh degree.

In tonal music, imitation at the fifth is associated with a change of key. A statement in the tonic is followed by a statement in the dominant. In this way imitation at the fifth leads the music away from the tonic key, causing tonal development and requiring further continuation.

IMITATION AT THE FIFTH IN TRIO SONATAS

In the trio sonatas we saw in the previous chapter, we "cut and pasted" the progression under the second entry. If the second entry imitates at the fifth, we can still cut and paste the progression, but we must also transpose it to the dominant. As before, sometimes we maintain the progression and its bass line intact, sometimes chord inversions are changed, sometimes substitute chords are used within the progression. Each statement of the theme "expresses" more or less the same progression, but the second time in the key of the dominant.

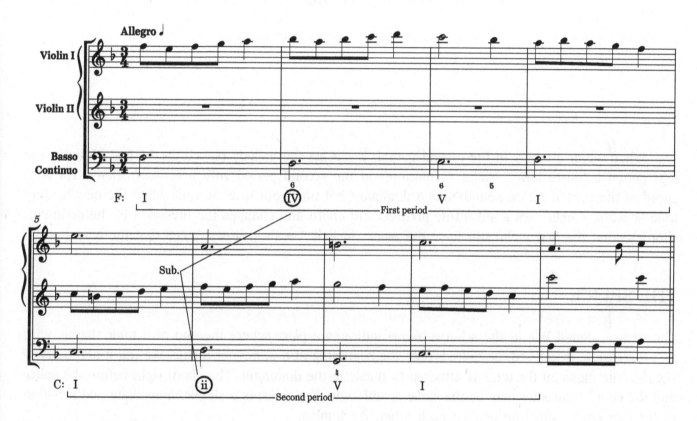

Example 7.1. (Corelli, op. 1, no. 1)

Sometimes, as in this example from a Corelli trio sonata, the composer just jumps to the new key. We can schematize the transposed repetition as follows.

Violin 1	Violin 1 (continues with new material)
	Violin 2 (repeats violin 1 melody a fourth below)
Progression ***********************	Progression in the dominant ***
.......Period 1 (in the tonic).......	....................Period 2 (in the dominant)....................

Example 7.2.

When violin 2 enters in the second period, it repeats the melody played by the first violin in the first period a fourth lower. Violin 1 continues in the second period with a countermelody. The first chord of the second period sounds like a dominant but turns out to be a tonic when the new leading tone appears. Corelli uses a substitute predominant chord and changes the inversion of the dominant chord so that the first violin can have the more "melodic" scale degrees 6–7–8 that the bass had.

THE SPLICE

The vertical dotted line in the schema above indicates a place where the end of a tonic theme, with its progression, is patched, or spliced, onto the beginning of a dominant theme. We call it a *T/D splice* because the music in the tonic is attached to music in the dominant. The chord right before the splice and the chord right after may be the same or different. The splice is a simple, immediate juxtaposition of the two keys, butted up against each other like lumber.

DIFFERENT TYPES OF SPLICE

1. *The simple splice:* Example 7.1 is an example of a simple splice, where the music in the two different keys is juxtaposed with different harmonies on either side of the splice: the tonic before the splice, and the dominant after.

2. *Weak tonicization:* In this kind of splice, the harmony on both sides of the dotted line is the same: the V chord at the end of the first period becomes the I of the next period. In the next two examples, the first period ends with a half cadence. The dominant harmony sneakily becomes the tonic of the new key, so there is no clear juxtaposition of tonic and dominant. Although we draw a dotted line where the two periods are joined together,

the splice itself is not clearly audible. The repetition of the same harmony contributes to a smooth joint; only the presence of the theme and the subsequent music convinces us that it is a new tonic. In example 7.3, Marcello has cut and pasted the progression but has changed the inversions of the chords, producing a new bass line so that the soprano can have the more "linear" scale degrees 3–2–1 in m. 7. In example 7.4, you are to complete the answering voice and the basso continuo (improvising or writing), substituting "you" for "I" in the text. Add a third voice if you feel like it.

Example 7.3. (Marcello, Psalm 7)

Example 7.4. (Thomas Augustine Arne, "The Judgement of Paris")

3. *The embellished splice:* Sometimes linear nonharmonic embellishments are sounded between the "T" and the "D" of the splice. In example 7.5, the tonic arrival occurs at the soprano G on the second beat of m. 3 and is followed by a little melodic "tag" that includes the leading tone of the new key. The new leading tone is not part of a real harmony (i.e., it does not have consonant support), and so there is no modulation, just an embellished splice.

Example 7.5. (Francesco Antonio Vallotti, "Laudate pueri, . . . for ever and ever, amen.") *Measures 12–28 are included for discussion in chapter 8.*

Here is an example in which the embellishment at the splice is a chromatic passing tone. There is no pivot chord or cadence preceding the thematic entrance in the new key, which would make a modulation (see the next section).

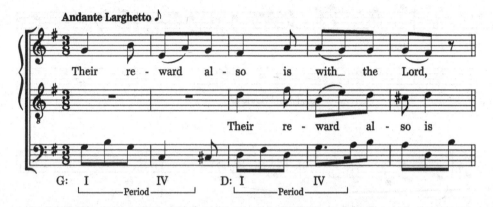

Example 7.6. (Handel, Foundling Hospital Anthem XVI: "Blessed are they that consider the poor") *What do you think happens next?*

NOT A SPLICE—THE MODULATION

If a modulation occurs before the new thematic entrance, the first note of the theme in the dominant will coincide with a harmonic arrival. The modulation fills a little space between the two periods; thus there is no splice. Nadia Boulanger used to liken modulation to a procession in which the king was the new tonic. He never entered alone, she said, but was preceded by courtiers, trumpets, and drums. Here the modulatory harmonies prepare for the arrival of the new tonic, and with it, the new theme. This is in contrast to the earlier examples in this chapter, where the new tonic was a peasant.

More elaborate modulations can occur within the melody of the first period, with pivot chords that make a convincing modulation to the new tonic. In the following examples, analyze the change of key.

Example 7.7. (Marcello, Psalm 9) *See "Note on Dorian and Mixolydian Key Signatures" later in this chapter. The return to the tonic has been included for discussion in chapter 8.*

Example 7.8. (Antonio Caldara) *Note that after the "interesting" line with the suspension has occurred in the bass, Caldara gives it to the soprano, so the bass will have to do something different. Improvise or write a bass in the second period.*

EXERCISE 7-A

1. *Writing:* In example 7.9, the figured bass is given for both periods. Notice the substitute chord. Compose a melody for the soprano over the first period, using the suggested rhythm or not. Imitate the melody a fourth lower in the alto over the second period (the moments of entry are indicated with arrows). Compose a countermelody for the soprano over the second period, using the suggested

rhythm of the first voice (or not). You are not allowed to use immediate note repetitions. What type of splice is it? Why? Explain briefly.

Example 7.9.

2. *Writing:* In example 7.10, the melody over the first period and the continuation over the second period are given for the soprano. Find the beginning of the second period (hint: transpose the first few notes of the melody up a fifth on a separate sheet, and try to fit this transposed melody against the first voice. Don't forget to add the required accidentals in the transposed version!). Write a bass line that is transposed exactly in the second period. Remember that the first period begins only when the first voice enters, not with the half rest.

Example 7.10.

IMITATION AT THE FIFTH IN THE MINOR MODE

To move from a major key to its dominant, you need to alter only one note (the new leading tone), but to go from a minor key to its minor dominant means altering three notes:

1. The old leading tone must be canceled to become the normal minor third degree of the new key.

2. The old sixth degree must be raised to become the new second degree.

3. The old fourth degree will have to be raised for the new dominant to sound like a dominant (if this new leading tone is approached from below, the old third degree will have to be raised as well to become the raised sixth degree of the ascending form of the melodic minor scale).

The above changes can take place within a modulation or just pop up in the new statement of the theme. In the minor, the chromatic introduction of the new leading tone is even less convincing than in the major (see example 7.6). For example, if you're in C minor, it's not enough to go F–F-sharp–G, because G will still sound like V (i.e., it will want to be major). Only a proper pivot will make the G appear persuasively as the new minor tonic.

In the following example by Vallotti (example 7.11), reprinted in Luigi Sabbatini's treatise, all of the necessary alterations are made at once at the end of m. 2: G-natural replaces G-sharp, F-sharp is introduced, and the new raised sixth and seventh degrees, C-sharp and D-sharp, are introduced. With the "steps" moving in quarter notes, the second half of the third beat of m. 2 can be considered as a neighbor and two passing tones, so there is no modulation, just an embellished splice. Nevertheless these notes, though not harmonically supported, suggest V/v strongly enough to make a convincing move to E minor.

You may feel that the harmonic progression from the end of m. 1 to the end of m. 2 is strange. If you consider it out of context and play it slowly, you hear $V^{6/5}$, i, and v^6 minor, apparently, in succession. This is perfectly normal in Baroque music that uses imitation at the fifth in the minor.

Example 7.11. (Vallotti, Confiteor, ". . . for ever and ever, amen") *Note that as in example 7.8, the continuation of the upper voice gets the "good" melody while the bass is reduced to roots.*

In the following excerpt from the "Christe" section of a Caldara Mass (example 7.12), the joint between the periods is a half cadence, as in examples 7.3 and 7.4. In minor keys, however, the chord at the half cadence is not the same as the first chord of the second period. Here the chord at the half cadence in the fourth measure is E major; at the onset of the next thematic entry, it is simply restated as an E minor chord. This is a "weak tonicization" in a minor key. It is different from examples 7.3 and 7.4 where the V chord is major and is simply repeated. You can improvise or write the second period (note the reharmonization of the beginning of the second period).

Example 7.12. (Caldara, "Christ have mercy on us")

In this example by Marcello, you are to complete the bass line in mm. 3–7. We have included the return to C minor, where the alto sounds a third entry, for discussion in the next chapter.

Example 7.13. (Marcello, "I have a sea in my eyes, and you have a rock in your heart") *See the "Note on Dorian and Mixolydian Key Signatures" below.*

NOTE ON DORIAN AND MIXOLYDIAN KEY SIGNATURES

In the eighteenth century, composers often used the old modal key signatures. For major keys, the Mixolydian signature was used, which has one sharp too few (or one flat too many). For instance, example 7.7, which is in A major, has only two sharps; the leading-tone is added as an accidental. For minor keys, the signature of the Dorian mode, which has one flat too few (or one sharp too many), would be used. Thus example 7.13 is in C minor, and the sixth degree is lowered by means of an accidental. In the minor, the modulation to the dominant "looks" smoother because the second degree of the dominant key is already raised in the key signature.

EXERCISE 7-B

1. *Writing:* Add a bass to example 7.14 ("He who eats of this bread shall live forever . . .").
2. *Writing:* The melody for the soprano (taken from example 6.4) over the first period is given in example 7.15. Imitate this melody a fourth below in the alto (the moment of entry is indicated with an arrow). Compose a bass line that is transposed exactly in the second period, using only dotted half notes. Write a continuation in the soprano, using mostly quarters, half notes, and dotted half notes. What type of splice have you written? Explain briefly.

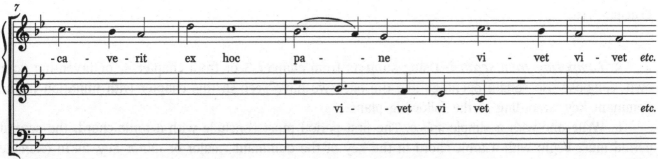

Example 7.14.

Example 7.15.

3. *Writing:* In example 7.16, the melody for the alto in the first period is given. Imitate this melody a fifth above in the soprano (the moment of entry is indicated with an arrow). Compose a bass line that is transposed exactly in the second period, using mostly eighth notes. Write a true modulation, using a pivot chord, before the entry of the soprano (in m. 3). Write a continuation in the alto over the second period, using a rhythm different from that of the bass line or the soprano.

Example 7.16.

4. *Composing from scratch:* Using subjects from chapter 3 or from chapter 4, or inventing your own, compose trio sonata openings like the ones we have seen in this chapter with imitation in the dominant key, according to the following plans:

a. Write one with a simple splice. The first period must conclude with a tonic chord, the second period must begin with a tonic chord in the key of the dominant (major or minor key, as in example 7.1).

b. Write one with a "weak tonicization" splice; in other words, the new key initially sounds like V (or v) of the old key (major or minor key, as in examples 7.3, 7.4, or 7.12).

c. Write one with an embellished splice, introducing the new leading tone as part of the "tag" between the periods (major key only), as in example 7.5.

d. Write one in a major key only, with a modulation during the first period in which the new leading tone is introduced chromatically, as in example 7.6.

e. Write one with a convincing modulation to the dominant, with the new thematic entry coinciding with a harmonic arrival in the new key (major or minor). You may model on example 7.7.

You may use one of the texts below or create your own.

"Never may my woes be relieved, since pity is fled"

"Oh fatal consequence of rage, by reason uncontroll'd"

"Anima dolorosa che vivendo tanto peni e tormenti . . ." ("Sorrowful soul, who, while you live, suffer and torment yourself . . .")

5. *Composing:* Write a trio sonata opening, using the "unpack the box" method.

- *Step 1:* Compose a cadential progression in four parts.

- *Step 2:* Choose one part other than the bass line and present it as a theme in the right hand over the bass line in the left hand. You may add embellishments to make the theme more interesting. This is your first period. Transpose your bass line and theme down a fourth or up a fifth and tack it on the end of the first period. This is your imitation at the fifth. Go back to your four-part harmonization and select one of the two hitherto unused melodies to use as a countermelody or compose a new one. Add that melody to your second entry (do not forget to transpose it) in the voice that sounded the first entry.

- *Step 3:* Add a free continuation in three parts that modulates back to the tonic key, followed by an authentic cadence. The process is illustrated in example 7.17.

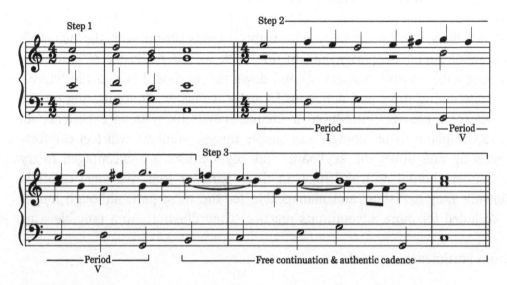

Example 7.17.

PARTIMENTO EXERCISES

WHAT IS PARTIMENTO?

Musicologist Friedrich Lippmann succinctly called partimento "the outline of a polyphonic composition, notated as a single voice with frequent changes of clefs, consisting partly of thorough-bass elements, partly of thematic statements, which can be used as a basis for a more or less improvised keyboard performance."[1]

The "polyphonic composition" in that definition is a piece that has been thought out by a good composer, but the student sees only the "notational shorthand"[2] that must be filled in. If the composer had ideas about what melodies should appear in the upper voices that are not shown, we don't know them, but often we can infer them from various evidence. Partimento is a bit like "color-by-number": a competent artist has made a picture and then removed all the color, leaving only outlines of areas containing numbers. These numbers identify the color you are to paint in those areas. Often you can't even tell what the picture is until you fill in the colors!

Over the figured or unfigured bass, one could accompany with block chords in the right hand, but some authors didn't approve of such chordal clunkiness. Marpurg said, "Although the counterparts should not be too elaborate and too highly embellished, they should not be allowed to become a mere figured bass exercise."[3] Likewise Mattheson derided organists "who first quite properly, without the slightest embellishment, perform the theme four times through on the entire keyboard in nothing but consonances and gentle thirds; then they begin again with the consequent just as circumspectly from its beginning; always producing the same tune; interposing nothing imitative or syncopating; but constantly only playing merely the concord, as if it were a thorough bass."[4]

WHY PARTIMENTO?

Partimento isn't just for keyboardists. It's for anybody who wants to experiment with the materials of Baroque music. Full realizations aren't necessary, and in this book we offer a range of partimento-related activities. Just playing subjects and answers up and down the keyboard is a tactile, visual, and aural way to experience alternating tonic and dominant forms of a melody. Concentrating on the difference between subject and tonal answer (introduced in chapter 10) is likewise an experience all music students can muster at the piano. After doing these simple things, students will feel comfortable enough to play two parts up and down the keyboard, and keyboardists are encouraged to try more elaborate realizations, either chordal or truly fugal, in three parts or four. We have carefully chosen the particular partimenti; they are short and manageable for the most part, although longer more complicated ones are included for more adventurous practice. They illustrate, in a tangible way, the concepts discussed.

What you can learn from partimento exercises:

1. You will be exercising your figured bass skills.

2. You will get fast at recognizing repeating passages in the bass. They are an invitation to put the same melodic material in the right hand.

3. You will have to remember the subject and the melody that accompanies it (i.e., the continuation from the second period), so you get used to thinking in two parts as a kind of unit.

4. Repetitions will take place in different keys, so you will learn to play both voices in different keys.

5. You are "coerced" into using correct rhythms and melodies, so you won't go off the rails stylistically.

6. You'll see how harmony and melody interact, how figures indicate melodic shapes (e.g., it's not just a sixth above the bass—it's part of the theme).

What you won't necessarily learn from partimento because these musical elements have already been provided for you by the good composer:

1. How to come up with an idiomatic harmonic progression and good harmonic rhythm

2. How to compose a good melody from scratch

3. Idiomatic rhythmic and melodic designs

You could of course use partimento exercises as models ("Renwick suggested that partimento anthologies such as the Langloz manuscript functioned as thesauruses of styles and patterns that had to be mastered by organists and composers"[5]), but you could just as well use composed pieces as models (and you should). The difference is that with partimento you are forced to "get under the hood" and think about alternative melodies, voice leading, chord members, how to arrange the registers, and so forth.

How to do partimento exercises:

1. In partimento, you never have to provide a voice below that (or those) given; so if there's a high line or duo, treat it as a "solo" or "duo." Just play it and add nothing.

2. Never change given figures. However, some basses are unfigured or only partially figured, so you have to do what feels right even if it means adding a figure. For instance, seventeenth-century theorists say that in major keys a "mi," the lower note of a melodic semitone, always gets a "6" (as you saw in the rule of the octave), and 6 generally follows 4/2, even if it's not notated.

3. When you see just the figure 2, 4/2 is often better than 5/2, and a fourth above the bass is best treated as part of a 6/4/3 or 6/4/2.

We suggest three methods for doing these exercises at the keyboard in three or four voices (or you can write out solutions).

Method 1: Given this partimento,

Example 7.18.

you can extract just the alternating tonic and dominant versions of the theme and play them up and down the whole keyboard from memory, as in example 7.19. The purpose of this is to exercise your memory and to get you used to the alternation of keys and to the different connections between the two versions of the theme.

Example 7.19.

Method 2: You can play the bass as written with clunky block chords in the right hand, like this:

Example 7.20.

Method 3: You can add a single voice above with good continuity, rhythmic variety, dissonance, and so on, obeying the rules of voice-leading and the chord content indicated by the figures. If you see a C figured ♭7/3, it would be best to have one of the "juicy" tendency notes above the bass (E or B-flat), but if you play the fifth (G), that's OK too.

Example 7.21.

EXERCISE 7-C

1. *Improvisation:* Here are some partimenti by Bernardo Pasquini that simply alternate tonic and dominant statements of the theme in the bass with a splice for you to use in one of the three methods above. Since the themes only appear in the bass and are accompanied right from the outset, the texture is not that of a fugue, but the fugal principle of successive transposed entries of a theme is at work. You might want to begin by adding dotted lines to indicate splices between themes.

Example 7.22. *This one has a "Mixolydian" key signature and is in effect in E major (all the Ds are sharped). The "theme" is four eighth notes long, and the step is an eighth note.*

Example 7.23. *This one is a little longer; the step is an eighth note.*

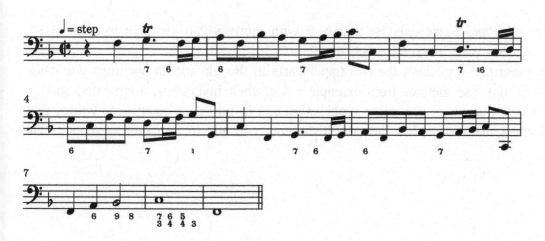

Example 7.24. *The theme is eight quarter notes long and the step is a quarter note.*

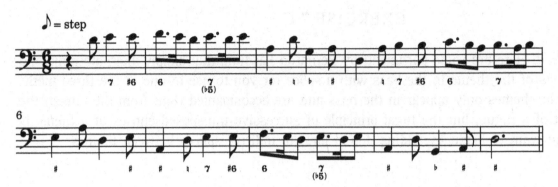

Example 7.25. *The step is the eighth note. This one has a "Dorian" key signature, so Pasquini has to write in the B-flats when the theme is in D minor (and we have added some in parentheses).*

2. *Writing or improvisation:* Go back to chapter 5, example 5.36b, and look for instances where the motive repeats at the fifth above or fourth below. Turn each of these instances into a trio sonata opening (where the imitation at the fifth above or fourth below is harmonized over the rule of the octave). Proceed as follows: (1) Assign the motive to one of the two upper voices and its imitation at the fifth above or fourth below to the other upper voice, over the ascending bass line; your imitation has to be in the key of the dominant, so think of the rule of the octave as being in the dominant by this point and add accidentals as needed. (2) If the first statement of the motive ends before the imitation enters, see if you can extend the motive in a way that the extension also works in imitation; if this is not possible, fill in free material. (3) Write or play a continuation in the first voice against the imitation in the second. (4) See if that continuation, or parts of it, could be imitated in the second voice (if there is space); if not, and there is space, compose or improvise another continuation in the second voice. (5) Continue each upper voice to the end of the passage. If you improvise this exercise (partimento), you need to make sure that you can play both the upper two parts in your right hand.

3. *Writing or improvisation:* Same exercise as no. 2, using the chart you came up with in exercise 5-I, no. 1.

4. *Writing or improvisation:* Same exercise as no. 2 with motives 2–6 given in example 5.37, using the charts you came up with in exercise 5-I, no. 2.

5. *Writing or improvisation:* Embellish the two upper parts in the trio sonata openings you came up with in nos. 2–4. You may use motives from example 5.4 or their inversions, augmented so that the sixteenth note is now a quarter or any other embellishments in mixed or equal note values that you can think of. You must make sure that the embellishments you add to the opening motive also work in imitation.

NOTES

1. Quoted in Sanguinetti, *The Art of Partimento*, p. 14.
2. Gingras, "Partimento Fugue in Eighteenth-Century Germany," p. 52.
3. Mann, *The Great Composer as Teacher and Student*, p. 201.
4. Mattheson, *Johann Mattheson's Der vollkommene Capellmeister*, III, 20, §97.
5. Gingras, "Partimento Fugue," p. 53.

8

REMODULATION AND A THIRD ENTRY

Back to the Tonic; The D/T Splice; Modulation and Remodulation; Splice Plus Modulation; Chord Factors in Splice Pairs; The Third Thematic Entry; The Retransition; Remodulation and Retransition in Minor Keys; Nonmodulating Themes; Partimento

BACK TO THE TONIC

Now that you have made thematic statements in the tonic and the dominant, what do you do next? In the last chapter we saw how composers simply cut to the dominant with a T/D splice (e.g., Corelli's example 7.1). Likewise, it is possible to cut straight back to the tonic with no ceremony.

THE D/T SPLICE

In this simple example by Marcello (example 8.1), the period consists of only a single harmony, and no modulation takes place. At the end of the first period, the first voice leaps up a fifth ("com-pren-") from the root of the first chord to the root of the second. In the corresponding place at the end of the second period, the second voice skips up a fourth, making a dominant-tonic (D/T) splice. The melodic alteration results from the fact that the distance from the tonic up to the dominant is not the same as the distance from the dominant up to the tonic. The pair of dotted lines shows the places, in both versions of the melody, where the alteration takes place.

Example 8.1. (Marcello, Salmo Quinto, "Thus, I understand you, holy and most just God")

V (progression)

I (progression)   **I** (Etc.)

Example 8.2.

For other examples of a T/D splice followed by a D/T splice (we call this a *splice pair*), see Corelli's example 7.1 and Marcello's example 7.13.

MODULATION AND THE D/T SPLICE

In example 7.7, in the previous chapter, Marcello modulated smoothly to the dominant using a pivot chord, vi becoming ii. To get back, however, he merely spliced the tonic (A major) onto the dominant. What is clever here is the way the melodies in m. 3 and in m. 6 resemble each other. Analyze the chord factors in the melodies in these measures—they provide a little preview of the melodic alteration known as "tonal answer" discussed in chapter 10.

MODULATION AND REMODULATION

When there is a simple or embellished splice, the moves to the dominant (from the first to the second period) and back to the tonic (from the second to the third period) are instantaneous. A modulation, on the other hand, adds an additional harmonic progression between periods. If you had a little modulatory music at the end of your first thematic statement, and you simply cut and paste the whole progression, including the move to the dominant, you will wind up in the dominant of the dominant (or the supertonic, depending on whether you make it major or not) because I is to V as V is to ii.

ii (Etc.?)

V (Progression + modulation)

I (Progression + modulation)

Example 8.3a.

This can happen in the course of a piece, but right at the beginning we don't want to get so far from the tonic. Most fugues alternate tonic and dominant key areas at the beginning. One way to regain the tonic is to substitute a different modulation after the basic progression in the second period. Because it modulates *back again* to the tonic, we call it a *re*modulation.

V (Progression + remodulation)

I (Progression + modulation)

I (Etc.)

Example 8.3b.

In this trio sonata by Jean-Baptiste Loeillet (example 8.4), the modulation and the remodulation use the same rhythms in the melodic part, but in the modulation a harmony is inserted on the last eighth of m. 2 that is completely different from the corresponding place at the end of m. 4. Since the chord inversions are different, the chord factors are different. So, even though the large-scale motions are I–V and V–I, there is no direct splice of corresponding elements.

Example 8.4. (Jean-Baptiste Loeillet, Trio Sonata, mm. 1–12) *The remodulation might be called a D/T splice, except for the passing seventh that restores the B-flat of the tonic key. See the rest of this piece in example 13.7.*

The remodulation takes us up a fourth. Loeillet uses this relationship in his next pair of entries (mm. 9–11). Compare the move from D minor to G minor in m. 11 to the joint between mm. 4 and 5, where the music went from C back to F. Another example in which the second set of entries reverses the order of the first is Vallotti's "Laudate Pueri" in example 7.5. Analyze the modulations in that example.

SPLICE PLUS MODULATION

Composers often make the remodulation sound very similar to the original modulation, as in this example by Vallotti (example 8.6a), in which the progression and the modulation/remodulation have been bracketed and labeled. Here there is a splice, shown by dotted lines, followed by a modulation confirming the new key. As in the Marcello example (example 8.1), the splice is the place where a specific harmonic and melodic alteration takes place between a tonic and a dominant. The modulation/remodulation pair consists of the two chords on either side of the splices, to which we add a progression that confirms the key. Each next theme enters at the tonic arrival in the new key, not immediately after the splice.

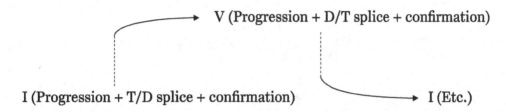

Example 8.5. (Diagram of example 8.6a)

Example 8.6a. (Vallotti, "Laudate Pueri") *The instrumental bass is to be doubled an octave lower, so the sung bass never actually crosses below. Note legal accented passing tones in mm. 2, 4, 6, 8, and 10. Deviations from strict style are marked by arrows.*

Because the chords are in a different relationship on either side of the two dotted lines, the melodic motions are different: the melodic ascending fifth in the alto (m. 4) is replaced by an ascending fourth in the soprano (m. 8, just as in Marcello's example 8.1); likewise, the descending minor second in the bass is replaced by a descending minor third (actually a major sixth ascending, to keep the line in a good register). In the first case, the pivot chord in the modulation is I in C that becomes IV in G, and in the second case it is I in G that becomes V in C.

Example 8.6b. *Note legal accented passing tones at the arrows.*

CHORD FACTORS IN SPLICE PAIRS

Although the harmonies across the two dotted lines are not in the same relationship, these two passages (mm. 4 and 8) sound quite similar for two reasons: (1) the same progression and melodies are sounded after the dotted line, and (2) we are hearing the same chord factors across the dotted lines. The bass goes from a root to a third in both cases, and the melody goes from a root to a root. At the first dotted line the tonic and dominant are spliced together; at the second, they are connected in reverse. The T/D splice and the D/T splice are in a reciprocal relationship. Not every V–I or I–V succession is a splice: there must be two corresponding moments in the music where the music in V and the music in I face each other across the dotted line, and the melodies *must have corresponding chord factors*. Either harmony can come first, but the second time, their relationships are reversed.

Example 8.6c.

There are a few commonplace patterns for melodic motions across splice pairs that are very widely used; these are shown in example 8.7. You should memorize them (the fifths of chords are not much used for reasons that become clear in the next chapter).

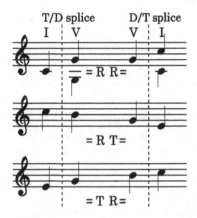

Example 8.7. (R = root; T = third)

THE THIRD THEMATIC ENTRY

Usually, the third entry coincides with the tonic arrival after either a splice, a remodulation, or both (memorize example 7.1, by Corelli, as an example of the first of these; example 8.4, by Loeillet, as an example of the second; and example 8.6a, by Vallotti, as an example of the third). The movements between the keys and the thematic entries occur periodically, so you know when to expect the next entry.

One of the most fundamental features of tonal music is the coincidence of harmonic arrival and thematic entry. Just as the dominant arrival heralded the entry of the second voice, the tonic arrival announces the third entry. It doesn't matter what register this third entry is in (in example 8.6a, by Vallotti, the two tonic entries are an octave apart; in the Kyrie by Isabella Leonarda, example 8.8 below, all four entries in the three upper voices occur on only two different notes).

Sometimes, if the first two entries are both in the tonic (i.e., imitation at the unison or octave, discussed in chapter 6), the third entry occurs as the first of a new pair of entries in another key. In example 6.4, after two entries, Steffani inserted a measure to modulate to the relative major; the arrival of the new tonic coincides with the third entry. In example 6.3, Marcello introduced the new pair of entries with the first degree of the dominant (A) as the fifth of the old tonic; this substitute chord makes an especially smooth modulation, since the new entry comes *before* the new tonic arrival!

EXERCISE 8-A

1. *Analysis:* The following beginning of a fugal section from a Kyrie movement by Isabella Leonarda starts in the fourth measure in the dominant key (the piece is in D minor with a Dorian key signature). Disregard the choral bass in mm. 40–42; it essentially doubles the continuo, but Leonarda

has embellished it with the rhythmic motives of the principal theme. Note that the second word, "eleison," makes an elision, the word overlapping with the next thematic entry. Label thematic entries, harmonies, and splices, and explain how the voices are joined (splice, modulation, remodulation, etc.). Draw dotted lines and label chord factors as we did in examples 8.6b and 8.6c.

Example 8.8. (Isabella Leonarda, Kyrie from Messa Concertata, op. 4)

2. *Analysis:* Analyze the imitative opening by Dietrich Buxtehude in example 8.9. Play the first measure of each entry straight through to get a feeling for the alternation of tonic and dominant as you move through the pitch space. Do a harmonic analysis, label thematic entries, label melodic

embellishments, and explain how the voices are joined (splice, modulation, remodulation, etc.). Draw dotted lines and label chord factors as we did in examples 8.6b and 8.6c.

Example 8.9. (Dietrich Buxtehude, "Benedicam Dominum")

3. *Composing from scratch:* Modeling on Vallotti's example 8.6a, compose a quartet opening containing three entries, the first in the tonic, the second in the dominant, and the third in the tonic again. *You must use the harmonies and chord-factor patterns shown in example 8.7* on either side of the splice that precedes the modulation/remodulation (shown with a dotted line).

THE RETRANSITION

The retransition has the same function as the remodulation, but it involves a longer or shorter section, causing the periods to be of different lengths. The retransition can contain new melodic and harmonic material. When there is a retransition, you don't know when to expect the third entry because there are no periods of equal length. When the extra material of a retransition is added, there is no direct correspondence between the ends of the periods.

In the following example by Vallotti (example 8.10a), the second thematic statement comes in after seven measures. We can parse those measures into a basic progression (tonic prolongation, mm. 1–4), a measure of modulating harmony (V/V, m. 5), and a confirming cadence (mm. 6–8). The tonic is not regained, however, until nine measures later because Vallotti has added two measures to make a retransition.

Example 8.10a. (Vallotti, "Laudate pueri")

The second entry goes right on to ii, which we said does not normally happen at the beginning of a piece. However, the ii moves smoothly on to V with the two "inserted" measures in the retransition (mm. 13 and 14) providing the music necessary to regain the tonic. Example 8.10b compares mm. 5–6, the modulation, with mm. 12–15, the retransition. Measure 13 has free melodic material, and it is followed by a repetition down a step of the figure from m. 12, now V of D, which is followed by the normal two measures of cadential confirmation in D.

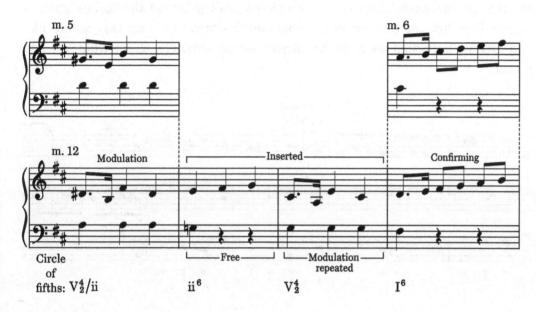

Example 8.10b.

This retransition sounds very natural for a number of reasons: (1) the modulatory m. 12 (V/V in the dominant) resolves not to E major but E minor, which helps get back to the tonic, D; (2) the free measure (m. 13) has the inversion of melodic material we heard in mm. 4 and 11; (3) we don't mind hearing the modulatory figure again in m. 14 because (4) mm. 12–15, taken together, make a circle of fifths progression V/ii–ii–V–I.

Another example you have seen that heads onward to ii after the dominant statement is example 7.5, mm. 6–7. There Vallotti uses a sequence of ascending fifths to regain the tonic.

REMODULATION AND RETRANSITION IN MINOR KEYS

In going back to the minor tonic, we have to undo all the alterations we made to get to the minor dominant: we have to get rid of the dominant's leading tone and restore the flat sixth degree of the tonic and its own leading tone. In example 8.11 by Corelli, the first two periods are three measures long. They are separated by embellished splices. The first violin's move from the third of the tonic to the root of the dominant is embellished with a passing tone, and the return splice (m. 7) is embellished with a chordal skip.

Clearly, Corelli wants these two brief passages to sound similar, and to this end he uses the same rhythm, which can be as important as pitch in our perceptions. Such tiny details warrant your close attention because they smooth over the structural joints, making the music flow unperturbed while changing keys. This sense of forward momentum is a crucial aspect of Baroque style. An unusual feature of this particular opening is the lack of strong harmonic arrival back in the tonic until the fourth note of the third entry in the bass. The theme sneaks in on the third scale degree and then realizes its cadential potential, so the modulation is not completed until *after* the theme has entered (as in example 6.3). In cases like this, the sudden major dominant harmony may initially sound like an applied dominant to its own iv, but when we hear the theme, we immediately accept whatever key it is sounded in as the tonic.

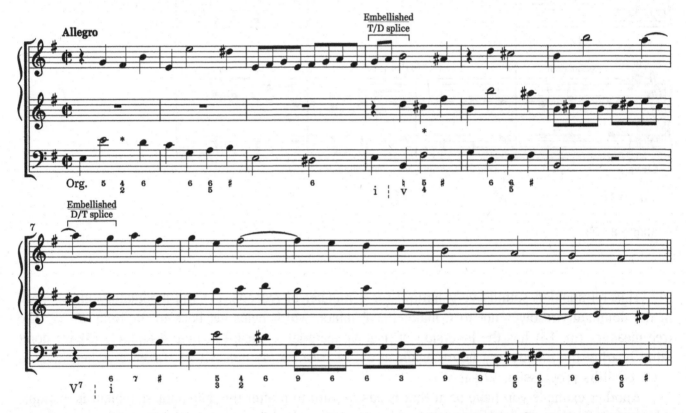

Example 8.11. (Corelli, Church Sonata, op. 3, no. 7, ii) *In the return to the tonic, Corelli first introduces the D-sharp as a NHT in m. 6. Note that the leap of a major seventh from the leading tone in mm. 2–3 is not in strict style. Note substitute chords at asterisks.*

Several of Bach's three-part inventions (called *sinfonias*) are in trio sonata texture. In this one (example 8.12), we have a fairly long retransition. It begins as if it would move another fifth away (the C-sharp in m. 8 corresponds to the F-sharp in m. 4), but Bach restores the tonic's flat sixth degree (F-natural) in m. 9. The surprising B-flat moves us toward D minor (B-flat and A are not in strict style, embellishing a 4–3 suspension over D). From there, it is easy to regain A minor, with a thematic entry in the bass.

The last measure of this retransition (m. 12) is technically unnecessary since A minor has been effectively regained and a tonic entry could occur there. So why does Bach wait another measure to bring in the bass? It could be that he wants to keep the music flowing in four-measure periods; it could be that he wants to precipitously lower the register of the upper voices; it could be he thinks it's humorous to repeat the soprano scale down from F in m. 11 in the middle voice in m. 12. We will see more "unnecessary retransitions" later on.

Example 8.12. (Bach, Sinfonia 13) *Remember that the hemiola in mm. 2–3 justifies the passing C on the apparent downbeat.*

EXERCISE 8-B

1. *Identification of terms:* Define and distinguish T/D splice, D/T splice, embellished splice, modulation, and retransition.

2. *Improvisation/keyboard harmony:* Play what would have happened if Vallotti had gone to D major in example 8.6a, m. 8; play a full period with a thematic entry in D. Play what would have happened if Vallotti had gone to E major in example 8.10a, mm. 12–13; play a full period with a thematic entry in E. Play what would have happened if Bach had actually gone to B minor in m. 9 of example 8.12; bring in a thematic entry in the bass on B, and improvise chords above, keeping sixteenths running in the upper voices.

3. *Writing (short):* The subject and basso continuo for three consecutive periods are given in example 8.13. Treat the bass as unfigured (in other words, you may add figures). Fill in the missing thematic entries. Provide a continuation in the soprano in m. 2. Use this continuation in the third period (in the tenor) and add a free soprano. Text: "Incostanza, e che pretendi" ("Fickleness, and what do you pretend?").

Example 8.13.

Example 8.14. (Handel)

4. *Writing (short):* The subject, the beginning of the continuation, and the basso continuo for three consecutive periods are given in example 8.14. Treat the bass as unfigured. The arrow shows where the second entry comes. Use your continuation from the soprano in the second period as the alto of the third period (the continuation might need some adjustments). Fill in a free soprano in the third period.

5. *Writing:* The subject and basso continuo (partially figured) for three periods are given in example 8.15. Fill in the answer at the fifth (in the alto) and the third entry (in the tenor). This time the answer needs to be followed by a retransition before the third entry can come in (to close the circle). The second period will thus be longer than the first (you can figure out how much longer by a careful analysis of the bass). As before, use the same or a slightly adjusted continuation in the second and third periods and add a free soprano line in the third period.

Example 8.15. (Fux)

6. *Writing (long):* In the given bass in example 8.16, find three periods and a retransition. Mattheson believes that writing two upper parts to a bass is the most difficult exercise because he sees the bass as most often dependent on the upper parts. Over the bass in example 8.16, compose a melody for the first violin or soprano over the first period; put the same melody, in the appropriate key, in the second violin or alto; compose a countermelody for the soprano; compose convincing music for the retransition. You may complete the last measures (the third period), and then you will add a third entry (for one of the instruments already in).

Example 8.16.

7. *Composing from scratch:* Using either of these subjects or any one from chapter 3: (1) harmonize it, (2) tack on a convincing modulation to the dominant (with a splice or not), (3) build a trio sonata opening with a free bass, consisting of three periods: the subject alone, the imitation at the fifth with a countermelody in the first voice (if you use a remodulation or retransition, label it), and a third entry in the tonic key in one of the upper voices. Add the same countermelody in the second and third period in the appropriate keys. Provide a harmonic analysis.

Example 8.17.

8. *Composing from scratch:* Compose as in no. 7 above, but use your own subject (consult chapter 17). Use one of the texts below or choose your own.

"A wondrous rapture must it be, the love of two souls plighted"

"The winds are blowing, the gusty winds"

"Chi vol haver felice e lieto il core" ("Whoever wishes to have a happy, joyful heart")

"Pleni sunt coeli et terra" ("Heaven and earth are full [of thy glory]")

NONMODULATING THEMES

As we have seen, the purpose of the modulation at the end of the theme is to permit the first note of the entrance in the dominant to overlap with the harmonic arrival in the dominant key. Not all themes do this. We have seen some themes that just stay in the tonic, with no modulation added at the end, but in these situations there is no overlap of the second theme entry with the harmonic arrival (e.g., Corelli, example 7.1; Marcello, example 8.1), just a jump to another chord that initially sounds like V.

However, it is possible to overlap *a tonic arrival with a dominant entry* because the first degree of the dominant scale is a chord factor of the tonic triad. This kind of overlap will only work as long as the second entrance is *above* the first (if it were *below*, the entrance would create an illegal 6/4 chord). In this example by Handel (example 8.18a), the first note of the second entry is the fifth of the F major chord at the tonic arrival. Compared to the first entry, where the first note was obviously the root, we would say that this entry has been reharmonized with a substitute chord (like the one we saw in example 6.3, m. 13).

Example 8.18a. (Handel, Wedding Anthem XIV) *Note that the continuo starts out independently but soon merely doubles the choral basses.*

Example 8.18a. *(Concluded)*

The use of such a joint between first and second entries requires a retransition before the third because there is no way to overlap a tonic note with the dominant arrival, as shown in example 8.18b. The tonic entry either causes an illegal 6/4 chord if the bass resolves correctly, or at the very least it makes a drastic deceptive resolution of the preceding V/V, with a strong "false relation" of the diminished fifth (shown with a dotted line in example 8.18c). The need for retransition means that the entries cannot occur periodically.

Example 8.18b. (What Handel didn't do)

Example 8.18c. (What Handel didn't do)

However, there are some adjustments that composers use to get around this problem, ones that make periodic entries possible after all. One is to delay the entrance a bit (often requiring a shorter step) so that the dominant arrival can be heard before the tonic chord (example 8.18d). Another example is the fourth entry in the first fugue in *WTC I* by Bach, shown in example 9.15.

Example 8.18d. (What Handel could have done)

Another sleight of hand is to make the resolution of the V/V deceptive to vi in only two voices, arriving on scale degrees 6 and 1 of the dominant, which are 3 and 5 of the tonic. During a short delay, these degrees can be quickly reinterpreted by the ear as members of the tonic triad (example 8.19).

Example 8.19. (Pasquini)

Example 8.20 is based in the same principle, but in the minor. The cadence to the dominant, A minor, is avoided altogether by the substitute G-natural, which leads down to F-natural, making the tonic return appear all the more natural. In these last two examples the third entry still has a kind of subdominant feel, but the assertion of the theme bullies us into accepting it as in the tonic.

Example 8.20. (Pasquini, "Fuga in basso continuo")

This final example, by Jan Dismas Zelenka, shows one more instance of a nonmodulating subject in which the dominant arrival is denied, still leading to periodic entries. We would expect the half-note D in m. 2 to imply an imminent arrival on C. However, the corresponding A in m. 4 is harmonized not in G but in C, making a "plagal" arrival, which is not really an arrival at all but which permits the entry on low C in the bass (scale degrees 2–1 in the dominant are of course also scale degrees 6–5 in the tonic).

Example 8.21. (Jan Dismas Zelenka, Miserere) *Instrumental parts have been omitted.*

PARTIMENTO

The following partimenti contain either embellished splices, modulations and remodulations, or retransitions, and so you must remember not only the tune in two keys but also the different endings that lead from one to another. Pasquini's examples 8.22 and 8.23 have modulations and remodulations of equal lengths, so the entries are periodic. (In many measures of example 8.22, although the step can be as short as the eighth note, you will want a single harmony for the entire measure.)

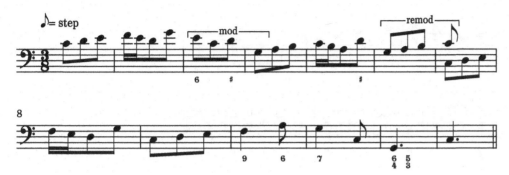

Example 8.22.

In example 8.23, the "7 6" under the third quarter-note beat refers to intervals above the first sixteenth note, although by the time the 6 comes the bass will have moved on; the last of the string of four sixteenths is a consonant echappée. Note that the theme in example 8.23 is five quarter notes long.

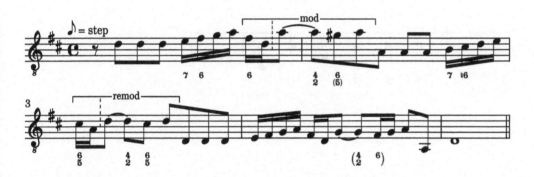

Example 8.23.

In examples 8.24a and 8.25, the modulation is built into the theme, and extra music (a retransition) is added to regain the tonic. In these three, note how Pasquini switches to the B-flat over the D to remain in the tonic at the end.

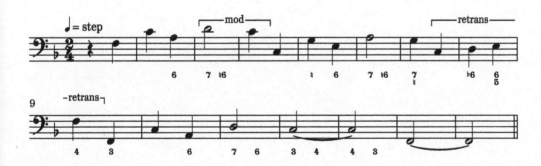

Example 8.24a.

Example 8.24b. (Another version)

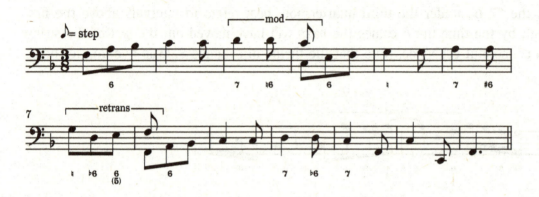

Example 8.25.

Example 8.26,[1] supposedly by J. S. Bach, starts out with a solo, then a duo, but after that the author has simply carried out method 2, using chords in the right hand. The theme in the dominant has a tacked-on retransition that lengthens the thematic statement. The fugue also contains added free material from time to time. The step is the quarter note except once.

Example 8.26. (J. S. Bach, Vorschriften und Grundsätze zum vierstimmigen Spielen des Generalbasses, no. 16)

Example 8.27, from the Langloz manuscript, also begins with soprano and alto entrances, so you don't need to add anything until bar 4, where the theme is sounded in the tenor (another solo occurs at the end of m. 8). The replacement of the figure C–A–C–D–E in m. 2 with G–E–F–G–A in m. 3 is a common way to accomplish a modulation/remodulation. The countermelody that is provided in the top line in mm. 2–3 can be reused if you are doing method 3.

Example 8.27. (Langloz no. 31)

NOTE

1. Gingras, "Partimento Fugue in Eighteenth-Century Germany," p. 55.

9

FUGUE EXPOSITION

Fugue versus Trio Sonata; The Subject as Bass; The SATB Exposition; The BTAS Exposition; The Countersubject; Other Orders of Entry; Basic Principles of Invertible Counterpoint; Vocal Ranges and Other Orders of Entry; Two Subjects or Answers in a Row; The Subject and Answer in Nonadjacent Voices; Partimento

FUGUE VERSUS TRIO SONATA

The trio sonata openings we looked at in the last chapter share a number of formal and contrapuntal principles with fugue openings: (1) both present a series of entries of the theme, (2) both present the theme in alternating tonic and dominant keys, and (3) in both, the initial theme moves to the dominant, either by an immediate T/D splice or a modulation or both. If the second entry is followed either by a D/T splice or a remodulation back to the tonic or both, the theme and its imitation at the fifth form a periodic structure; otherwise the second entry can be followed by a retransition of a different length, in which case the theme and its imitation are nonperiodic.

A fugue differs from a trio sonata in that there is most often no independent bass line. In a fugue, the theme functions both as the principal melody and as the bass. (Many pieces called fugues do have independent bass lines, however. For instance, Sabbatini calls all of Vallotti's examples in previous chapters "fugues," and many vocal fugues, like those found in Bach cantatas, have independent basses.)

From now on we will call the first tonic statement of the theme the "subject" and its imitation at the fifth the "answer." The essence of a fugue opening is the alternation between subject and answer, usually in adjacent voices.

THE SUBJECT AS BASS

Because there is no independent bass line, the thematic material (subject, countermelodies, etc.) must be able to function as a bass. To be usable as a bass, the theme(s) cannot contain the fifth chord factor because illegal 6/4 chords are likely to result. Take Vallotti's example 8.6 or Leonarda's Kyrie (example 8.8)—in both, the melody starts on the fifth chord factor. If these subjects were to appear in the bass, the first note would be part of a 6/4 chord, unusable in this position (i.e., not passing, arpeggiating, or cadential). Similarly, a long second degree before the tonic arrival cannot be harmonized, as it usually is when it's in the soprano, with ii–V but must be harmonized with vii^6 or V$^{6/4/3}$. When the subject is used as a bass line, it can be figured (as in partimento), and a continuo player can improvise chords above it.

EXERCISE 9-A

1. *Analysis:* Look back at the subjects in chapter 3 and decide which could be used successfully as bass lines. Why might a subject not be suitable as a bass?

2. *Improvisation and keyboard harmony:* Harmonize those that can work as bass lines. Do you find yourself harmonizing them the same way as when they were soprano lines?

3. *Writing (short):* Select the ones that make good bass lines, copy them in a low register, and write three-part chords above.

THE SATB EXPOSITION

In a fugue, the exposition often contains as many thematic entries as there are vocal or instrumental parts. The simplest way to structure an exposition is to use the theme as a bass line throughout the exposition. This means the lines enter from the top down: the soprano starts, the alto then serves as "bass" to the soprano, then the tenor serves as "bass" to the soprano-alto duo, and finally the bass enters.

Fugue expositions with entries in the order SATB are very common. Baroque composers were used to working with figured bass, and for them the easiest thing would be to repeat the harmonic progression when the same bass line repeats—albeit in alternating keys. Another reason might be that our ear tends to be drawn to the highest voice of a polyphonic passage, and if the voices of a fugue enter in the order SATB, there is a nice tension between our attraction to the theme in each new voice and our tendency to follow the soprano. The subject and answer are always clearly recognizable in the lowest voice, whereas the top voice always presents new material. If a countermelody is reused (see "The Countersubject" later in the chapter), it will first appear in the top voice (above the answer) and then move to the inner voices.

Example 9.2 schematizes the four voices of example 9.1 entering in the order SATB, with the subject and answer always appearing as the bass line. The subject and answer are marked in example 9.2 as "I—" and "V—," respectively. The end of the subject moves to the dominant, and the answer is followed by a retransition. The third entry does not end with a tonic arrival, as we might expect.

Example 9.1. (Bach [Krebs?], Eight Short Preludes and Fugues, no. 7, BWV 559) *The first chord shown in the example is actually the end of the prelude. Note that the countermelodies that follow after each subject and answer start with the same suspension (mm. 7–8, 13–15, 18–20). Are other parts of the countermelodies repeated?*

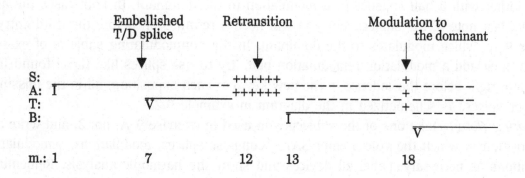

Example 9.2.

Before the fourth entry, instead of duplicating the splice, Bach composed a modulation to the dominant by reharmonizing the B (at the asterisk in example 9.1) and changing the end of the subject. The effect is to have a shorter time interval than that between the first two entries.

Note how the first retransition changes the minor third, G, of the dominant key, to the new leading tone, G-sharp, to modulate back to the tonic (see the discussion of this technique in chapter 8). Remember that we call this a retransition (rather than a remodulation) because it is longer than the move to the dominant at the end of the previous subject. Do a harmonic analysis of the entire excerpt. Are the subject and answer harmonized the same way?

EXERCISE 9-B

1. *Analysis:* Analyze the fugue exposition in example 9.3. Provide a harmonic analysis, label the subjects and answers, and explain the joints between the voices (i.e., splice, modulation, retransition, etc.).

Example 9.3. (Bach, "Lobet den Herrn," BWV 230, mm. 99–104)

2. *Writing (short):* The subjects in examples 9.4a–e are taken from chorales. Choose one or more to use as the basis for a four-part SATB exposition. Example 9.4a ends with a half cadence; example 9.4b ends either with a half cadence or a modulation to the dominant. In both cases the answer can enter on the last note of the subject, but you will need a retransition before the third entry; likewise in example 9.4c, which modulates to the dominant. In the nonmodulating subjects of examples 9.4d and e, you must add a modulation/remodulation pair. Try to use splices like those found in Vallotti's example 8.6a, right before the cadence in the new key. For each exposition, fill in the missing material in the upper voices, as schematized in the diagram in example 9.2.

3. *Writing (long):* Take one of the subjects you used in exercise 9-A, no. 2, and write a four-part fugue exposition in which the voices enter SATB. Compose splices, modulations, remodulations, and/ or retransitions as necessary. Label all devices and show the harmonic analysis. Remember to look for opportunities to use suspensions between the subject and the countermelodies.

Example 9.4a. ("Befiehl du deine Wege")

Example 9.4b. ("Ein feste Burg ist unser Gott")

Example 9.4c. ("Ermuntre dich, mein schwacher Geist")

Example 9.4d. ("Allein Gott in der Höh' sei Ehr")

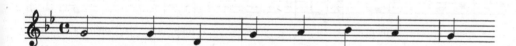

Example 9.4e. ("Der Herr ist mein getreuer Hirt")

THE BTAS EXPOSITION

The four entries in the following fugue opening (example 9.5) follow the order from lowest to highest voice (BTAS). This is a nonmodulating theme: the third scale degree, E, following the end of the subject makes a good combination with the fifth scale degree G with which the answer starts. There is a retransition (marked in m. 7) before the third entry.

Example 9.5. (Fux, Magnificat K. 97, "For ever and ever, amen") *(1) The answer in m. 4 shortens the first note value from a half note to a quarter, a standard variant. (2) The A in the tenor of m.6 seems to enter on a dissonance against the G in the bass; this is possible because A is a chord factor and G is part of a suspension, prepared on the first beat, dissonant on the second beat (when A enters), and resolving on the third beat (prep/diss/res are labeled in the example). (3) At the start of the third entry (m. 8) the F in the bass is a reharmonization of the first note—C would have been a root in m. 1; now it is a fifth (like the G in m. 4). There is one deviation from strict style, marked by an arrow in the bass of m. 11.*

Notice the repeating melody (bracketed in the bass of mm. 5–7) sounded with the later entries, as bracketed in mm. 9–11 (tenor) and 12–14 (alto). This is a reused *countermelody* because it is regularly repeated against all the subjects and answers in the exposition, forming a characteristic duo. It often happens, as here, that the characteristic motive of the countermelody begins after the subject has started.

THE COUNTERSUBJECT

A countermelody (continuation) that *regularly* accompanies the subject is called a *countersubject*. The version of the countermelody (continuation) that accompanies the answer is transposed and can be called a *counteranswer*. It is possible to write a fugue with a subject and many different countermelodies, but it is economical to reuse the same countermelody to the subject. Once you have a good two-voice combination, why not reuse it?

The issues in composing a countersubject include *independence* (melodic, rhythmic, contour); *continuity* (how it connects to the end of the preceding theme); *uniformity* (similarity to the subject); *good two-part writing* (variety of intervals, clear harmony); and *invertibility* of the combination (so that either melody can appear as bass). In the following passages, we shall see all of these issues addressed.

Mattheson presents a detailed discussion of a countersubject from Kuhnau's Clavier-Übung (shown in example 9.6 and discussed earlier in example 4.27a). He says, "The notes of the first theme are of one value; but beginning with the little rest disrupts the uniformity nicely. . . . The author chooses a second theme or countertheme that descends after the preceding subject had ascended. . . . This countertheme consists only of notes which are different in value from the preceding ones. Here the *vis rhythmica*, the effect of the rhythm, is very distinct. . . . The first theme *walks* stepwise; the second, however, *runs* and *leaps*."[1]

Example 9.6. (Kuhnau)

Marpurg recognizes the need for uniformity as well as variety and seems to issue contradictory statements. On the one hand, he suggests drawing the motives of the countersubject from the subject itself: "It goes without saying that the kind of simple counterpoint chosen [for the countermelody] for the beginning is used until the end. Often the subjects are such that one can borrow portions from them to form a countermelody by way of imitating and transposing . . . figures from the theme itself. Such countermelodies doubtlessly cohere best with the subject."[2]

On the other hand, he emphasizes independence of the voices: "All voices . . . must have a good melody, and none must predominate."[3] He emphasizes rhythmic independence in particular: "Although the countermelody should not be too curly or too colorfully checkered, it should not form thoroughbass-style passages either. . . . In order to avoid this mistake it is necessary that one voice always moves against another, be it through shifts [syncopations] or passing or neighbor notes, as the circumstances permit."[4]

He maintains that voices should work well together even as they compete: "In all types of musical pieces one part has to fit well with another, if a beautiful whole is to arise from it, which is to be observed in a fugue in particular."[5] He says all the voices should be equal in importance: "The larger the number of voices in a fugue, the fewer florid figures the countermelody permits. . . . Yet in a fugue all voices compete with each other and none has preference over another as is the case in other genres."[6]

Marpurg suggests preceding the entry of a subject with a rest, which both sets off the theme and provides independence from the other voices: "One puts the rest in that voice in which the theme will soon afterwards enter."[7] Both Mattheson and Marpurg like the entry of the principal tune to occur against a suspension. Mattheson speaks of "those good suspensions and syncopations which, so to speak, are the soul of fugues."[8] Marpurg likes the first note of the subject to be the agent in a suspension, probably because it makes the new entrance seem to "interrupt" the continuous flow of the preceding voice.[9]

EXERCISE 9-C

1. *Analysis:* Evaluate Fux's countermelody in example 9.5 in terms of Marpurg's criteria for good countersubjects.

2. *Composing or improvisation (short):* Add countermelodies to examples 9.7a–d. When thinking harmonically, treat the subject as an unfigured bass (i.e., add your own figures). In the first two, the answers overlap with a half cadence, and the answers continue on to ii. Note that the last measure of the subject in examples 9.7c and 9.7d is incomplete; you must complete the measure somehow—in these examples we can expect a splice or an embellished splice or a very fast modulation!

Example 9.7. (Sabbatini)

3. *Composing (long):* Using the subject given in example 9.9 compose a fugue exposition based on the schema in example 9.8. There is a typical splice before each entry. The alto entry is shown with an arrow. The splices should all be mirror images of each other, thus the entries will be periodic.

Soprano	S	CA	FC	FC
Alto	—	A	CS	FC
Tenor	—	—	S	CA
Bass	—	—	—	A

Example 9.8. (S = subject, A = answer, CS = countersubject, CA= counteranswer, FC= free counterpoint).

Example 9.9. (Langloz manuscript)

OTHER ORDERS OF ENTRY

The two orders discussed so far (SATB and BTAS) alone are not sufficient for making an interesting piece. Mattheson says, "Now as concerns [the term] 'artful alternation' [of subjects and answers], we do not understand by it the old trodden path, straight from top to bottom, or from bottom to top . . . but we mean such an arrangement and division whereby the theme occurs sometimes in this, sometimes in that place, be it high or low, without rank and order."[10] However, in order to have more flexibility in ordering your entries and at the same time use a countersubject, both of your principal thematic tunes (subject, countersubject) must be usable as bass lines. For this to be the case, the S/CS combination must be invertible.

BASIC PRINCIPLES OF INVERTIBLE COUNTERPOINT

If you want to reuse your countersubject *and* have a different order of entries (ASBT, say), then both your countersubject (dotted line) and subject (solid line) must be able to sound as bass lines.

```
                           S_____ ---------
             A_____  -------------
                                        T ____
                           B_____ --------
```

Example 9.10.

In the schema above, the countersubject appears as the bass line below the answers in the soprano and the tenor, but at the third entry the subject appears in the bass, so both the subject and countersubject work as upper lines and as bass lines. When we exchange the relative positions of the two tunes—in other words by "inverting" them—we can think of the process as transposing the upper voice down an octave or the lower voice up an octave, and we call it "inverting the combination at the octave."

We start with a two-voice combination: two melodies, one above the other. When we take the melody that was above (call it A) in the original combination and put it below the other (call it B), the intervals by which the two voices are transposed (X and Y) are related in the following way: *The sum of the absolute values of X and Y equals the interval of inversion plus 1.*

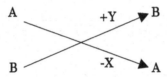

Example 9.11a.

Thus in invertible counterpoint at the octave (IC8), if we move A down an octave (X = –8) and leave B where it was (transposed at the unison so Y = 1), we add the absolute value of these two numbers together to get 9, which is 8 (the interval of inversion) plus 1.

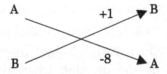

Example 9.11b.

If we transpose A down a fifth and B up a fourth (–5 and +4), we still get 9, so the combination has been inverted at the octave again, but the whole combination has been transposed.

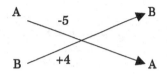

Example 9.11c.

Invertible counterpoint changes the vertical-interval relationships in the combination. If in example 9.11d the vertical interval between the first note of melody A and the first of melody B were a sixth, when we invert at the octave, the first notes in the inverted combination would form a third. Thus *corresponding intervals also add up to the interval of inversion plus 1* (6 + 3 = 9).

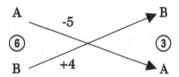

Example 9.11d.

In *invertible counterpoint at the octave,* the vertical intervals in the original combination are transformed according to this chart:

Table 9.1

Original	1	2	3	4	5	6	7	8
Inverted	8	7	6	5	4	3	2	1

Note that the corresponding intervals always sum to 9. The dissonances of second and seventh map onto each other, so they will work the same in both versions; the perfect consonances of octave and unison map onto each other and thus have to be treated the same way, likewise the imperfect intervals of a third and a sixth. The only problem interval is the fifth, which might appear as a consonance in the original but which will become a dissonant fourth in the inverted combination. For this reason we can never have the fifth chord factor in either the subject or the countersubject, unless it is treated in the ways discussed in chapter 4.

Since a fourth in the original becomes a fifth in the inverted combination, it is impossible to use dissonant cadential 6/4 chords in the original; the dissonance disappears when inverted and the resulting consonant tonic chord sounds bad when following a predominant chord. Because cadences are standardized formulas, we often break out of invertible counterpoint at the cadence.

The following exposition by Angelo Predieri (reprinted by Giovanni Battista ["Padre"] Martini) has entries ASBT. (The rest of this movement appears in example 13.12.)

Example 9.12a. (Angelo Predieri, Exposition, mm. 1–11) *Note the Dorian key signature. The first text syllable of the countersubject, the "A-" of "Amen," enters on the last note of the subject, eliding with the counteranswer and making the answer seem to interrupt the flow of the first voice. In his discussion, Martini points out the use of different melodic intervals at the joints between the subject and the following counteranswer and between the answer and the following countersubject. These are splices, indicated as always by dotted lines. In the alto of m. 3, the interval between the last note of the subject and the first note of the counteranswer is a descending second. In the soprano of m. 5, the interval between the last note of the answer and the first note of the countersubject is a descending third. In m. 7, the joint between the subject in the bass and the following counteranswer is again a descending second, and so on. Analyze the harmonies and the chord factors across the splices. Note how Predieri avoids the cadences to A minor in mm. 4 and 8; such cadences are discussed in chapter 13. The avoided cadence functions as a remodulation.*

The subject/countersubject pair is inverted at the octave: the A/CA pair appears in mm. 3–4 with the CA in the lower voice; then the S/CS pair appears in mm. 5–6 with the subject in the lower voice. If we analyze the chord factors in each of these pairs, we see that for the most part the two melodies exchange thirds and roots—no fifth occurs, so there are no 6/4 chords. Remember example 3.13, in which it was suggested that outer voices employ roots and thirds complementarily? Where do the fifths of chords finally occur? Examples 9.12b and c below show pairs from example 9.12a. The harmonies are shown without inversion. The ends of the examples have different harmonizations.

Example 9.12b.

Example 9.12c.

EXERCISE 9-D

1. *Analysis:* Go back to exercise 9-B, no. 2. Are your subject/countersubject pairs invertible? (Switch the positions of the two voices and see what happens.)

2. *Writing:* If they are not, compose new countersubjects that are. Do you like them as well as your first ones? Better?

3. *Writing:* Write countersubjects to the subjects in example 9.13 so that the combination is invertible at the octave.

4. *Writing (long):* Compose ASBT expositions using solutions from no. 3 above that you and your teacher think are successful.

Example 9.13a.

And   He   shall   reign   for   e - ver   and   e - ver

Example 9.13b.

Example 9.13c.

Example 9.13d.

cru - ci - fix - us

Example 9.13e.

Example 9.13f.

Example 9.13g.

VOCAL RANGES AND OTHER ORDERS OF ENTRY

We mentioned in chapter 7 that in a trio sonata, imitation at the fifth allows the subject and answer to appear comfortably within the corresponding vocal ranges of the two upper parts because the vocal ranges in any pair of adjacent voices lie roughly a fourth or fifth apart, as schematized below. Note that the ranges of adjacent voices overlap by about an octave (shaded areas represent the shared octave). If necessary, the boundaries of each vocal range may be extended by one step on either side.[11]

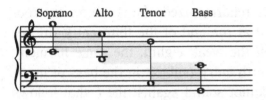

Example 9.14. (Vocal ranges)

In the common SATB model, the four entries alternate in presenting the subject and the answer, with each entry starting a fourth or fifth below the previous one. As a result, the subject and answer occupy roughly the same place within the vocal range of the voice in which they appear. For instance, in example 9.3, the first entry uses the upper octave of the soprano range, the answer uses the upper octave of the alto range, the third entry uses the upper octave of the tenor range, and the fourth entry uses the upper octave of the bass range.

Marpurg explains that in a four-part fugue there are twenty-four different possible orders in which the four parts can enter.[12] However, from among these twenty-four possibilities, the following six are the ones most commonly used: SATB, ASBT, ATBS, TASB, TBSA, BTAS. All of these combinations start with an adjacent pair of voices, which means that there is not too much space between the voices in a thin, two-voice texture, and it means that the subject may be followed by the answer in a corresponding vocal range. In addition, all later pairs of entries also involve either adjacent voices or the bass and soprano, so any pair of later entries will again combine the subject and answer or vice versa. In other words, these six orders of entry allow for the succession of subject–answer–subject–answer, and for good spacing.

On the other hand, in expositions with BTSA, SABT, ASTB, ATSB, TABS, and TBAS entries, the second and third entries occur in voices that will normally use imitation at the octave (unless the composer decides to make one of the voices sing at the other extreme of its register—see example 9.16 below). Four-part fugues almost never start with the first two entries in the outer voices (SBTA, SBAT, BSTA, BSAT) because of the general desire for close voicing when there are only two voices; nor do they start with an outer and an inner voice (STAB, STBA, TSAB, TSBA, BATS, BAST, ABTS, ABST), which would normally result in the first duo imitating at the octave. Exceptions to this will be discussed below. So much for the properties of the twenty-four possibilities.

TWO SUBJECTS OR ANSWERS IN A ROW

Marpurg says: "Although ordinarily the entries of the voices alternate between subject and answer . . . extraordinarily they can be made to imitate at the octave, so that the subject or answer appears in different voices twice in a row."[13] In the following example (example 9.15), the subject appears in the alto, and then the answer in the soprano is followed by another answer in the tenor (sub/ans/ ans). The soprano and tenor entries occupy the same position within the respective "vocal" ranges. The subject is nonmodulating (we already discussed a nonmodulating subject in chapter 8 in Handel's Wedding Anthem XIV, example 8.18a) so the first note, G, of the answer enters as the fifth of the $I^{6/3}$ triad. When the second answer enters in m. 4, the first note is reharmonized: the G is now the root of the chord with the third above. There is a remodulation to I at the end of the third entry (m. 5). When the first notes of the second and third entries sound on the weak eighth, the same harmony has sounded on the downbeat (long brackets); however, the fourth entry (subject in the bass of m. 5) is different. The B in the tenor on the third quarter of m. 5 cannot sound against the C that follows in the bass (first note of fourth entry). So Bach speeds up to an eighth-note harmonic rhythm (two short brackets) for a different harmony when the fourth voice enters.

Example 9.15. (Bach, WTC I, fugue in C major, mm. 1–6) *Note that Bach momentarily tonicizes C major at the beginning of m. 4, although the entry is otherwise in the key of the dominant. This example contains many deviations from strict style, like the parallel ninths at the end of m. 5 (arrow).*

For an interesting case study, compare Bach's fugue from the first violin sonata in G minor, mm. 1–4, with his fugue in G minor for lautenwerck, mm. 1–4, based on the same theme. Which one has a retransition? Why?

THE SUBJECT AND ANSWER IN NONADJACENT VOICES

Sometimes composers have subjects and answers alternate, regardless of the actual order of vocal entries. In those orders that "skip over" one voice (S followed by T, T by S, A by B, or B by A, where one would normally have two subjects or two answers in a row), the composer must demand that one voice sing in a "wrong" register. In the following example, the subject in the tenor is actually in the alto range. Hence the soprano can follow with the answer; the answer in the soprano is followed by the subject in the bass, with an unusually big distance between the parts. We have marked the retransition in mm. 6–7 that brings us back to the tonic key.

The following fugue (Example 9.17), perhaps by Giovanni Battista Pergolesi, uses the order of entry STAB, while successive entries alternate between the subject and answer. This is because the opening subject occupies the lower part of the soprano range, while the tenor is in a very high range; in the third entry the alto subject sounds in the same register as the original subject in the soprano.

Example 9.16. (Handel, Anthem II, "In the Lord put I my Trust") *Note that Handel's retransition restores the flat sixth degree of the tonic.*

Example 9.17. (Giovanni Battista Pergolesi, "Dixit," Psalm 109) *The subject ends with a modulation, the answer with a retransition that is shorter.*

EXERCISE 9-E

1. *Writing (long):* Compose a fugue exposition based on the diagram below, using the given subject.

Table 9.2

Soprano	—	A	CS	FC
Alto	S	CA	FC	FC
Tenor	—	—	—	A
Bass	—	—	S	CA

Your subject/countersubject combination must be invertible at the octave, and the countersubject must obey the criteria set forth by Mattheson and Marpurg. Do not use sixteenth notes. Suspensions or seventh chords are possible with this combination; you are encouraged to use them. The group of four eighth notes at the end of the subject constitutes an embellished splice. This splice will require some adjustments when going from the A/CA version to the S/CS version. You must keep the same rhythm in both versions. The entries are periodic (the soprano entry is shown with an arrow). Provide a Roman numeral analysis and circle the adjustments at the splice in the countersubject and counteranswer.

Example 9.18. (Adapted from Langloz Manuscript)

2. *Composing from scratch:* Take a few subjects from chapter 3 (you may transpose the given material in order to accommodate ranges), and prepare a four-voice exposition for each. Choose a different order of entry for each from among the following: BTAS, ATBS, TASB, or TBSA. Use the appropriate splices, modulations, and so on, as needed. Label all devices and write out the harmonic analysis.

PARTIMENTO

These partimenti look a little more like fugal thematic expositions because they begin by adding one voice after another and because they have a countermelody that you can reuse against every statement of the theme. For method 1 (described on p. 131), you should start by playing the subject and answer through all the registers; then you can add the countermelody and play *both* over the whole keyboard (subject + countersubject, answer + counteranswer). Be sure you know what note to start the countermelody on (or what vertical interval it makes with the theme) and how to connect the end of the theme to the countermelody because this connection must be altered at the splice, sometimes even with a remodulation. When you play the duos over the whole keyboard, you have to break off the voice that just sounded the countermelody and concentrate on the voice with the new countermelody.

In this demonstration of method 1, you are given the partimento by Pasquini shown in example 9.19. The versions of the theme are spliced together (dotted line), and you are to play the alternating versions of the theme (i.e., subject and answer), accompanying them with their countermelodies as shown in example 9.20. We have invented an altered countermelody at the splice in m. 9 that makes a smooth line and a "diagonal splice" (in mm. 6, 9, 12, etc., the harmonic rhythm is the dotted quarter note). Memorize this one, beginning an octave or two higher.

Example 9.19. (Pasquini)

Example 9.20. (Pasquini)

In example 9.21a Pasquini again starts with "solo" lines; you don't add anything until he marks "tutti." In example 9.21b he provides a triple-meter version of the same subject. In both examples, the step is the eighth note.

Example 9.21a. (Pasquini)

Example 9.21b. (Pasquini)

In example 9.22 the first three entries are in the order AST. The theme first sounds in the alto and is followed by a countermelody beneath the soprano. When the tenor enters, the countermelody should appear above, in the soprano, so the combination in mm. 2–3 is invertible at the octave. Some alteration will be necessitated by the figures in m. 4, and perhaps other little adjustments as well. How much of the subject can you put above the bass at *entra il soggetto* in m. 6?

Example 9.22. (Pasquini)

In example 9.23 the dominant form of the theme comes first; after the tonic form, there is a one-bar modulation. When you do method 2, note the emphasis on the subdominant in bars 7–8.

Example 9.23. (Pasquini)

The partimento fugue shown in example 9.24 also begins with soprano and alto entries and has a reusable countermelody. The tonic statement is eight quarters long, but the dominant statement is lengthened by two beats to provide a retransition. The lines from m. 10 (fourth quarter) to m. 12 (third quarter) in treble clef can be treated as "soli."

Example 9.24. (Langloz Manuscript, no. 11)

Example 9.25 shows an unfigured partimento by Fenaroli. The "tutti" begins in m. 17. Note how in m. 15 the countermelody borrows the rhythm of the theme.

Example 9.25. (Fenaroli, Partimenti, book 5, no. 7, Gj 1416)

Example 9.25. *(Concluded)*

NOTES

1. Mattheson, *Der vollkommene Capellmeister*, III, 23, §§18–20.
2. Marpurg, *Abhandlung von der Fuge*, V, §3, p. 148.
3. Marpurg, §4, p. 149.
4. Marpurg, §5, pp. 149–50.
5. Marpurg, §3, p. 148.
6. Marpurg, §4, p. 149.
7. Marpurg, §6, p. 150.
8. Mattheson, *Der vollkommene Capellmeister*, III, 20, §87.
9. Marpurg, *Abhandlung von der Fuge*, V, §2, pp. 147–48: "This countermelody does not always have to be consonant nor always dissonant with the entrance of the theme. We know that as soon as there is a convenient place for the theme to enter, one should not wait for another. If it happens that the theme can enter on a suspension, that is excellent. If this is not possible, then the entrance will happen on a consonance."
10. Mattheson, *Der vollkommene Capellmeister*, III, 20, §106.
11. On "collateral ranges" in the Renaissance, see Schubert, *Modal Counterpoint*, pp. 208–9.
12. Marpurg, *Abhandlung von der Fuge*, IV, §7, p. 96.
13. Marpurg, IV, §7, p. 96.

10

TONAL ANSWER

Real Answer versus Tonal Answer; Moving the Splice; Tonic Scale and Dominant Scale; Other Alterations and Scale Degrees; Reciprocity and Types of Subject; Analyzing Melodies; Writing Tonal Answers; When to Use Real Answer; Countersubject and Counteranswer; Diagonal Splice; Tonal Answer and Harmonic Progression; Partimento

REAL ANSWER VERSUS TONAL ANSWER

All the versions of the theme you have seen up to this point are in the tonic or the dominant. The latter versions are simply transpositions of the theme: they duplicate, in the key of the dominant, exactly what the theme did in the tonic. We saw that often they are introduced by a modulation and followed by a splice or a remodulation that prepares the next entry back in the tonic. We called the statements in the dominant "answers" in the previous chapter. They are often called "real answers" to distinguish them from "tonal" answers, which are melodically altered versions of the subject in the tonic.

Composers started altering the transposed theme around 1600.[1] Mattheson brilliantly articulates the reasons for this: he describes fugal imitation as trying to maintain three "qualities of reiteration": (1) trying to keep the subject and answer within the range of an octave, (2) trying to limit starting notes to the tonic and dominant, and (3) trying to make the subject and answer "as alike and similar as can only be done with good style."[2] He says that to accommodate these needs, we alter in the least conspicuous way.

The first of these reasons might seem pretty abstract: who cares about the sum of the ranges of the two tunes? But try this experiment: if somebody sings an ascending fifth and then you imitate, singing an ascending fifth from their second note, it can seem unnatural and difficult. That's because the resulting ninth sounds dissonant with respect to the first note in your memory. It would be more natural for you to sing up a fourth, wouldn't it?

The second reason, to limit starting notes to the tonic and dominant, might seem more reasonable, insisting on keeping the piece in a tonal area bounded by just two keys. We have already seen that if we simply repeat the motion from the first entry to the second, the third entry would come on the supertonic (example 8.3a), and we would spin out around the circle of fifths.

The third reason is completely reasonable—of course we want the tunes to sound the same, otherwise they wouldn't be "reiterating"! The problem is reconciling all these reasons, and Mattheson leads us through the details with an example:

> Now anyone who would want to choose the Dorian mode, or D minor, and would want to make a fugue out of the first phrase of the familiar hymn "Vater unser," etc., while observing the similarity of the intervals as well as the correct opening pitch in the answer, would stay too close to the original tune and would have to exceed the boundaries of the mode in an intolerable way.[3]

What he means is that if you start your answer on D and maintain exact transposition, you will end on G, which exceeds "the boundaries of the mode," which are A–A (in the plagal Dorian mode). From a tonal point of view, this results in a harmonic arrival on the subdominant, which is not a member of the all-important T/D axis.

Example 10.1a. ("Vater unser") "Dux" means leader, or subject; "comes" means follower or answer.

Mattheson goes on: "However, if he wants to avoid this, as is appropriate, then he has to have the answer enter with a foreign note . . . so that the same intervals, i.e., thirds, whole-tones and semitones, are preserved. And that is not much good either."[4] The "foreign note" is E, which could not overlap with the dux's ending on D, necessitating a modulation or transition of some kind.

Example 10.1b.

"Or otherwise, he must change the interval of the descending third into a second, thus preserving the two main qualities of the answer and violating only the third, least important quality, namely the precise similarity of its intervals, just a little in one single place."[5] In other words, the overall motion from the beginning to the end must be from A down to D in the subject and from D down to A in the answer, and the alteration must be very discreet. In this way all entries can overlap with arrivals (example 10.1c).

Example 10.1c.

The importance of the "bounds of the mode" and filling the octave are a remnant of modal theory (Mattheson seems to equate Dorian and D minor). Each mode has two forms, the *authentic* and the *plagal*. In the authentic mode, the octave extends from the final (tonic) to the final and divides at the fifth; in the plagal, it extends from the fifth (dominant) to the fifth and divides at the final (tonic). The simplest way to explain tonal answer is to base it on corresponding parts of these octave scales. If the subject goes from the "middle" note to one extreme of the authentic mode, the answer will go from the "middle" note to the extreme of the plagal mode. Thus in "Vater unser" (see example 10.1a), an authentic melody, the distance from the "middle" of the authentic mode (A in the Dorian) down to the final (D) is different from the "middle" of the plagal mode (D in the Hypodorian) down to the lower extreme (A). For Mattheson, fitting the tune into the mode is more important than preserving *all* melodic intervals. The intervals that must be preserved all come after the splice, that is, after the adjusted interval: in general, we can say that on either side of the splice, the exact intervals are maintained.

MOVING THE SPLICE

Another way to understand the difference between subject and tonal answer is to consider that we're just moving the splice between real answers that we saw in chapter 8 (e.g., examples 8.1, 8.6b and c). The theme does not recur in an exact transposition of its original form, as in real answer; rather, a melodic interval at the beginning of the subject changes in the answer version of the theme. We can now identify with a splice the interval that makes Mattheson's subject different from his answer. The alteration occurs for "tonal" reason—in other words, to get from the tonic to the dominant and from the dominant to the tonic. In the above example of "Vater unser," we place a dotted line between A and F in the subject version of the tune and between D and C in the answer version. Instead of having the splice *between* the entries, it now occurs *within* the melody.

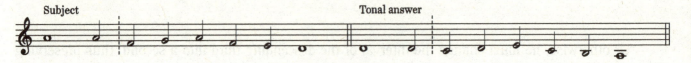

Example 10.2.

Moving the splice can make the transitions between keys much smoother: the muss and fuss (albeit the often beautiful muss and fuss) of modulation, retransition, and so on are eliminated. And it allows the important degrees of tonic and dominant to shine out in the melodies as starting notes, ending notes, high notes, and low notes, in both the subject and answer versions (these notes are stressed in the melodies by almost all Baroque composers).

In this little partimento by Pasquini we see an awkward use of real answer that could be improved by the use of tonal answer. The subject is exactly one measure long, and the return to the tonic (A minor) in the third entry is accomplished with a change of harmonic progression at the beginning of m. 3 compared to the beginning of m. 2 (example 10.3a). The B after the splice in m. 2 is the "foreign note" Mattheson didn't like. It would have been much smoother to use a tonal answer, answering E–A with A–E, as shown in example 10.3b, where the first two notes are the dominant and tonic scale degrees answered by the tonic and dominant scale degrees. Does it bother you that the harmonic functions are different in the answer?

Example 10.3a. (Pasquini)

Example 10.3b.

Play the subjects and their tonal answers in examples 10.4, 10.8a, and 10.8b up and down the keyboard (as in method 1 of the partimento exercises) to get a feel for the smooth back-and-forth of keys.

TONIC SCALE AND DOMINANT SCALE

In the next four sections we focus on analyzing the difference between a subject and its tonal answer. Example 10.4 shows the subject and answer from a fugue by Bach, whose first four notes are like the "Vater unser" tune used by Mattheson. You can put in the dotted line that shows the splice where the answer differs from the subject. The subject makes a clear harmonic arrival in C minor (on scale degree 3), and likewise the answer arrives on scale degree 3 of the dominant. But is the whole answer in the dominant? In order to understand which notes belong to which keys and where the splice is, we have to analyze the "scale degrees" of the melodies.

Example 10.4. (Bach, *WTC II*, fugue in C minor)

To describe the difference between a subject and its tonal answer, when we have both in front of us, we reckon in terms of two scales. This method, which recalls the plagal and authentic scales Matteson was thinking of, is a kind of amalgam of similar systems of scales proposed by Marpurg and André Gédalge.[6] The normal scale of the key can be laid out against a scale built up from the dominant note as shown in the following example.

"Degrees"	1	2	3	4	5	6	7	8
Tonic scale	C	D	Eb	F	G	Ab	Bb	C
Dominant scale	G	A(♮)	Bb	C	D	Eb	F	G

Example 10.5a.

We suspect that the subject begins with "1 of D" and not "5 of T" for two reasons: we know that there is an alteration, and we know that subjects rarely begin on "5 of T." Mapping the theme from example 10.4 onto these scales, we move, at the moment of the alteration, to the *opposite* scale to reckon all notes. Thus we go from the first degree of the dominant scale to "3 of T," meaning the third degree of the tonic scale. We know from looking at the answer that the melody from then on sounds exactly the same in both subject and answer version, so the rest of the subject stays in the tonic scale. We can plot the motion of the first four notes of the subject on the chart with arrows.

"Degrees"	1	2	3	4	5	6	7	8
Tonic scale	C	D	Eb →	F →	G	Ab	Bb	C
Dominant scale	G ↘	A(♮)	Bb	C	D	Eb	F	G

Example 10.5b. (The subject)

What's nice about this method is that the path of the answer will be the *mirror image* of that of the subject, even though the intervals are different. From "1" of the tonic scale we go diagonally down instead of up. The diagonal line *is* the splice, after which the intervals are all exactly the same.

"Degrees"	1	2	3	4	5	6	7	8
Tonic scale	C	D	E♭	F	G	A♭	B♭	C
Dominant scale	G	A(♮)	B♭	C	D	E♭	F	G

Example 10.5c. (The answer)

Each note has two identifiers: the scale from which the note is taken (tonic or dominant), which we place below a line like the denominator in a fraction (with letters, not numbers), and the degree of the relevant scale, which we place above. Thus the subject consists of

$$\frac{1}{D} \quad\vdots\quad \frac{3 \quad 4 \quad 5}{T}$$

Example 10.6a. (Pronounced "one of the dominant, three four five of the tonic")

and the answer:

$$\frac{1}{T} \quad\vdots\quad \frac{3 \quad 4 \quad 5}{D}$$

Example 10.6b. (Pronounced "one of the tonic, three four five of the dominant")

As always, the dotted line shows the D/T and T/D splices. The third note in the answer is a C, but we do not confuse this C, which is the fourth degree of the dominant, with the C that is the first degree of the tonic because *as long as the melodies are exact transpositions of each other, we stay in the same "scale."*

This method of reckoning notes may seem cumbersome, but it is completely reliable when dealing with multiple alterations (see "Multiple Splices" in chapter 17), and it is very simple: all the "numerators" in examples 10.6a and b are the same in the two versions, and all the "denominators" are opposites. The double meaning of notes is essential to switching back and forth between keys. Using "scales" of the type shown in example 10.5, analyze the scale degrees in the original "Vater unser" subject and in example 10.1c.

Important: It is essential that the segments of the melody on either side of the splice sound the same, that is, they must have the *same semitone positions*. This will ensure that the two melodies, subject and answer, sound "as alike and similar as can only be done with good style" in spite of the alteration, which is "just a little in one single place," as Mattheson said.

OTHER ALTERATIONS AND SCALE DEGREES

Marpurg likewise explains that if the *dux* (the leading voice) modulates to the dominant, the *comes* (the following voice) must be altered in order to return to the tonic. But his description of the alteration differs a little from Mattheson's. Marpurg says it "happens in two ways: (A) via skipping a scale degree. This happens in the larger half of the octave. (B) via repeating a scale degree; i.e., if one plays a note twice. This happens in the smaller half of the octave."[7] By "larger half of the octave," Marpurg refers to the fifth span from tonic up to dominant (degrees 1–2–3–4–5); the "smaller half" is the fourth span from dominant up to tonic (degrees 5–6–7–8).

A melody that illustrates the first way (A) is a subject by Pachelbel based on the chorale "Vom Himmel hoch." The chorale melody is the subject, filling the smaller half of the octave from D down to A; the answer, fitting in the larger half of the octave, must "skip" a scale degree to get from A down to D.

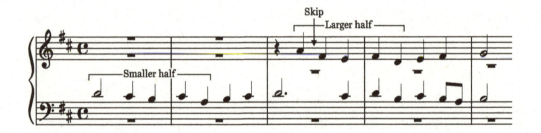

Example 10.7. (Pachelbel, "Vom Himmel hoch") A descending fourth outline is replaced by a descending fifth outline.

Here are two subjects (example 10.8) that illustrate Marpurg's principle of "playing a note twice" in the "smaller half of the octave." The fugue from which Mattheson's subject is taken (example 10.8a) is in G minor with a "Dorian" signature. We analyze the splice in the subject as 1/D–4/T and the splice in the answer as 1/T–4/D. Example 10.8b, from a Handel keyboard fugue, illustrates the same principle. Add dotted lines and scale degrees to the Handel.

Example 10.8a. (Mattheson)

Example 10.8b. (Handel)

RECIPROCITY AND TYPES OF SUBJECT

Now that we have two different versions of the theme, we might wonder if one is melodically better than the other. Here are two strikingly similar fugue subjects and answers in which the first two pitches exchange degrees 1 and 3 but of the opposite scales.

Example 10.9a. (J. K. F. Fischer, "Ariadne," 20)

Example 10.9b. (Bach, Cantata 21 ". . . for He is the help of my countenance and my God")

You can see that Fischer's subject is Bach's answer. *Either version can be the subject, either one the answer.* They are in a reciprocal relationship. The subject and the answer move between the tonic and the dominant scales in mirror motions. Which of the two versions is more appealing depends on the nature of the melodic material itself. We find that in repertoire, when 1 of one scale goes to 3 of the other, the first note is more often the dominant (as in the Bach example above). One reason some composers might prefer the subject to begin with the dominant note in this context is that all the notes can outline the tonic triad, as in example 10.9b, and the bulk of the tune is in the tonic. We "know" from examining both subject and answer that the first note is really something else, but the fifth scale degree can be part of the tonic triad, while the tonic note can't be part of a dominant triad. Fischer's subject mixes in notes of different triads and is perhaps not as clear tonally as the Bach. Sing both.

Other types of subjects feature different degrees across the dotted line, and in them, too, certain orders predominate in the repertoire. For instance, when 1 of one scale goes to 6 of the other, the subject version of the tune is usually the one beginning with the dominant note. Subjects and their tonal answers are not always equally beautiful or clear. Some subjects are altered in a way that may make them less likable, while, on the other hand, many tonal answers go completely unnoticed—the listener just thinks, "There's that theme again."

ANALYZING MELODIES

At the beginning of a subject (for now) you must assume the first note to be "scale degree" 1 of either the tonic or the dominant scale. For now we will only see pieces that start with the tonic or dominant note of the key.

EXERCISE 10-A

1. *Analysis:* Label the scale degrees around the splices in these fugue subjects and tonal answers. In order to find a splice, you have to compare the subject and the answer and find the melodic interval that is altered in the answer. On one side of the splice you will have one scale, on the other side, the other. On both sides you will have the same "degrees." That is, you will label the degrees with the same two numbers in both cases, but the letters indicating the scales will be reversed. You may want to make a chart for the scales of the tonic and dominant. Disregard the countermelodies and the harmonies for now (remember that tonal answer "degrees" are completely abstract).

Example 10.10a. (Fux, Omnis terra, K. 183)

Example 10.10b. (Handel, Israel in Egypt)

Example 10.10c. (Handel, Samson) *The subject in the alto and the tonal answer in the tenor occupy adjacent octave ranges, and the countermelody in the alto remains in the same range as the subject.*

Example 10.10d. (Fux, Salve Regina, K. 257)

Example 10.10e. (Handel, Duet XIV)

Example 10.10f. (Handel, Duet X)

See also Bach Cantata 71, vii (example 11.15) and Handel "And with His Stripes" (example 11.2a).

Example 10.10g. (Fux, Accurrite fideles animae)

Example 10.10h. (de la Guerre, Gigue from Suite in A minor)

WRITING TONAL ANSWERS

In the preceding pages we have tried to explain how to spot and analyze tonal answers when you can see both the subject and answer. (If we didn't see both versions, we might assume the piece had a "real" answer.) In this section we will suggest how to *compose* a tonal answer from a tune you have found or invented.

Tonal answer is generally used when there is a clear and direct succession between an important note of the tonic scale and one of the dominant scale in the "head" of the subject (i.e., the very beginning). *Limitations:* for the moment, we only allow scale degree 1 to be used before the splice and 1, 3, and 6 after the splice. These are the most common degrees, and we want to keep things simple, so we have blacked out scale degrees 2, 4, 5, and 7.

"Degrees"	1	2	3	4	5	6	7	8
Tonic scale	D	E	F	G	A	B♭	C	D
Dominant scale	A	B	C	D	E	F	G	A

Example 10.11. (For D minor)

In the exercises above you have seen examples of 1/D going to 1/T, 3/T, and 6/T (and vice versa, 1/T going to 1/D, 3/D, and 6/D), and for the moment those are the only possibilities allowed. *Exceptions:* (1) often degree 3 is inserted between degrees 1 and 5 (see example 10.12), and (2) when the second note is degree 4 passing down to degree 3, we can consider degree 4 as an embellishment of the motion from 1/D to 3/T; this becomes a repeated note in the "smaller half" of the octave (see example 10.8).

Occasionally surprising variants occur, as in this example, where Vallotti has embellished the splice with a sixteenth note in two quite different ways. He clearly prefers rhythm to contour, motion to a repeated note. Recall Corelli in example 8.11.

Example 10.12. (Vallotti) *Compare the rest of subject and answer.*

WHEN TO USE REAL ANSWER

As you will see when you know a lot of music, any subject can get a real answer, but for the moment we want to explore the world of tonal answer. The subjects in the exercise below are designed to "require" a tonal answer because they contain a clear opposition between members of the two scales in the "head" of the subject. In general, we say that when a subject only rises from 1 to 2, or 3, or 4, it takes a real answer, even if afterward a 5 occurs because it is too late by then. This is a fuzzy area.

EXERCISE 10-B

Sometimes there is more than one "right answer," but you should try to find the one that Mattheson and Marpurg would like.

1. *Writing (short):* Write the answer to the given subjects. Indicate the splices and tonic and dominant scale degrees.

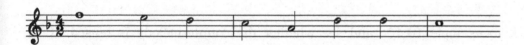

Example 10.13a.

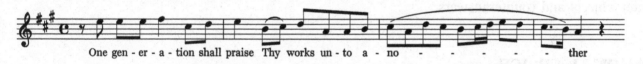

One gen - er - a - tion shall praise Thy works un - to a - no - - - - ther

Example 10.13b.

Example 10.13c.

2. *Improvisation:* Play the subjects and answers from no. 1 above, up and down the whole keyboard, as in partimento exercise method 1.

COUNTERSUBJECT AND COUNTERANSWER

When a tonal answer is used, a countermelody that accompanies both subject and answer must be altered accordingly. In chapter 8, we saw that a splice affects the harmonic progression as a whole. For instance, in example 8.6b we saw a splice in the modulation/remodulation pair that affected both the bass and the melody. With tonal answer the splice is an integral part of the theme, and any reused countermelody will be affected by the splice in the subject and answer as well. However, the alteration does not change the chord factors used on either side of the splice (example 8.6c).

In example 10.10g, the D/T splice occurs at the same moment in the answer (between "veni" and "veni") and in the counteranswer (after the four sixteenth notes in "coronaberis"). The T/D splice takes place in the corresponding places in the following subject/countersubject pair (between the fourth and fifth measures of the example). Label "scale degrees" and chord factors in both countermelodies. Remember: *countersubject is to counteranswer as subject is to answer.*

EXERCISE 10-C

1. *Analysis:* Go back to example 10.10c and see whether the countermelody is reused. If so, how is it altered? Label the scale degrees of the countersubject and counteranswer. Do the same for examples 11.2a and 11.15 in the next chapter.

2. *Composing (short):* Using the subjects and answers you wrote in exercise 10-B, compose countersubjects and counteranswers.

DIAGONAL SPLICE

The alterations do not always take place in the subject and countersubject simultaneously. In the following example the T/D splice in the answer occurs at the bar line between mm. 2 and 3; the counteranswer has an embellished splice, and the actual change of interval occurs three sixteenths earlier, so we say the splice is "diagonal." The two versions of the four-sixteenth motive (m. 2 and m. 4) have been bracketed.

Example 10.14. (Bach, C major Overture, fugue, beginning) *Only the string parts are shown. Oboes and bassoons, not shown here, double the violins and bass in the exposition.*

We can analyze the countersubject and counteranswer in the same way we do the subject and answer, using the two scales. The overall motion in the CA is from 3/T to 1/D (example 10.15a), while in the CS it's from 3/D to 1/T (example 10.15c). Three sixteenth notes embellish the splice. The CA complements the answer the same way the CS complements the subject: in both combinations, 3s and 1s are exchanged. Because T and D are reversed in the two versions, the CA's overall motion (E–G) is the retrograde of the subject's, and the CS's (B–C) is the retrograde of the answer's. In this case these "degrees" are also roots and thirds of chords, and as we mentioned in chapter 3, we like to see them exchanged in outer voices, alternating vertical thirds and sixths.

This particular embellishment, frequently found, is an amazingly elegant solution. Imagine what would happen if the splices in the countermelodies were to occur at the same time as those in the themes (i.e., if we straightened out the dotted line). If the counteranswer (example 10.15a) were to serve as the model, then the countersubject would appear as in example 10.15b. The result would be a rather inelegant repeated C going into the third beat; this is perfectly legal, but the forward motion and sense of direction would suffer. If the countersubject (example 10.15c) were the model, then the counteranswer would leap up a third at the splice (example 10.15d). Again, this would sound awkward, even though perfectly legal.

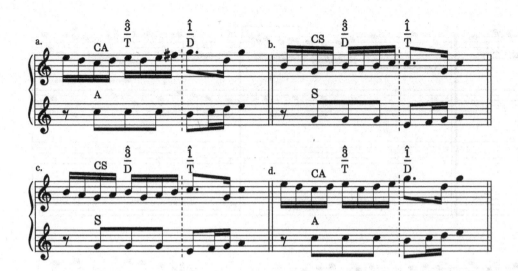

Example 10.15.

An interesting feature of this particular theme/countermelody pair is that the second groups of four sixteenth notes of the countermelodies are diminished versions of the themes they accompany, both in the subject version and the answer version. This illustrates Marpurg's suggestion, quoted in chapter 9 in our discussion of countersubject, that the material of the countermelodies be drawn from the theme.[8] Here (example 10.16) it is a transposed version of the third through seventh notes of the theme.

Example 10.16.

Often the countermelody begins *after* the splice, so it does not need to be altered, just transposed to fit the rest of the answer. Then, strictly speaking, it need not be called a counteranswer, it may simply be called a countermelody. Example 10.19 has such a countermelody.

EXERCISE 10-D

1. *Composing:* For each of the subjects given in example 10.17, compose a countersubject, write the tonal answer (the point of entry is indicated by the arrow), and compose a counteranswer.

2. *Composing:* Same as question 1, but compose countermelodies that are invertible at the octave.

Example 10.17. (Arrows indicate point of entry of the answer)

3. *Composing:* For each given subject in examples 10.18a–c, compose a fugal exposition in four parts. This exercise is based on contemporary practice. Mattheson reports: "We read about Lully that in his fugues and choruses he wrote down nothing but the mere entries of the voices where they should begin with the theme. But the rest he had his assistants fill in. In this way they doubtlessly learned so much that afterwards they were able to find these entries on their own. Let us do the same."[9]

You will have to write a tonal answer to the given subject and compose a countermelody that will be used consistently throughout your exposition. Your subject/countersubject combination may have to be invertible at the octave. Use sixteenth notes sparingly. You should use suspensions or seventh chords when it is possible. Indicate the splices with a dotted line. Label the tonic and dominant scale degrees for the first three entries (label only the first two notes after the splice), both for the subject (or answer) and for the countermelody (the splice might not take place at the same time in the S and the CS). You must keep the same rhythm in both the S/CS and A/CA versions (including at the splice). The entries are periodic (the second entry is shown with an arrow). Provide a Roman numeral analysis.

Example 10.18a. *The order of entry in this fugue exposition is BTAS. You only have to write up to the first few notes of the fourth entry in this exercise.*

Example 10.18b. *The order of entry in this fugue exposition is SATB.*

Example 10.18c. *The order of entry in this fugue exposition is ASBT.*

TONAL ANSWER AND HARMONIC PROGRESSION

THE PROBLEM WITH SCALE DEGREE 6

When we analyze tonal answer, we assign the pitches before and after the splice to the degrees of the scales of the tonic and dominant. In most of the examples we have looked at so far, the harmonies before and after the splice are the tonic and dominant harmonies themselves. But this need not always be the case. When 1 of one scale is followed by 6 of the other scale, the harmonization cannot involve the tonic and dominant. In the following subject by J. K. F. Fischer, shown in example 10.19a (fourth entry in the bass), the harmony before the splice is V followed by vi—and not I—after the splice. The tonal answer, shown at example 10.19b as it appears in the second entry, is harmonized as I followed by I^6 (or sometimes iii)—and not V—after the splice.

Example 10.19a. (Fischer, F Major Fugue, mm. 15–19)

Example 10.19b. (Fischer, F Major Fugue, mm. 5–9) *For another example, see Bach example 11.15, where the iii harmonization is used for 6/D.*

If the tonal answer in example 10.19b is harmonized I–iii across the splice, then the first two notes of the subject (example 10.19a) and answer (example 10.19b) represent the same chord factors (roots) in the respective harmonies, as labeled in the examples. If, on the other hand, the tonal answer is harmonized with I before and I^6 after the splice, the chord factor of the second note is different from the one of the second note in the subject. As a result, the second note of the answer is *reharmonized.* Perhaps both versions of the theme can be thought of as using substitute chords (vi for I and iii for V).

ALTERNATIVES TO HARMONIC CUT AND PASTE

As we have insisted, the "scale degree" method only explains melodic alterations. The numbers are independent of harmony (they are not chord factors), and they are even independent of the key of the music—they are not always scale degrees in the actual key of the music. We assume that in the Bach example 10.14 all the notes after the first one in the subject will be harmonized in the tonic, and that all the notes after the first one in the answer will be harmonized in the dominant. That is in fact what Bach does, but many examples employ reharmonization.

It is possible to harmonize in ways that don't reflect at all the abstract scales by which we label the notes. In example 10.20, the answer enters as part of a progression in the tonic key, even though we analyze the first note of the answer as "1 of D." This is because the end of the subject does not modulate to the dominant. The third entry begins on "1 of T" but it's actually part of a vii^6 harmony in the key of the dominant. We are in the key of the dominant at this point (rather than back in the tonic key) because there has been a modulation to the dominant during m. 5.

Example 10.20. (Graun, "Christus hat uns ein Vorbild gelassen" ["Christ has left us a role model"]) *See example 11.3 for another reharmonization of "1 of T."*

As this example illustrates, the subject–answer relationships articulate the pillars of the tonal space independently of the local harmonies. Melodic transposition at the fifth, keys, and chords are in a flexible relationship. When we listen to the subject as it appears in the bass at the very beginning of the movement, we probably hear the first three beats of m. 2 as 6–2–5 in the tonic. That's in the part of the subject whose "scale degrees" are "supposed" to be in the dominant. In the corresponding place of the third entry, Graun harmonizes these pitches as 6–2–5 in the tonic: in m. 7, the first three beats use IV–vii⁶(?)–I in the tonic key.

EXERCISE 10-E

1. *Analysis:* Go back to Exercise 10-A and analyze the harmonic progressions. Show the degrees in all T/D and D/T splices. Which examples use reharmonization?

2. *Writing:* Use tonal answers and countersubjects/counteranswers from this chapter to write four-part fugue expositions following the model just discussed.

PARTIMENTO

In these exercises tonal answers allow for periodic entries, without modulation/remodulation or transitions. In all of them, you are to try to reuse the countermelody. In the first example, by Pasquini, you could make up a countermelody that doesn't begin until after the splice (dotted line) in m. 2, so you will never have to alter it but merely transpose it.

Example 10.21. (Pasquini)

In example 10.22, the theme enters against a suspension (as in example 10.20), and the combination is invertible at the octave if altered appropriately at the splice. At the end Pasquini shows (with little vertical lines) a place to put the theme in an upper voice (should it be a subject or an answer?), making a little stretto over the pedal.

Example 10.22. (Pasquini)

The last four eighths of the theme in example 10.23 are a very common way to substitute a filled-in fifth (B-flat–F, the "larger half of the octave," in mm. 2 and 4) for a filled-in fourth (F–B-flat, the "smaller half," in mm. 1 and 3). Unusually, Pasquini's answer is in the subdominant! If you reuse the countermelody shown in bar 2, how will you alter it, if at all?

Example 10.23. (Pasquini)

In the following exercise, the treble-clef music in mm. 10–13 can be played as "soli."[10]

Example 10.24. (Langloz Manuscript, no. 24)

In the following example, Handel assumes you can figure out that the answer is tonal and not real (how?). His system for indicating entries above the bass is to show with a capital letter the voice that has the theme, and the first note of the entry (c with a single horizontal line over it means middle C, and with two lines C an octave higher). Thus "A f-" means the alto enters on F above middle C, and "C c= " means the *cantus* (soprano) enters on C above middle C. Harmonies change often on the eighth note.

Example 10.25. (Handel)

NOTES

1. For a thorough discussion of the origins of tonal answer, see Walker, *Theories of Fugue from the Age of Josquin to the Age of Bach*, pp. 64–76.

2. Mattheson, *Der vollkommene Capellmeister*, III, 20, §47.

3. Mattheson, §51.

4. Mattheson, §52.

5. Mattheson, §53.

6. Marpurg, *Abhandlung von der Fuge*, III, §1, p. 31; Gédalge, *Traité de la fugue*, pp. 20–28.

7. Marpurg, *Abhandlung von der Fuge*, III, §3, p. 34.

8. Marpurg, V, §3, p. 148.

9. Mattheson, *Der vollkommene Capellmeister*, III, 19, §41.

10. Renwick, *The Langloz Manuscript*, p. 57.

11

THEMATIC PRESENTATIONS

Summary of Chapters 5–10; The Exposition; Simple Fugues; Some Aspects of Musical Variety; Multiple Fugues; The First Type of Double Fugue; How to Avoid Periodicity in the First Type of Double Fugue; A Lesson from Mattheson; The Second Type of Double Fugue; The Third Type of Double Fugue; Invertibility in Double Fugues; Triple and Quadruple Fugues; Permutation Fugue; Invertibility in Triple and Quadruple Fugues; Unpacking Harmonic "Boxes" Part II; Partimento

SUMMARY OF CHAPTERS 5–10

We have seen how, in a ground bass piece, the harmonic progression forms a period that is repeated with different melodic surfaces. Then we saw how a repeating harmonic progression can support imitation at the octave or unison in a trio sonata or invention. Similarly, a trio sonata with imitation at the fifth can be made by repeating the progression in the dominant. The idea of periodic repetition applies to fugues as well, as we have seen, although modulations, remodulations, and so on can prevent periodicity. Tonal answer enables us to have periodic entries in alternating tonic and dominant keys by making the splice between keys an integral part of the theme.

In this chapter we will look at several ways of structuring expositions and other thematic presentations on the larger scale. The basic types to be covered here are simple fugues, multiple fugues (double, triple, quadruple), and permutation fugues. Until now you have only seen little sections of a piece. A basic principle of this book is that a whole piece is built out of these small units (subject/countermelody pair, remodulation, episode, etc.). In this chapter you will be looking at complete pieces (albeit short ones) for the first time. Consequently, longer analytical commentary is offered.

THE EXPOSITION

Some theorists believe that the exposition is complete when each voice has sounded the theme. Under that definition, the number of entries in the exposition equals the number of voices. Thus in a four-voice fugue, the exposition will contain four thematic statements, one by each voice. So when one voice then sounds the theme again, as often happens, these writers call this last entry "redundant." In this book we will refer to thematic sections as "theme groups" that may contain *any number of entries*, from one on up. Although these tend to alternate with nonthematic episodes (discussed in chapter 12), some fugues consist of nothing but thematic presentations (they are "all exposition"). In this chapter we will see examples of such fugues.

SIMPLE FUGUES

A simple fugue contains a single theme that recurs; no other melody (i.e., a countermelody) recurs. Here is a fugue by J. K. F. Fischer whose subject you saw in example 10.9a. Except for two beats of retransition in m. 4, subjects and answers recur every six beats. With no countersubject, Fischer has taken pains to keep inventing new countermelodies. Such fugues are fairly rare.

Example 11.1. (J. K. F. Fischer, "Ariadne Musica," 20) *Because there are two splices, indicated in the first subject and answer, the subjects and answer are, in effect, nonmodulating—such multiple splices are discussed in chapter 17. Deviations from strict style are noted by arrows. Note especially the extra-long dissonance in m. 11.*

SOME ASPECTS OF MUSICAL VARIETY

Let us consider how a composer works within such a restrictive atmosphere, where a single theme is constantly sounding, recurring at regular time intervals, and where there are no episodes. How can the composer keep the listener's interest? What devices can be used to add contrast and variety and give shape to the piece as a whole? Here are most of the devices we have found:

Texture: The composer can change the number of sounding voices so that the texture thickens and thins out.

Register: The sounding voices may be at their upper or lower extremes or far apart. Highest and lowest notes are often structurally significant.

Spacing: The voices that sound may be close together or far apart.

Competition: If the countermelodies are more interesting than the subject, the repetitions of the subject will be less noticeable and boring.

Overlap: The interest in the countermelody can be further stimulated by having it seem to flow right through a thematic entry, which consequently is heard as interrupting. The first voice can be in the middle of a suspension or a run of sixteenth notes when the second statement jumps in.

Modulation: The thematic statements can appear in different keys, even in the opposite mode (i.e., changing from major mode to minor mode or vice versa). We label these entries according to the form of the melody (subject or answer) and the key of the longer segment (see example 11.2a).

Other techniques include stretto, melodic inversion, various double counterpoints, and so on, whose discussion is covered in chapters 18 and 19.

EXERCISE 11-A

1. *Analysis:* Discuss the six means of achieving musical variety listed above as they are used (or not) in Fischer's example 11.1.

2. *Analysis:* Discuss the six means of achieving musical variety listed above as they are used in another fugue in this chapter.

MULTIPLE FUGUES

Multiple fugues contain two or more themes that recur. Two themes make a double fugue, three a triple fugue, four a quadruple fugue, and so on. Most fugues have countersubjects, and if the countersubject is considered as a second theme, these fugues are called *double*. Not all authors agree on this meaning of the term *double fugue*; the differences in definitions depend on when the different themes are presented. There are three meanings for the term *double fugue*, which we classify as follows:

Type 1: For some authors, the term means a fugue with a countersubject. The idea is that if the countermelody is reused, it can be given equal importance with the theme. Mattheson's use of the term *double* is derived from the fact that the theme and countermelody must be able to exchange positions, in other words, that their combination is invertible through *double* counterpoint, usually at the octave. Mattheson calls Kuhnau's examples 9.6 and 11.4d double fugues. Example 11.2a by Handel is another.

Type 2: For other authors, a double fugue is one in which the presentation of the countermelody occurs simultaneously with the presentation of the theme. Sabbatini calls Vallotti's fugue in example 11.5 a double fugue of this type.

Type 3: Finally, some fugues introduce a new subject late in the piece, often with its own exposition, eventually weaving the original subject and this later one together. Since such fugues often have a countersubject, the late theme is often the third or even the fourth, and such fugues must, strictly speaking, be called triple or quadruple or quintuple. Bach's C-sharp minor fugue from *WTC I* and the "St. Anne" organ fugue are famous examples. This concept seems to have been introduced after the eighteenth century. Example 11.7 is an example.

What all these meanings have in common is the idea of a second, perhaps subordinate, theme that is combined with the principal theme. Whether the answer is tonal or real is immaterial.

THE FIRST TYPE OF DOUBLE FUGUE

Our example of this type is example 11.2a, from Handel's *Messiah* (25). First, we will give an overview of all the thematic presentations, pointing out entries in other keys. After the first five, entries occur in keys other than the tonic and dominant. This is quite normal in longer fugues, as the changes of key provide contrast. In m. 31, we have the subject form starting on F that moves to the key of B-flat minor (labeled S^{iv}). This entry requires a modulation to get to the next subject entry on C. Measures 43–47 modulate to E-flat, and in m. 48 we have a subject entry in that key (S^{vii}). This is followed by an unnecessary transition (mm. 52–54) leading to a subject in A-flat (S^{iii}). Measures 59–62 consist of free material that confirms A-flat using a new motive that was introduced in m. 47. Measure 63 starts a subject in the tonic, whose first note is the third degree of A-flat (so III supports 1/D). From then on we have only subjects and answers in the tonic and dominant keys.

Handel uses a single countermelody that has an importance equal to that of the theme (in fact, it's heard more often than the theme). This countermelody (bracketed) only begins over the fourth note of the subject or answer; thus it does not participate in the splice. The countermelody often appears to be sounded alone, without the theme. However, a close look reveals that the line that often accompanies this countermelody is in fact very similar to the fourth to seventh notes of the end of the subject ("stripes we are heal-"). Like notes 4–7, the notes in this facsimile (or extension, labeled in mm. 16–18) span a fourth over two measures. The difference between the two versions is that the original spans a diminished fourth, while the facsimile spans a perfect fourth with a chromatic passing tone that makes an applied dominant. Handel often extends the word "healed" by linking the extension to the last note of the subject, which means that the two statements of the countermelody can sound in immediate succession a fourth apart. Once, they are even sung in the same voice line, the soprano (mm. 39–43).

This fugue is not quite wholly thematic; in addition to modulations and other passages mentioned above, it contains one longish sequential episode (mm. 71–78; see chapter 12 for discussion of episodes).

Example 11.2a. The first type of double fugue (Handel, "And with His Stripes," Messiah, 25). *Doubling instrumental parts omitted. The original countermelody contains a deviation from strict style (marked with an arrow) but Handel later alters the melodies that make this crunch: in m. 24 he alters the rhythm of the bass line, and at m. 66 he initiates a new version of the countermelody that occurs again in m. 70. The fugue ends with a half cadence because it is followed immediately by another movement in F major.*

Example 11.2a. *(Continued)*

Example 11.2a. *(Continued)*

Example 11.2a. *(Continued)*

Example 11.2a. *(Concluded)*

HOW TO AVOID PERIODICITY IN THE FIRST TYPE OF DOUBLE FUGUE

We have discussed the fact that themes can appear at regular time intervals. On the one hand, this is good; it permits the listener to anticipate the next event and makes the music flow along smoothly, as in a dance. It also means the composer never has to invent new music—everything is governed by the theme and its harmonization(s). A fugue with regularly recurring entries can be very beautiful (see Bach in example 11.15; see also *WTC II*, 9).

On the other hand, periodic repetition can be boring. Mattheson has clearly heard enough of it and recommends the element of surprise: The theme should enter at a surprising time, in a surprising voice, or with a surprising harmonization. (See his discussion of example 11.4 below.) If there is no need for a remodulation, how can the composer break up the time spans between entries?

One way, discussed in the next chapter, is to insert episodes. Another is to insert an *unnecessary transition*, a little bit of music that flows seamlessly out of one thematic statement and into the next; it is neither a modulation nor a remodulation, and it is too short to be an episode, which usually contains sequential material. From an analytical point of view, the only way to tell if a transition is necessary is to leave it out and see if the next thematic entrance fits. In example 11.2a, if you play the subject in the tenor on the second half note of m. 9, it sounds fine (obviously, you have to change the continuations of the soprano and alto to accommodate this entry). The cancellation of the B-natural and introduction of E-natural in m. 10 make a better transition to F minor, but they are not strictly necessary. Likewise, the bass entry could happen on the second beat of m. 16 (corresponding to the alto entry in m. 5), so mm. 16 (second half)–19 (first half) are unnecessary. If we play the entries as described, we get a fully periodic presentation of the theme, as shown in example 11.2b. We haven't completely ruined Handel's music, but a lot of the élan of the original is lost.

Example 11.2b. (Handel's thematic material presented periodically)

Looking ahead to the next entry in the same movement, the soprano could enter with the subject on C in m. 23, but instead Handel interjects the same music as at mm. 16–19, down a fourth, and has the soprano sound the *answer* in m. 25. What did Handel want? The higher entrance of the answer? Two answers in a row? The two statements of the countermelody? To keep us in suspense? All these elements are bound together, and we can't say which came first in his mind. But as to whether we should call the remodulation necessary or not, we decide on the basis of the next entry; because an F could not sound in m. 23, we say it is necessary.

The music of the "unnecessary" transition is only unnecessary from a harmonic point of view; it may serve a registral, rhythmic, motivic, or other function. It is often the mere prolongation of a single harmony. Such a prolongation might be made by the expansion of a chord, bringing the melodic material into a different register, or extending the phrase length.

Another way to change the time interval between thematic entries is to overlap the head of one theme with the cadence of the preceding one, *compressing* the amount of time expected. This elision does not shorten the time interval enough to be called stretto, although it is similar in principle. A type that is frequently found involves a theme that starts 1/T–3/D, where the first note is reharmonized as the fourth scale degree of the dominant key (it functions as either the fifth of vii/V or the seventh of V/V). Example 11.3, a partimento fugue by Pasquini, illustrates this in m. 6.

Example 11.3. (a partimento by Pasquini) *Time intervals are indicated below the score. The little lines in measures 14–15 indicate the possibility of adding a theme in an upper voice over the pedal. Should it be a subject or an answer?*

A LESSON FROM MATTHESON

Mattheson shows how a beginner who "wants to imitate a good author and learn the art from him" might set about composing a double fugue of the first type. He proposes a subject (example 11.4a) that comes from a piece already composed. "I would then try, without consulting the model any further (by covering the rest with a piece of paper), to see how I might succeed with the countermelody." He proposes example 11.4b and comments: "First, I do not like at all the general pause (*) and the ridiculous interruption (†) at the end of the fourth measure: for it looks like little or nothing else were to follow. Meanwhile, most people would do it just this way." He also doesn't like the fifth on the downbeat of the third measure because when it is inverted at the octave it will become a fourth, "which is not tolerable." He also finds in the countermelody "neither life nor rhythmic differentiation, since both melodies are almost the same in these respects. I would now improve these three deficiencies in the following way: (example 11.4c)."[1]

Although this solves one rhythmic problem, it introduces another—all the notes in the countermelody are of the same value! Also, he doesn't like the connection between the subject and countermelody, and he doesn't like the vertical intervals between answer and countermelody: "There is neither contrary motion nor variety in the intervals, which consist of *nothing but* thirds, which become *nothing but* sixths upon inversion: one has to guard oneself very well against this *nothing but*."[2]

Finally he shows what Kuhnau, the "good author" whom he wanted to imitate, had done in the first place (example 11.4d), and adds his commentary (numbers correspond to numbers in the score). He says that

1. The joint between subject and countermelody is "cohesive" (however, note that this same link is not necessary in the second voice—see the soprano in m. 4, where rhythmic continuity is assured by the alto).

2. The alternating thirds and sixths are "beautiful," likewise the contrary motion and the variety of rhythms.

3. Full cadences, which would stop the flow of music, are avoided through the use of dissonance ("whoever does not understand this is stuck all the time." Compare example 11.4b).

4. An "interlude" prepares the entry of the bass (we would call this an unnecessary retransition). He observes that "one should not always burst in with the subject in another voice, without ceremony, right after finishing the subject in the first voice, but first consider place and time."

5. The entry of the bass sounds "quite strange and somewhat unexpected" because of the sixth above and because of the delay caused by the interlude. He approves of the countermelody being concealed in the inner part—we would have expected to hear it in the upper voice.[3]

Example 11.4.

THE SECOND TYPE OF DOUBLE FUGUE

In the second type, the subject and countersubject are sounded together right from the start. However, how do we know which is the subject and which is the countersubject? We'll call the first one to enter the subject, unless we have some reason to know that the other tune is the subject (e.g., it was sounded elsewhere in the piece). It is also fairly common for one of the tunes to move more slowly than the other, and that might make us want to call that one the subject. It might be more accurate to call the two tunes "subject 1" and "subject 2." This method of labeling is very useful in the third type of multiple fugue, which often has three or more themes, which we call subjects 1, 2, 3, and so on.

In the second type of double fugue, then, you can think of the "subject" as consisting of two voices, and likewise the answer. We can thus refer to the subject pair and the answer pair. In this short excerpt from a Vallotti fugue (example 11.5), both subjects carry the same text. The subjects are nonmodulating, so there is a modulation added after the tonic arrival in m. 4, followed by the real answer in both entering voices. When the pair of subjects is sounded in the lower voices, their positions are reversed—they have been inverted at the octave.

Example 11.5. (Vallotti, Type 2 double fugue) *The second note of the first subject is the fifth of the V chord, so a 6/4 chord occurs in the inverted combination on the downbeat of m. 6. Vallotti has indicated that the continuo player should play the B-flat above the G, softening the bad effect a bit (by and large, Vallotti uses 6/4s very freely).*

Example 11.6. (Handel, Anthem VII, another example of a type 2 double fugue) *Doubling instrumental parts omitted. A fragmentary third theme, similar to the second, might make this a triple fugue.*

Example 11.6. *(Concluded)*

In the above example of a type 2 double fugue (example 11.6), the two subjects have consecutive contrasting phrases of text. Handel dramatically introduces the first subject with three parts in unison ("Thou art the glory of their strength"), then the second subject appears in the bass of a full-textured homorhythmic setting ("Alleluja"). After that a "normal" double fugue exposition occurs (mm. 6–13) with the two subjects sounding together (note the unnecessary transition in m. 10). This short but intense piece contains some devices discussed in later chapters: a sequence (chapter 12), a stretto (chapter 18), and a pedal (chapter 19).

THE THIRD TYPE OF DOUBLE FUGUE

Most double fugues of this type actually turn out to be triple fugues because they often contain a countersubject in the exposition before the late entry of a new subject. In example 11.7, the new subject is introduced quite early, along with the third entry of the first subject. The second violins sneak it in at m. 11, and it sounds again in the basses at m. 16. This short fugue is quite dense in ideas, and we will refer to it again in our discussions of invertible counterpoint at the twelfth (chapter 16), melodic and mirror inversion (chapter 19), and rhythmic augmentation (chapter 19).

Example 11.7. (Handel, Anthem IV, "Declare his honour," type 3 double fugue) *Bassoon and contrabass parts omitted. Disregard circled notes for now—they will be discussed in chapter 16.*

Example 11.7. *(Continued)*

Example 11.7. *(Concluded)*

INVERTIBILITY IN DOUBLE FUGUES

When we have only two tunes to repeat in combination, we can ensure that either one can work as a bass line by avoiding the fifths of chords. The two themes from "And with His stripes" are shown in example 11.8a. Handel's first subject contains no fifths, and the second subject (or countersubject) contains only one, marked with an asterisk. This note is sometimes part of the "vii–V" idiom when in the bass, sometimes the fifth of V (when it is in an upper part), and sometimes Handel alters the melody to get rid of it altogether (see mm. 50 and 81 in example 11.2a).

In example 11.5, from Vallotti, the second note of the upper subject is the fifth of a V chord. (The chord factors are analyzed in example 11.8b.) When this note appears in the bass (m. 6), the upper parts make a simple 6/4 chord, although Vallotti asks the continuo player to add the seventh (he writes 6/4/3 over the continuo), softening the bad effect of the 6/4.

In Handel's "Declare His honour" (example 11.7), we have a striking alternation of roots and thirds. The two notes marked with asterisks in example 11.8c are reharmonized as fifths only when they appear in an upper part (the first violin in mm. 16–17).

Example 11.8a. (From Handel, example 11.2a)

Example 11.8b. (From Vallotti, example 11.5)

Example 11.8c. (From Handel, example 11.7) *The alternate harmonization, which occurs transposed in mm. 16–17 of example 11.7, is shown in parentheses here.*

EXERCISE 11-B

1. *Analysis:* Consider the soprano and alto in mm. 6–8 of example 11.5. Which notes are new chord factors that were missing in the opening duo? How do the rhythms of these parts match/complement those of the subjects in the tenor and bass?

2. *Analysis:* Analyze the following keyboard fugue excerpt. Bracket and label the thematic material using the following abbreviations: subject (S), answer (A), countersubject (CS), and counteranswer (CA). If it is a double fugue of the second (or third) type, label the subjects and answers using S1/A1 and S2/A2. Indicate which type of thematic presentation is used (e.g., double fugue of the third type). If there is a tonal answer, indicate the splices using dotted lines and label the tonic and dominant scale degrees (label only the first two notes after the splice). Do a Roman numeral analysis and label cadences. Make a diagram showing the order of entries.

Example 11.9. (Handel, Opening of the Fugue in G minor, G. 264) Deviations from strict style are circled. Note the legal ap in m. 3.

3. *Composing (short):* Here is a double fugue of the second type, which takes a real answer (example 11.10). Given the subject and countermelody, (a) copy the melodies into the alto and bass, transposed appropriately, and (b) add continuations to the given melodies in the first two voices, modeling on Example 11.5, and try to add missing chord factors and complementary rhythms.

Example 11.10.

Example 11.11.

4. *Composing (short):* Above is a double fugue of the second type whose subject takes a tonal answer (example 11.11). Given the pair of melodies and the beginning of the answer pair, (a) continue the answer pair in the bass and soprano, and (b) add continuations to the given melodies in the tenor and alto as above.

5. *Composing (short):* Take one of the exercises you wrote in nos. 3 or 4 and add unnecessary transitions.

6. *Composing (long):* Use a theme/countermelody pair you composed in exercise 10-C question 2 to compose the opening of a double fugue of the second type, in other words, with both tunes heard at the outset. The two melodies should not start exactly together. Bring in the other pair of voices at the appropriate time, and then compose free continuations to the two voices that started.

7. *Composing (long):* For each of the subjects given in example 11.12, find the answer; compose a countermelody (if the answer is tonal, you must compose both a countersubject and a counteranswer, or you must delay the entrance of the countermelody so that it does not participate in the splice);

arrange these materials into the opening of either a double fugue of the first type or of the second type; finally, add unnecessary transitions if you like.

Example 11.12.

TRIPLE AND QUADRUPLE FUGUES

Triple and quadruple fugues involve combining more melodies. Rameau gives an example in the *Traité* of a motet that "contains four different fugues," meaning that four themes are eventually woven together.[4] As noted, some multiple fugues have subjects that are introduced later on (so they would be classed along with double fugues of the third type), but we will focus here on triple and quadruple fugues in which all the subjects following the first one are introduced immediately as countersubjects. Furthermore, rather than study triple fugue as a separate, simpler entity, we will jump to a special kind of quadruple fugue in which all of the themes following the first are introduced in order as successive countermelodies in the exposition. It is called a *permutation fugue* because the themes are "rotated" systematically through the voice parts.[5]

PERMUTATION FUGUE

In a permutation fugue, the countermelodies are the other parts of a full harmonization of the subject and answer, and *all of them* are reused. They rotate through the voices one after the other. We call the melodies that accompany the subject CS1, CS2, and CS3 and the melodies that accompany the answer CA1, CA2, CA3. We put dotted lines in *all* the parts at each splice. A permutation fugue can be schematized thus:

Table 11.1

S	CA1	CS2	CA3	S	CA1	CS2
	A	CS1	CA2	CS3	A	CS1
		S	CA1	CS2	CA3	S
			A	CS1	CA2	CS3

You can see by reading horizontally that the theme is followed in each voice by countermelodies 1, 2, and 3, but alternating answer versions with subject versions. Looking vertically, you can see that each column after the third contains the same four melodies, but rotated.

Here is a little section from Johann Christoph Friedrich Bach's motet "Wachet auf!" with all of the melodies of the permutation fugue labeled. It may seem counterintuitive to break off the subject in the middle of the second beat of each measure, but remember that we define the countermelody as beginning exactly at the moment of the next thematic entry. This break is the boundary of the period (here the period is only four eighths long and contains only two chords). The exposition (which consists of all the music during the four entries) is a nice example of opening up the space bounded by E-flats and B-flats from bottom to top (one person can try singing subjects and answers directly, one after the other).

Example 11.13. (Johann Christoph Friedrich Bach, "[Zion's] heart leaps for joy").

Consider the four-part section in mm. 183 (fourth eighth)–184. At the joint between the two measures, we can put dotted lines and label the scale degrees of the notes in the melodies as they cross the D/T splice. The same can be done to the period that follows in mm. 184–185 (T/D splice). The notes immediately on either side of the splices are shown in example 11.14a. Note that the first note of countermelody 3 is not used consistently, so we have labeled it "X" in the diagram. The bass in mm. 184–185 has the same pitch classes as the subject, but with melodic direction reversed and with different words and rhythm, so we call it a "pseudo-subject."

We can replace note names with the "scale degrees" that we use to explain tonal answer.

	m. 183–184			m. 184–185	
Answer	B♭	E♭	CS1	E♭	D
CA1	B♭	G	CS2	G	F
CA2	D	B♭	CS3	X	B♭
CA3	X	E♭	Pseudo-subject	(E♭	B♭)

Example 11.14a.

	m. 183–184			m. 184–185	
Answer	1/D	1/T	CS1	1/T	3/D
CA1	1/D	3/T	CS2	3/T	5/D
CA2	3/D	5/T	CS3	X	1/D
CA3	X	1/T	Pseudo-subject	(1/T	1/D)

Example 11.14b.

INVERTIBILITY IN TRIPLE AND QUADRUPLE FUGUES

You notice in example 11.14b that we are using a degree (5) that we had "blacked out" in the previous chapter. We blacked it out there because it is, for the moment, not allowed in the subject or first countersubject because of the danger of bad 6/4 chords. "Scale degree" 5 is often going to end up being harmonized as the fifth of the tonic chord (otherwise it would be read as "1 of D"). It is only OK to use 5 in an inner part, as in example 11.13, where CA2 appears in the tenor in mm. 183–184, or as part of an idiom, as when V^6/4–V occurs in example 11.13 at the beginning of m. 183 (see discussion of arpeggiated six-four chord in chapter 4).

The 6/4 is obviously more of a problem when four melodies have to be usable as bass lines than when, as in a double fugue, two tunes can be composed that contain almost nothing but thirds and roots, as shown in example 11.8c. Since all of the countermelodies will at one time or another occur in the bass, there is a great danger of illegal 6/4 chords. That is, when we have *four* melodies that are to be regularly reused, how can we write complete triads (as Mattheson urged us to), yet at the same time have themes that can appear in the bass? Composers have five ways to deal with this problem. They can:

- Use 6/4 chords *very* freely, as Vallotti and Rameau often do.

- Add a free instrumental bass that "fixes" the 6/4 chords by sounding a root or third below (see example 11.15 by Bach).

- Never let the theme(s) with the fifth chord factor appear in the bass; in this case not all the possible permutations will be used.

- Change the offending note(s), altering the theme slightly.

Example 11.15. (Bach, Cantata 71, "Muss täglich von neuem dich, Joseph, erfreuen" ["You must daily rejoice anew, Joseph"]) Note the deviation from strict style at the arrows.

Example 11.15. *(Continued)*

Example 11.15. *(Concluded)*

- Use an interval other than the octave to invert the melodies. It's because of inversion at the octave that vertical fifths become fourths. In chapter 16 we will see that if the offending melody is inverted at the twelfth, the fifth chord factor will become the root.

J. S. Bach wrote a lot of permutation fugues in his youth. Example 11.15 shows one from Cantata 71. The fifths of chords in the soprano and bass have been labeled. Note that the fifths in the soprano in mm. 7 and 8 result from a reharmonization caused by the free bass. Otherwise the instrumental bass is a "basso seguente" doubling the alto in the third and fourth quarter notes of m. 9, then doubling the tenor, then in m. 13 following the sung bass part. Asterisked notes are "free" deviations from the sung bass that "fix" illegal or otherwise awkward 6/4 chords.

UNPACKING HARMONIC "BOXES" PART II

You saw in example 11.14 that subject "boxes" alternate with answer "boxes"; the boxes remind us of the principle of Rameau's canon in chapter 2, in which a harmonic progression has its parts strung out. The difference is that in Rameau's canon the progression was exactly the same each time it was sounded—there was only one box; whereas here (example 11.16), T/D statements alternate with D/T statements. Imagine writing the two boxes first, then stringing their melodies out in alternation, like this:

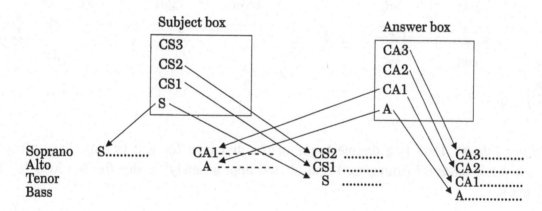

Example 11.16.

EXERCISE 11-C

1. *Analysis:* Here is another section of the same motet ("Wachet auf!") by J. C. F. Bach, also a permutation fugue. Label all the melodies in it (S, CA1, CS2, etc.); put the dotted line at each splice in each voice, label the scale degrees on either side of the splice, and analyze. Beware, there are some surprising deviations from the simple norms of permutation fugue. Explain substitute chords in m. 253. Why did Bach do that?

Example 11.17. (J. C. F. Bach)

2. *Writing (short):* Here is a double fugue of the first type for you to make into a triple fugue by adding the *same material* (transposed and altered appropriately) under the brackets labeled with a question mark.

Example 11.18.

3. *Composing (long):* Example 11.19 shows the two harmonic boxes from a triple fugue that uses a real answer, from an early cantata by J. S. Bach. String out the melodies to make a permutation-fugue exposition as schematized in example 11.16. Remember that you may start with any voice (moving melodies into appropriate registers), and that any melody may appear in any voice. If countermelody 2 appears in the bass, Bach alters the first note as shown (circled notes). You may add a free fourth voice if you like. Be sure to respect the given ranges. Remember that countermelody 1 connects to a *transposed version* of countermelody 2! After you have made seven entries of the theme, compare your answer with Bach's.

Example 11.19. (Bach, Cantata 71, "Dein Alter sei wie deine Jugend") *Note deviation from strict style at the arrow.*

4. *Composing (long):* Write a three-part permutation fugue exposition using the three melodies in example 11.20. Which melody is the best subject? What is the required order of entries? Do you need a transition and/or retransition? Show the Roman numerals.

Example 11.20. (Vivaldi, transcribed by J. S. Bach, BWV 596)

5. *Composing (long):* Compose a permutation fugue opening in three voices using the combination given in example 11.21. Write a third melody in the subject box. All three melodies should work as bass lines (fifth chord factors should be avoided or used idiomatically). Write out the answer box. Choose and identify which of these three melodies will be used as your subject/answer (S/A), first countermelody (CS1/CA1), and second countermelody (CS2/CA2). Your subject should start with scale degrees 1 or 5. Your choice should also take into account issues of continuity: for example, S has to be followed by CA1, and then by CS2. Every voice must sing all three melodies at least once.

Example 11.21.

PARTIMENTO

In this exercise (example 11.22), the countersubject begins right away, so it is a double fugue of the second type (Handel calls the countermelody "contrasubj" even when it's what we would call a counteranswer). The countermelody begins after the splice, so it need never be altered, only transposed. Try reversing the positions of the voices of the opening duo to see if it is invertible. Handel uses the same shorthand for upper-voice entries that you saw in example 10.25.

Example 11.22. (Handel)

NOTES

1. Mattheson, *Der vollkommene Capellmeister*, III, 23, §§40–42.
2. Mattheson, §43.
3. Mattheson, §45.
4. Rameau, *Traité de l'harmonie réduite à ses principes naturels*, III, chap. 44, p. 356.
5. The term was invented by Werner Neumann (1938).

12

SEQUENCES AND EPISODES

Sequences with One-Chord Models; Two-Chord Models; Multichord Models; Harmonic Smudge; Realizing Sequentially; Canons in Sequences; Ways to Harmonize the Suspension Chain; Sequences in Themes; Sequences in Episodes; Deriving Motives from the Subject and Countersubject; Using Sequences to Modulate; Joining Two Sequences; Partimento

Sequences contain a unit of music called a *model* and one or more transposed repetitions of that model. The model consists of some characteristic motivic material and may contain a single harmony or several harmonies. Because of the predictable repetition of motive and harmony, sequences are a nice means of prolonging or stretching out a section of a piece. There are many different types of sequence; you should memorize all the sequences discussed in this chapter.

Sometimes sequences occur within the theme but almost always occur in contrasting episodes. Episodes are nonthematic sections used to provide contrast and to make a smooth transition to another key. When you want to have entries in keys other than the tonic and dominant, you can write a free modulatory passage or you can use sequences to get to the new key. Modulations are less noticeable when the sequences contain applied dominants to get there. In this chapter, we will use only *ascending chromaticism* because that is the only kind available in strict style. If you and your teacher want to use descending chromaticism in sequences, refer to chapter 15. What follows are lists of all possible sequence types with one-chord and two-chord models, although not all of them are to be found in Baroque repertoire (these, like those mentioned in nos. 4 and 5 below, are simply named but have no examples associated with them).

SEQUENCES WITH ONE-CHORD MODELS

One-chord models are all quite rare, especially root position chords moving in parallel, which are barely acceptable. Parallel 6/3 chords are the exception, occurring fairly commonly.

   1. *Descending steps in parallel 6/3 chords, with or without 7–6 suspensions.* In example 12.1 (from the end of m. 3 through m. 5), the parallel descending 6/3 chords occur without suspensions. Note that the first chord is the goal of the cadence (D major in root position, at the asterisk), while the sequence consists of parallel 6/3 chords beginning with B minor (this substitution is a "harmonic smudge," discussed below). Note also the speeding up of the harmonic rhythm in the first two chords of m. 5, where only part of the longer motive is sounded.

Example 12.1. (Handel, Trio Sonata, op. 2, no. 1, i, mm. 1–6) *Note the accented passing tone on the second beat of the first measure marked with an arrow, not allowed in strict style.*

   For a similar example, see Handel in example 6.17, m. 3. For two examples of the same progression with embellishing 7–6 suspensions, see example 9.1, mm. 15–17 and 20–22.

   2. *Ascending steps.* This type of sequence is very rare. The harmonies are all in root position, moving in parallel. The motive that is repeated in the right hand in example 12.2 consists of a leap from the third to the fifth of each chord. The "parallel fifths" (that you see if you reduce the example to three parts) are not offensive because they occur on weak beats.

Example 12.2. (Bach, Invention 1, mm. 5–6)

The same type of sequence appears in the next example. This time all chords are in first inversion.

Example 12.3. (Bach, Organ fugue in G major, BWV 541, mm. 48–49)

3. *Descending thirds*. In example 12.4, third and fourth quarter, the motives in all three voices are repeated.

Example 12.4. (Bach, WTC I, D major fugue, no. 5, m. 17)

4. *Ascending thirds.*
5. *Descending fourths (ascending fifths).*
6. *Ascending fourths (descending fifths)*. In example 12.5 the motives are repeated with every chord. Note that offensive parallel fifths are avoided because the chord at the onset of each beat is incomplete; the fifth chord factors occur later in the pattern, as in example 12.3.

Example 12.5. (Bach, D major fugue, WTC I, m. 24)

TWO-CHORD MODELS

In one-chord models, the name of the sequence is the interval between successive roots. In two-chord models, the name of the sequence is the interval between the first chord of the model and the first chord of the repetition; we do not specify the relationship of the in-between chord.

1. *Descending steps with an embellishing chord in between.* When the descending steps progression is embellished by a chord a fifth below the first one, it is equivalent to what is commonly called the *descending circle of fifths.* The following sequences are based on two-chord models because the voice-leading patterns repeat every two chords.

Example 12.6. (Bach, "Lobet den Herrn," BWV 230, mm. 117–124, continuo omitted) *The sequence is by descending steps (= descending circle of fifths). The model (mm. 120–121) is repeated (mm. 122–123) a second lower. The voice-leading patterns in the soprano and bass are repeated in the same voices every two measures and thus encompass two chords (m. 123 in the soprano is an embellished transposition of m. 121; disregard the alto and tenor for now).*

Example 12.7. (Bach, D major fugue, WTC I, mm. 5–7) *Descending steps or circle-of-fifths sequence. The motives in the soprano and tenor are repeated after two chords. The two-chord model is restated a second below.*

You have seen other examples in keyboard pieces in examples 6.15, mm. 3–4, and 6.16, mm. 7–10.

2. *Ascending steps with an embellishing chord in between.* The root of the embellishing chord can be a third below the first chord or a fourth below, resulting in a descending third + ascending fourth model (example 12.8a) or descending fourth + ascending fifth model (example 12.8c), respectively. The former is often realized with the same bass note held (hence the name "5–6 progression," example 12.8b). The latter has roots a fifth apart, so it is also called the *ascending circle of fifths*.

Example 12.8. *Abstract representation of root progression via ascending seconds with embellishing chords: (a) "5–6 in root position," (b) "5–6 progression," and (c) "circle of ascending fifths."*

In the trio sonata opening by Loeillet shown in example 8.4, the episode that follows the exposition in m. 5 uses an ascending 5–6 sequence with applied dominants. It is called a *chromatic ascending 5–6 sequence* because the bass of the 5–6 progression ascends chromatically (A–B-flat–B-natural–C–C-sharp–D). Every other note (the bass of the 6 chord) is an applied leading tone. The motive is taken from the end of the answer form of the theme and includes the remodulation (motion up a fourth) from the end of m. 4. The two-chord model lasts four quarters. Label the chord factors in the top voice and bass. The sequence ends in D minor; m. 8 contains a 7–6 sequence in faster harmonic rhythm, leading to a cadence to D minor in m. 9. Compare Handel's speeding up before the cadence in example 12.1; in both cases the goal of the cadence coincides with the onset of another thematic statement.

We have seen an ascending circle-of-fifths sequence in Vallotti's example 7.5. Here's another example from a Handel concerto grosso (example 12.9, mm. 21–22). The same eighth-note motive, when inverted, can be used in a *descending* circle-of-fifths sequence! In mm. 30–33, each measure contains three chords of the descending circle of fifths, then starts over.

Example 12.9. (Handel, Concerto Grosso, op. 6, no. 6, ii) *Roots have been labeled in the two sequences. Analyze the chord factors of the two four-note motives, original and inverted, in the two sequences. This is an example of a sequence with an embedded progression, a "sequence-within-a-sequence," discussed in chapter 15. Descending chromaticism is a feature of free style.*

3. *Descending thirds with an embellishing chord in between.* The in-between chord is usually a fourth below the first chord, as in the famous Pachelbel "Canon" (example 12.10). The sequence accounts for the first six chords in each ground bass period. The upper voices form a canon at the unison over the repeating bass periods in the same way that the trio sonatas in chapter 6 did. Analyze the chord factors in the first violin.

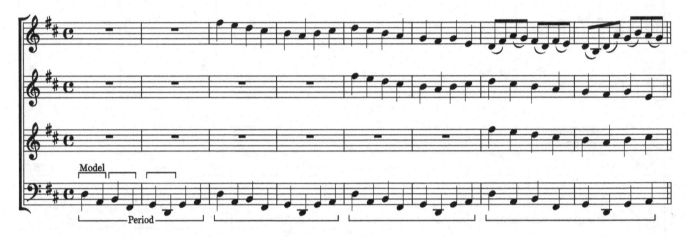

Example 12.10. (Pachelbel, "Canon," mm. 1–8)

The same sequence type occurs in example 12.12 (Bach, "Lobet den Herrn," BWV 230, mm. 156–161). The opening of Corelli's trio sonata in example 12.24 starts out like a descending-thirds sequence, but continues as a simple 7–6 stepwise descent; however, the motivic material shows us that the model is two chords long.

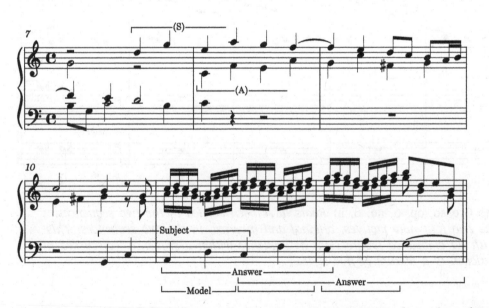

Example 12.11. (Pachelbel, fugue 1 in C major, mm. 7–12) *Note how the subject and answer are elided in the bass.*

4. *Ascending thirds with an embellishing chord in between.* The embellishing chord is usually a fourth above the first chord. In example 12.11, the sequence that starts at the beginning of m. 11 and lasts through the second beat of m. 12 uses the answer form of the theme in the bass, which sounds the roots of the harmonic progression. The motives in the upper parts repeat every two chords.

5. *Descending fourths (ascending fifths) with an embellishing chord in between.*

6. *Ascending fourths (descending fifths) with an embellishing chord in between.*

MULTICHORD MODELS

Often entire progressions of three or more chords are repeated sequentially. There are so many possibilities that we have no names for them other than the name of the overall motion from the first chord of the model to the first chord of the first repetition.

Bach presents the same descending-third sequence twice in "Lobet den Herrn" (example 12.12). The second time (mm. 156–161) it is the simple two-chord model, as seen above in the Pachelbel progression, with dissonant suspensions, but the first time (mm. 146–151), it has a third, embellishing harmony added between the first two chords of the model.

Example 12.12. (Bach, "Lobet den Herrn," BWV 230, mm. 141–165) *Roots in mm. 146–151 are CDG, ABE, FGC.*

The following sequence (example 12.13) is by ascending steps; the intermediate chords are in a pattern that rises a step, then a fourth, then a step; thus we hear IV–V–I with the I becoming IV of the next unit. But the model is actually four chords long because we don't recapture the *same motive in the same voice* until four beats have passed. Note that the repetition of the model is incomplete. (Chord factors have been labeled in the example.)

Example 12.13. (Caldara, "Caro mea vere est cibus") *The example starts with a short circle-of-fifths progression with a canon in the upper parts. Note that the harmonic rhythm is retarded at the end to emphasize the important arrival on A minor.*

A multichord model can be made to function in different types of sequence. In his G-sharp minor fugue from *WTC I* (18), Bach extracts a motive from the subject (scale degrees 3–4–5–1, of the dominant key, mm. 2–3) and uses it in two different sequences. The first (mm. 8–10) is by ascending thirds; the second (mm. 12–14) is by descending thirds. The difference is in the connection between the units; in the first case the bass rises a fifth to the third of the next chord (m. 9), while in the second, the bass stays on the same note to become the third of the next chord (m. 13).

HARMONIC SMUDGE

Sometimes, to move more smoothly into a sequence, the composer replaces the first chord of the sequence. This substitute chord (usually a third away from the expected chord and sharing two notes with the expected chord), sounds acceptable looking both backward and forward. We call it a "harmonic smudge." It enables you to begin the sequence with a substitute chord. See example 12.1 at the asterisk.

Another example of a harmonic smudge is to be found in Loeillet's trio sonata (example 8.4). The motive at the end of m. 4 is the one that is used in the sequence, but its chord factors are not the same as at the end of the next measure. Describe the substitution.

Chords whose roots are related by thirds can often be confused and may function the same way. In example 12.28, the vertical fifth on the downbeat of m. 5 sounds like the third and seventh of an F harmony, but might also be taken for the root and fifth of an A minor harmony. The chord on the downbeat of m. 5 is a smudge.

REALIZING SEQUENTIALLY

Strictly speaking, *realizing sequentially* means that the motives that make up each harmony must be the same in the model and in each repetition. This means that they must have *the same chord factors in all the corresponding places*. Test this by labeling the chord factors in the sequences shown in examples 12.1 through 12.12. Find deviations in the sequence in Handel's Anthem VII in example 11.6, mm. 15–18. Find the deviations in the following sequence.

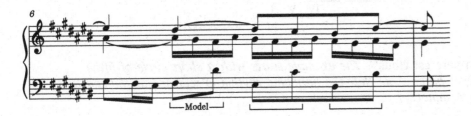

Example 12.14. (Bach, C-sharp major fugue, WTC I, m. 6) *Why do you think Bach did not continue as he began?*

CANONS IN SEQUENCES

When realizing the voice-leading sequentially, the texture can be rendered more interesting by distributing the repeated motives among two or even more voices to form canons. In the following descending circle-of-fifths sequence, Handel has the second violin imitate the first a fifth below. The motives have the same chord factors in the corresponding harmonies. Label the chord factors.

Example 12.15 (Handel, Trio Sonata, op. 2, no. 5, ii, mm. 42–44)

In the following example (example 12.16), the sequence is built from two motives derived from the counteranswer. In the counteranswer (example 12.16a) these motives are joined to make one beautiful seamless melody. However, to help us see how they are put together in canon, we break them apart and give them separate brackets and labels, as in example 12.16b. The model of the sequence, however, is four chords long because we don't recapture the *same motive in the same voice* until eight beats have passed. The root progression consists of an ascending fourth followed by an ascending second (it is the same type of sequence as in the Caldara passage of example 12.13; like Caldara, Bach makes frequent use of applied dominants). Label the chord factors in motives a and b in bass and soprano.

Example 12.16a. (Bach, "Sicut locutus est," *Magnificat* 11, mm. 1–8)

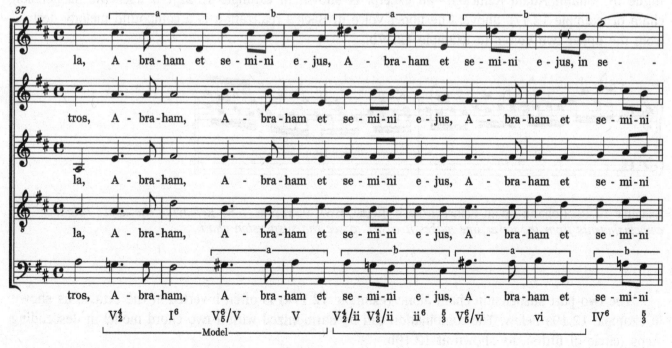

Example 12.16b. (Bach, "Sicut locutus est," *Magnificat* 11, mm. 37–41)

We have already encountered examples of canons in sequences in examples by Vallotti, example 7.5; Loeillet, example 8.4; Bach, example 12.6; Handel, example 12.9; and Caldara, example 12.13. Look at those examples: label the two halves of the motive in the two canonic voices, and label chord factors.

WAYS TO HARMONIZE THE SUSPENSION CHAIN

The *suspension chain* is a voice-leading pattern that no Baroque piece can be without. It consists of two descending stepwise melodies, one syncopated, the other not (example 12.17a). This rudimentary canon at the quarter note can be used in a sequence with a one-chord model, as shown at 12.17b, where the sequence is realized in three voices. If this realization were inverted at the octave (with the top line moved down an octave into the bass), 4–5 and 2–3 suspensions would result, with root position chords on successive weak beats. We almost never find this inversion.

Example 12.17.

The following sequence (example 12.18), in two parts, is from a fugue by Bach (based on a fugue by Johann Adam Reincken—an excerpt is shown in example 12.22). It uses the suspension chain of example 12.17b above. The upper voice in Bach's realization is a compound melody derived from the upper two voices in example 12.17b.

Example 12.18. (Johann Adam Reincken/Bach, fugue, BWV 965, mm. 7–8) *Removing the upper neighbor embellishments from the lower line makes it easier to see the suspension chain.*

The two-part suspension chain alone (example 12.17a) is often inverted at the octave, as shown in example 12.19a below. The combination can be harmonized with a two-chord model in descending steps (circle of fifths), as shown at 12.19b.

Example 12.19.

Example 12.20. (Reincken/Bach, fugue, m. 44–45)

Bach uses this sequence in the same fugue based on Reincken (example 12.20).

The same two-part suspension chain can be combined with yet another bass to form a sequence with a four-chord model, as shown in the following example.

Example 12.21.

Reincken's fugue, which served as a model for Bach, uses the same harmonization in example 12.22 (Bach does not use it).

Example 12.22. (Reincken, fugue, mm. 27–28)

Another harmonization of the chain is shown in example 12.23. Essentially, the two upper parts are identical with those of example 12.22 above. But the bass line starts out a third lower. Starting at the asterisk, the upper two parts are reharmonized with a chromatically ascending bass line (again ending on A). Starting at the double asterisk, the upper two-part combination is reharmonized with a cadential progression, also ending on A. Reincken uses this altered progression to confirm the tonic key of A minor.

Example 12.23. (Reincken, fugue, mm. 19–20)

SEQUENCES IN THEMES

Sequences are used in both themes and episodes, the two large building blocks of all Baroque music. We shall discuss each of the two situations in turn.

1. *Sequences in trio sonata, invention, and fugue subjects.* Sequences may appear in various places within the themes. The theme of Pachelbel's "Canon" (example 12.10) consists of a sequence and a cadence. In the following example the sequence also occurs at the beginning of the subject. The motives in the bass and violin 1 are repeated as indicated by the brackets (note that the sequence is by descending thirds but the register of the motives is not consistently descending—the second

motive is up a sixth instead of down a third). The subject closes with a cadential progression. When the answer enters, the two upper parts form a canon (rearranged in register) over the repeated period in the bass.

Example 12.24. (Corelli, Trio Sonata op. 3, no. 3, Largo, mm. 1–8)

In Handel's trio sonata opening shown previously in example 12.1, the sequence occurs in the second half of the subject, following a harmonic progression that first cadences in i (in m. 2) and then in III (in m. 3).

The following beginning of a two-part invention contains a sequence (example 12.25). The model in m. 1 is three quarters long and is repeated in m. 2 one step higher. Both the subject (right hand) and countersubject (left hand) repeat their motivic material, except for the first note in the left hand of m. 2. This small alteration affects the harmonic progression as well, seeming to split the first beat of m. 2 into two chords. Note that when Bach inverts the combination in mm. 5–6, the first note in the right hand of m. 5 is changed to A-flat. Bach does this to avoid a dissonant vertical fourth; in two parts we more easily accept a 6/4 chord if we do not hear the actual fourth attacked on the strong beat.

Example 12.25. (Bach, Two-Part Invention in F Minor, mm. 1–6) *The chord on the downbeat of the second measure is either an inserted iv chord or a ii⁶.*

2. *Sequences in chorale preludes.* It is common to harmonize stepwise motion in a chorale tune with a sequence. In example 5.23 (Pachelbel) the descending notes F-sharp–E–D in the top voice are harmonized with chords on B–E–A–D–G.

SEQUENCES IN EPISODES

Episodes provide contrast between thematic statements, and they may contain fewer than the total number of voices in the fugue. We have called them *nonthematic*, but actually their motivic material is most often derived from either the subject or countersubject, so they sound like they belong in the piece, even though they have a fresh sound.

DERIVING MOTIVES FROM THE SUBJECT AND COUNTERSUBJECT

Marpurg says:

> [The episode] must flow from the character of the theme. . . . But where does one take the passages for the episodes from? From the theme and the countermelody with which the theme is already combined. . . . And if the theme is not such that one can borrow anything suitable from it, one invents good melodic progressions which go well with the character and [rhythmic and melodic] motion of the theme. . . . The episodes do not need to use all voices. One can let one or two voices disappear gradually one after another, or together, in order to reintroduce the theme even more emphatically and clearly afterwards, especially if it is to appear in an inner voice.[1]

In example 7.5 by Vallotti, the exposition of mm. 1–6 is followed by an episode (called *divertimento* in Italian) that starts off with a sequence in mm. 6–9. The motive with which the episode opens (alto in mm. 6–7) is taken from the end of the subject and the beginning of the countersubject. The episode starts at m. 7 but the sequence starts already with the onset of the ascending motive in m. 6—in other words, at the end of the answer. The model of the sequence is two measures long (mm. 6–7) and consists of an ascending fifth progression. Vallotti takes the opportunity to add upper parts that make a canon with the motive. The alto part, starting in m. 6, is imitated at the upper fifth, starting in the soprano of m. 7. Note that because in the sequence the two vocal parts repeat the same voice-leading motions, they repeat the same chord factors. This same sequence recurs in mm. 21–24 at the end of the second pair of entries. Compare m. 4 with m. 21.

USING SEQUENCES TO MODULATE

Episodes are commonly used to move from one key area to another because they provide pivot chords that facilitate the introduction of the new pitches of the next key. Very often the modulation takes place during the sequence, as in mm. 3–4 of example 12.26. The motives in the soprano and bass are repeated every half measure. The sequence modulates to the dominant key in m. 4, where Bach introduces the new leading tone F-sharp at the second repetition of the model. If you play the sequence with and without the new leading tone you will get a sense of how smoothly the modulation takes place. How is the motive in the right hand of the sequence derived from the subject? How is the motivic material in the left hand of the sequence derived from the subject?

Example 12.26. (Bach, Two-part Invention in C major, mm. 1–4)

The reason we often find a harmonic smudge at the beginning of a modulating sequence may be twofold. On the one hand, it may be a matter of the length of the necessary sequence. For instance, to get from C major to G major around a descending circle of fifths will require six chords (C, F, B, E, A, D major, and G); if each chord lasts a long time (due to motivic material), this may be too long, and substituting A minor (vi) for C (or compressing the two chords into a single beat, as Handel did in example 12.1, m. 3) will shorten things considerably. On the other hand, how long a sequence is and where it starts and stops may also have to do with melodic starting and stopping points. How much melodic ground is to be covered?

JOINING TWO SEQUENCES

Composers often string together two sequences in a row (e.g., Handel, example 12.1, Loeillet, example 8.4). In the following example by Bach (example 12.27), the first sequence occurs in mm. 5–6 where both hands repeat the same melodic material successively a third below (descending third sequence). Measure 9 projects another sequence, again with both hands sharing the same motive. The sequence again descends by thirds (as in mm. 5–6), but this time three times as fast. Note that the example tonicizes/modulates to the dominant twice. The first tonization occurs in mm. 7–8, with the introduction of the new leading tone (B-natural). At the end of m. 8, Bach quickly returns to the tonic key by replacing the new leading tone with the old fourth scale degree B-flat. The sequence in m. 9 moves again to the dominant key, which is then confirmed by the following cadential progression. (You can see the rest of this piece in example 13.11.)

Example 12.27. (Bach, Two-Part Invention in F Major, mm. 1–12) *The sequence is actually part of a larger canon with which the piece starts: from the very beginning, the left hand imitates the right hand a measure later and an octave below. The canon breaks off in m. 7, leading into a new canon that starts with the right hand of m. 8, which is imitated by the left hand in the following measure a ninth below. This canon breaks off with the second beat of the right hand in m. 10.*

When Bach uses two sequences in a row, he often chooses a faster harmonic rhythm for the second one that, as in the previous example, is often of the same type as the first. In the next example (example 12.28), Bach also uses two sequences in a row. The first one, in mm. 3–4, is by descending steps (or circle of fifths) with a harmonic rhythm in half notes, as illustrated underneath the excerpt. (Note that the left hand does not present an exact motivic repetition.) The sequence that follows in mm. 5–6 moves faster (in quarters) and leads to a cadence in the relative major.

Example 12.28. (Bach, Two-Part Invention in A Minor, mm. 1–6)

Remember that in sequential patterns the following are permitted:

- You may double the leading tone.

- You may use a diminished triad in root position (vii° in major and minor, ii° in minor).

- The fifth of the diminished triad may ascend.

EXERCISE 12-A

1. *Improvisation and keyboard harmony:* Continue Caldara's sequence in example 12.13. What keys does this take you to? What accidentals do you need to add? Can you make it back to F major?

2. *Composing (short):* Go back to chapter 5, take any two commonplace sixteenth-note motives, and use them in a circle-of-fifths sequence, ascending or descending. You may write just one line and add a bass, use the motive in the bass and add just a top part, or add two parts in canon with the bass. For instance, given these motives:

Example 12.29a.

You could write the soprano, or the alto, or both, above the bass. If you write both, with the motive switching from voice to voice, you are writing a canon like that in example 12.16b—be sure the links between the motives are the same.

Example 12.29b.

3. *Composing (short)*: Add two parts in canon above the bass of the "5–6 progression" shown in example 12.8b. In your canon, the motive you choose in one of the upper parts above the first note in the bass is to be imitated in the other upper part over the second note in the bass, and so forth. If you continue the progression until the bass reaches again the tonic, you have a version of the rule of the octave with canon.

4. *Composing (short)*: Same exercise as no. 3 but this time choose a motive in one of the upper parts over the first *two* notes in the bass and imitate that motive in the other upper part over the third and fourth notes of the bass, and so forth.

5. *Composing (short)*: In how many different ways can the motive shown in example 12.30 be placed in canon above the "5–6 progression" shown in example 12.8b? You may do this exercise an octave lower.

Example 12.30.

6. *Composing (short):* Use the motive shown in example 12.30 or 12.31 or take any theme or countermelody from any musical excerpt in chapters 5–12 that was not used in a sequence and extract a motive that can be used for a sequence. Write a sequence in three parts in which the two upper parts form a canon (using the motive). Use one of the sequence types discussed so far and write out at least two repetitions of the model.

Example 12.31.

7. *Composing (short):* Using the sequences in questions 2 through 6 and in example 12.37 below, write a sequence that modulates (a) from a major key to its relative minor, (b) to the dominant key (major or minor), and (c) using ascending chromaticism or applied dominants to a distinct key of your choice. For instance, use the tune in example 12.32 in canon with itself to modulate from C minor to A-flat major. Use the sequence with a multi-chord model in mm. 38–49 of example 12.37 in some of your modulations.

Example 12.32. (Original melody from Handel, Messiah, 25)

8. *Composing (long):* Reincken's fugues are totally thematic. Bach, feeling the anxiety of influence, wrote "improved" versions of Reincken's pieces in which he added voices and episodes. We have already seen examples from one of these fugues above. Here is the opening of a fugal gigue by Reincken (example 12.33).

- Label the thematic entries with brackets. Identify and analyze the splices.

- Choose some motivic material from the subject and write a sequence in two parts in which the two parts form a canon. Name the sequence type, label the chord factors, and provide Roman numerals.

- Take the corresponding motivic material from the answer and write a different kind of sequence in two parts in which the two parts form a canon. Name the sequence type, label chord factors, and provide Roman numerals.

Example 12.33. (Reincken, fugal gigue in A major)

9. *Composing (short):* Here is a two-voice combination (example 12.34) to which you are to add two entirely different sequential bass lines (i.e., do not write the same progression with just different inversions). Name sequence types.

Example 12.34.

10. *Analysis:* Identify all sequence types in this excerpt from a gigue by Baldassare Galuppi (example 12.35).

Example 12.35. (Baldassare Galuppi, Gigue from Sonata in D Major, mm. 1–20)

11. *Analysis:* Identify the sequence types in the following excerpts (examples 12.36 through 12.38).

Example 12.36. (Strozzi, from Arie op. 8)

Example 12.37. (Fenaroli, *Partimenti*, Book II, No. 8, Gj 1324, mm. 37–71)

Example 12.38. (Marianna Martinez, Allegro from Sonata No. 3 in E major, mm. 70–84)

PARTIMENTO

In this example from the Langloz Manuscript (example 12.39), the sequences come in episodes between thematic entries. This fugue uses "real" answers, but note the alteration between the third and fourth notes of the countermelody, which serves the modulation and remodulation later in the piece. (The fourth between soprano and alto on the fourth beat of m. 2 is two notes of a 6/4/2 chord, not approached in strict style.)

Example 12.39. (Langloz Manuscript, no. 1)

In the following exercise by Handel (example 12.40), the sequence is built into the theme. The theme in the tonic is five half notes long, but the statement in the dominant is six half notes long because the alto needs an extra unit of the sequence to get down to the third of G (the alto B and the continuation of the soprano and alto are not shown but should be assumed). Handel indicates in which upper voice, C (for "cantus" or soprano), A, or T a theme could be sounded, and on what note it should start (d with one line is the D above middle C, two lines means an octave higher). Try to reuse the countermelody Handel has suggested.

Example 12.40. (Handel)

In this partimento by Fenaroli (example 12.41) the sequence is also built into the theme. The score is only partially figured, so you will have to add many figures. A fairly elaborate multi-chord sequence begins in m. 12 for you to analyze and memorize. Find other sequences in this fugue. Look at the pattern in mm. 20 (third beat)–22 (fourth beat). Can you put a theme above?

Example 12.41. (Fenaroli, Partimenti, Gj 1394)

Example 12.41. (*Concluded*)

Here is the bass line from a short section of the prelude from Bach's Suite for Lautenwerck BWV 997 (example 12.42). It contains sequences with multi-chord models for you to realize and analyze. For fun, look up the score and see what Bach did!

Example 12.42. (Bach, Suite for Lautenwerck BWV 997, Prelude, mm. 21–29)

This Fenaroli fugue is unfigured (example 12.43). In the episodes you will find several sequences with multi-chord models. The "grace notes" are appoggiaturas in free style (see chapter 14) that may be dissonant and are to be played as eighth notes on the beat.

Example 12.43. (Fenaroli, *Partimenti*, Gj 1385)

Example 12.43. *(Continued)*

Example 12.43. *(Continued)*

Example 12.43. *(Concluded)*

NOTE

1. Marpurg, *Abhandlung von der Fuge*, VI, §1, §3, p. 151; §6, p. 152.

13

LAYING OUT A WHOLE PIECE

Cadences; Mattheson on Cadences in Fugue; Placement of Formal Cadences; Placement of Subordinate Cadences; Joining Sections; Modulating by Means of Successive Entries; Fragmentary Entries; Motivic Unity; Case Studies of Modeling

We can think of the construction of a whole piece as an assembly of elements that may have been composed separately. The two primary elements of longer pieces are thematic statements (often in groups) and episodes (you have already composed these separately). Of lesser magnitude, but very important, are so-called unnecessary transitions and cadences. The transitions are freely composed, and you will have to rely on your intuitions and your ear to compose them. But cadences are conventionalized formulas, of which we give several examples here to memorize and use.

CADENCES

AUTHENTIC CADENCES

It is important to distinguish between authentic cadences and other harmonic arrivals. Harmonic arrivals are often very strongly felt but lack the important characteristic motions of the true *authentic cadence*. The "vii⁶" cadence, also called a *contrapuntal cadence*, makes a clear arrival, but it is not as strong as an authentic cadence (it can become authentic by the bass moving up from scale degree 2 to the root of the dominant chord on the weak part of the beat). An authentic cadence must have scale degrees 5–1 in the bass. Occasionally, the V enjoys an arpeggiation, which slightly weakens the cadential effect (see example 8.10, mm. 7–8). The tonic goal must sound on a strong step, and V normally lasts at least a full step. A *perfect authentic cadence* ends with scale degree 1 in the highest voice (often 7 moves to 8 and 2 moves to 1 so that the root of the goal harmony is tripled); an *imperfect authentic cadence* has scale degrees 3 or 5 in the soprano. Only an authentic cadence can end a piece, and it's usually perfect.

Authentic cadences can be divided into two large classes, depending on how much thematic material is used "in" the cadence and depending on the context in which the cadence occurs: (1) *formal cadences*, which arrest the forward momentum of themes or sequences—they are just plopped in, and they momentarily displace the motives that provide continuity (Loeillet's trio sonata, in examples 8.4 and 13.7, is a good example) and (2) *subordinate cadences*, which occur within complete themes or sequences, that is, within some ongoing process, and so they are subordinate to them, weakened by the continuity that these impose. Bach's G-sharp minor fugue from *WTC I* is a good example of cadences occurring within both theme and sequence.

FORMAL CADENCES

These are always authentic cadences, and they are likely to consist of standardized melodic clichés, like the cadential suspension (example 13.lb) or the dotted eighth + trill + sixteenth-note anticipation. Such cadences are used to contribute to the overall sense of shape: they put a stop to forward motion; they provide a respite from the obsessive repetition of characteristic features; and they divide the piece into segments. By articulating the longer spans, they contribute to the sense of form.

Example 13.1 shows a few of the many different formulas that are commonly used. Cadential formulas are truly commonplace in a way that the other examples in your commonplace book are not. These are like punctuation—just as nobody invents new punctuation marks, so nobody tries to be original in a cadence. Note which ones start (on the previous strong beat) on predominant chords, which on tonic, and which on dominant.

Example 13.1.

Sometimes a small fragment of the theme is found within the cadence. If it is not preceded or followed by the other members of the theme, the cadence can still be called formal. In Bach's B-flat minor fugue from *WTC I*, the alto notes in mm. 24–25 are recognizable as notes 3–5 of the subject (example 13.2). However, this is but a fragment; the rest of the cadence is standard issue, and a complete thematic statement then begins at the harmonic arrival. Note that although many authors recommend putting a rest before the first note of a new entry (see Marpurg's remarks in chapter 20), one often hears the goal note in a cadence becoming the first note of the subject.

Example 13.2. (Bach, B-flat minor fugue, *WTC I*, mm. 23–26) *Note deviations from strict style.*

EMBELLISHING THE ARRIVAL

One way to keep the motion going on through the authentic cadence in the middle of a piece is to put a 4–3 suspension or a 9–8 suspension as an embellishment over the harmonic goal. These suspensions continue the forward momentum beyond the cadence but do not necessarily weaken the sense of arrival. Indeed, sometimes they can be thought of as heightening it.

AVOIDED CADENCES

In an avoided cadence, something unexpected happens just as we arrive at the harmonic goal or just before. Marpurg gives some ways to avoid the authentic cadence altogether (the first five of these avoided cadences are illustrated in example 13.3):

1. Use a *half cadence* instead (phrase ends on V).

2. Use a *plagal cadence* instead (the root position tonic is approached by IV or ii$^{6/5}$ or even V$^{4/2}$).

3. Use a *Phrygian cadence* instead (6–5 in the bass in the minor).

"Furthermore," he says, "the full cadence can be interrupted or avoided in three ways":

4. Via a changed progression of the bass (V–vi).

5. Through changing the final chord (e.g., vi^6, V/ii, I^6, V/vi in various inversions, V/V, and V/IV, all in various inversions)

6. By simply omitting the final note

"Such an interrupted or avoided or, as one usually says, evaded cadence is called with one name, a pretend cadence." He says that the purpose of these pretend cadences is to keep the music moving for a long time and that they are "of the greatest necessity in a fugue for the uninterrupted continuation of a harmonic fabric."[1]

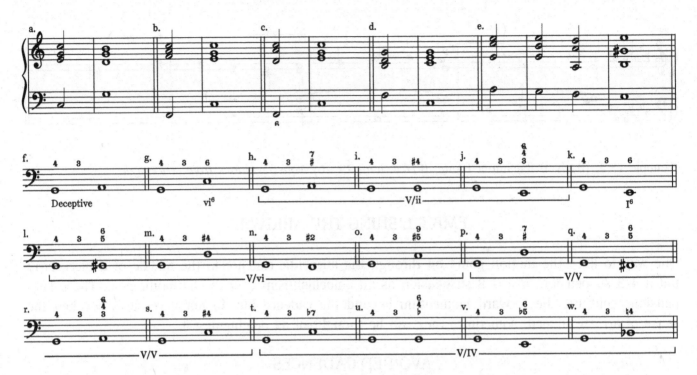

Example 13.3. (Illustrations of Marpurg's definitions 1–5 above) *Example a is a half cadence. Examples b–d illustrate plagal cadences with an unusual resolution of V⁴/²; example e is a Phrygian cadence; f is a deceptive cadence; examples g–w illustrate other harmonic substitutions. Note that in f–w Marpurg puts the 4–3 figures over the dominant chord to intensify the anticipation of a cadence.*

Example 13.4. (Some other examples of avoided cadences) *In example c, Marpurg veers off to other keys after a dominant chord; he puts the whole 7–6/4–5/4 cadential setup over the note he wants you to hear as a dominant.*

Often a suspension from the previous chord creates a seventh over the goal note, as in example 13.4b, m. 2. Also, the dominant can be transformed into a minor chord, as at the asterisks in mm. 2–4 of example 13.4c, so that the next chord, the expected tonic, becomes a dominant seventh chord. You can see this also in Predieri's example 9.12a, which has the whole cadential setup aimed toward A minor in m. 8, then turns back to D minor in m. 9. In the C-sharp minor fugue from *WTC II*, Bach sets up the 7/#3–6/4–5/4 in mm. 10–11 as if heading for F-sharp minor but then introduces the lowered leading tone (E-natural) in m. 11; a similar avoided cadence occurs with the A-natural in the bass in m. 12, where you might expect A-sharp. (Measure 4 seems to lead to E major, so the entrance of the subject in m. 5 is a surprise.)

FINAL PLAGAL CADENCES

A final plagal cadence is not really a cadence but a way to stop *after* the final authentic cadence of the piece. It uses IV to embellish I, and usually occurs when the tonic scale degree is prolonged. It is often associated with the word "Amen" in hymns. Handel's example 11.6 really ends with the authentic cadence in m. 26, and a plagal cadence is tacked on in mm. 27–29.

SUBORDINATE CADENCES

Sometimes the cadence either contains a part of a complete thematic statement or is part of a sequence. Such cadences are more or less overwhelmed by the momentum of the motivic material. In the C-sharp minor fugue from *WTC II*, the subject can be divided into three phrases: a (first half of m. 1), b (second half of m. 1), and c (first half of m. 2). Phrase a has cadence potential as scale degrees 4–5–1 (embellished), which Bach exploits at the end of m. 14 and at the beginning of m. 20. Phrase c also has cadential potential as scale degrees 4–2–3 (embellished), which Bach exploits at the beginning of m. 13 and in the alto voice in the fast circle-of-fifths sequence in mm. 18–19. Thus cadences can potentially be made to coincide with different parts of the subject.

In example 13.2, we saw a formal cadence in Bach's B-flat minor fugue from *WTC I*. However, in the same piece there is a cadence that overlaps with the beginning of a complete statement of the theme, and thus it is an example of a subordinate cadence.

Example 13.5. (Bach, B-flat minor fugue, *WTC I*, mm. 51–56) *The theme here is a hybrid version of the theme; i.e., a mixture of both subject and answer—see chapter 17.*

MATTHESON ON CADENCES IN FUGUE

Mattheson says:

> The very best is to arrange the theme in such a way that one rather avoids formal closure altogether and to set its boundaries such that no real interruption takes place, since points of rest are not at all at home in fugues and contrapuntal pieces, but are such strangers that they can hardly appear . . . before the entire chase has come to an end. I deliberately

choose the comparison with hunting because the chase has nothing to do with resting and standing still. My esteemed friend Walther says that the fugue takes its name from *fugando* because one voice, so to speak, chases the other.[2]

Mattheson seems to think that what we have called formal cadences are to be avoided until the end of the piece. He proposes two types of harmonic arrival that are appropriate during the course of a fugue: (1) a tonic arrival in which the melody avoids the tonic scale degree and in which the rhythmic activity is strongly maintained and (2) an arrival in which a substitute harmony appears or the tonic chord appears in inversion. He distinguishes between harmonic arrivals in a melody and full-textured avoided cadences: "The former take place willfully and deliberately in the single melody; the latter, on the other hand, occur with the constraint of the artistry and almost necessarily with full harmony. The first serve for a more convenient, uninterrupted continuation of the texture to come; the second only for the extension, expansion, and prolongation of what is then present."[3]

He gives an example of the first type in which the B at the downbeat of the fourth measure represents a tonic arrival, but because it is embedded in ongoing rhythmic motion and because it is not the tonic scale degree, the cadential effect is weakened.

Example 13.6. (Mattheson) *This subject and countersubject are taken from the second movement of Bach's Violin Sonata no. 3. The subject is used by Marpurg in a discussion of stretto (see examples 18.3 and 18.4). Note that the descending chromaticism in the counteranswer is only available in free style.*

EXERCISE 13-A

1. *Improvisation and keyboard harmony:* Play Marpurg's different avoided cadence types in examples 13.3 and 13.4c in all keys. Improvise a progression in which you set up the 7/#3–6/4–5/4 and then surprise the listener with what happens next, using one of Marpurg's devices. Let other members of the class say which evasion you used.

2. *Composing (short):* Using the model cadences in example 13.1, compose a middle voice that could be used as the head of a subject; the middle of a subject; the end of a subject. Then, to compose the rest of the subject, consult chapter 17, "Writing an Original Subject."

PLACEMENT OF FORMAL CADENCES

Usually we find cadences preparing new thematic statements and/or new contrapuntal devices, such as stretto. Loeillet's trio sonata in example 8.4 shows the cadence (in m. 9) punctuating the string of two sequences (in mm. 5–8), followed by thematic statements in new keys. Other examples in which a formal cadence is placed between a sequence and a thematic entry include examples 7.5 (Vallotti), 12.1 (Handel), and 12.2 (Bach).

Example 13.7 now shows the rest of Loeillet's piece (mm. 13–24). The G minor harmony in m. 13 is the beginning of another episode. Analyze the sequence(s) in this episode, which concludes with a cadence to D minor in m. 18. What is the origin of the motivic material in the sequence(s)? Another sequential episode follows; analyze the passage in mm. 19–22. At the end of m. 22, Loeillet has a surprise for us, a short progression in the parallel minor leading to the final cadence at the end of m. 23.

Example 13.7. (Loeillet, trio sonata, mm. 13–24) *Note that the last chord has no figures in the continuo. Should the player play an A-flat, A-natural, or no third at all?*

PLACEMENT OF SUBORDINATE CADENCES

In the C-sharp minor fugue from *WTC II*, Bach could have introduced a new thematic statement on the second half of m. 14 in the key of B major, or on the downbeat of m. 19 in G-sharp minor. As it is, these harmonic arrivals are bypassed on the way to the thematic statements in G-sharp minor (m. 17) and E major (m. 20), respectively. Bach's choice of which arrivals to make structural, in other words, stopping altogether or introducing a theme or a new contrapuntal procedure, is not based on key alone but on pacing (is it too early to hear the theme?) and register (is the right hand in the right register for an entry?).

JOINING SECTIONS

The smoothest joints between sections maintain a continuous sense of melodic direction, rhythmic density, and harmonic pacing. Sometimes, however, some rupture takes place, of register, rhythm, and so on. Sections are usually elided (i.e., the last note of one section coincides with the first note of the next) as when thematic statements occur at points of harmonic arrival (whether cadences or not). The following paragraphs describe and illustrate ways to link the three building blocks discussed above: theme groups, sequences, and cadences.

1. *Theme group to sequence.* This occurs very frequently: After the expository section, the sequence develops motives from the theme group and can move to new keys. The link is facilitated if the motive that is used in the sequence is based on the end of the subject. Then the end of the last statement of the subject is elided with the beginning of the sequence, so the joint seems very smooth, as in Loeillet's trio sonata (example 8.4, end of m. 4). The end of the theme that makes the return from D to T is used as the motive for the 5–6 sequence. The E rising to the F would, if it were part of the 5–6 sequence, be a fifth rising to a root (an A minor chord going to an F-major chord in first inversion), but here the first chord is not right for the sequence. It is a C-major chord, so the E is the third. Thus the motive is right but the chord is a harmonic "smudge" (see chapter 12). Another example is Vallotti's "Laudate Pueri" in example 7.5. Of this example, Sabbatini says, "It should be remarked that, out of the last beats of the Subject and Answer, the Author fashions his elegant *Divertimenti* [episodes]."[4]

2. *Theme group to cadence.* In Predieri's little "Et in saecula" fugue (example 9.12), an authentic cadence is placed after the initial theme group (5 entries) in mm. 1–11. This cadence contains both the subject in the soprano and the countersubject in the tenor, so it is a subordinate cadence. It is accomplished by means of the free bass in mm. 9–11. The rest of this fugue is shown in example 13.12.

Since most themes end with some kind of harmonic arrival, it might be considered redundant to end an expository section with an added authentic cadence. However, if the harmonic arrival is as weak as Marpurg and Mattheson suggest, then some cadential punctuation might be appropriate. In Bach's E-flat major fugue from *WTC II*, mm. 26–28, the end of the answer makes its usual descending-thirds sequence (I–vi–IV in B-flat major) leading to a long cadence after the fourth entry (IV–V–I in B-flat in mm. 28–30). As often happens, this particular cadence precedes a new contrapuntal device, in this case a stretto.

3. *Theme group to theme group.* Calling this a link might seem silly, since we have said that theme groups can contain any number of entries. Nonetheless, it is meaningful if we consider that the thematic material may be presented in a new way. Thus if the composer follows a series of normal entries with a series of inverted entries (sometimes called a *counterfugue*), we might regard the two sections as separate thematic sections. In Handel's anthem in example 11.7, a second exposition in mirror inversion begins in mm. 21–22 (compare with mm. 10–11).

4. *Sequence to theme group.* If the sequence of an episode uses the head motive from the theme, the sequence can lead directly into a new thematic statement by eliding the last repetition of the sequence model with the beginning of the new thematic statement. For a famous example, see mm. 9–12 from Bach's C minor fugue from *WTC I* (example 16.18). The sequence descends by fifths (with applied dominants) from the third beat of m. 9 to the third beat of m. 11, with the two upper parts moving in canon. The end of the sequence in m. 11 is, at the same time, the beginning of the new thematic statement in the soprano in the relative major key. The moment when the last member of the sequence turns from a fragment into a full thematic statement is a wonderful surprise. It seems at first like it will be just another move around the circle of fifths from E-flat to A-flat, but then we say, "Oops, that was the head of the subject."

5. *Sequence to cadence.* This kind of link occurs frequently. The cadence gives a little relief from the repeating motive in the sequence, and it confirms the harmonic arrival (often in a new key) in preparation for a thematic statement. We have already seen a sequence connected smoothly to a cadence in Loeillet's trio sonata (example 8.4, mm. 8–9). However, in Bach's motet "Lobet den Herrn" (example 12.12, mm. 152–155), the F that would normally follow out of the sequence in the soprano on the downbeat of m. 152 is sounded an octave higher, so the line can descend 4–3–2–1 in the soprano to the cadence. This cadence could be the final cadence of the piece, but it is immediately followed by the same sequence again, forming the extended blocks necessary to end such a long piece.

6. *Sequence to sequence.* We have seen many examples of two sequences in a row in which the second one moves at a faster harmonic rhythm than the first, although the reverse is also possible. The purpose of these pairs of sequences seems often to be a matter of registral exploration. For instance, take the sequences or series of cadences in the C-sharp minor fugue from *WTC II*, mm. 9–16: at first they go down, in mm. 9–13, then they are followed by an ascent in mm. 13–16. See also the pair of sequences in the C major fugue from *WTC II*, mm. 55–64.

7. *Cadence to theme group.* This is a very frequent formula, as we have said (Loeillet, example 8.4; Vallotti, example 7.5). The new entry usually arrives on the goal note or a fraction of a step later. The new entry most often begins with the root of the goal harmony, but it may also begin with another chord factor. In Bach's B major fugue from *WTC II* we see both types. In mm. 26–29, the cadence is to F-sharp and the next entry is in F-sharp. However, at a later point, Bach cadences to E (mm. 59–61) and introduces an entry on the third of the E major chord, in the key of G-sharp minor (S^{vi}). This is especially clever because the first three notes of the subject in G-sharp minor outline an E major chord!

8. *Cadence to sequence.* Loeillet (example 13.7) follows the cadence in m. 12 with another sequence rather than a thematic statement; he has already had four thematic entries and needs some contrast, so he uses the end of his theme in the sequence. However, the same technique can also be particularly effective if the sequence uses the head of the subject; we have the impression that

a thematic statement is coming, only to be foiled, and to say, "Oops, I thought it was the theme." Measures 51–68 from the C major fugue, *WTC II*, are a good example. A thematic statement in the tonic (mm. 51–55) ends with a subordinate authentic cadence to the dominant. A thematic statement appears to begin in that key in m. 55, but it turns out that Bach only uses the opening motive of the theme for the two-chord model of an ascending stepwise sequence (mm. 55–60). This sequence is followed, as mentioned before, by a descending sequence (mm. 61–64), an irregular harmonization of a 7–6 chain, leading to a deceptive cadence (m. 68).

9. *Cadence to cadence.* Sometimes cadences are sounded one after the other. Such a string of cadences has the same effect as a nonthematic, episodic section. You have seen two cadences in a row in Vallotti's "Laudate Pueri" in example 7.5. In mm. 10–11 the sequence ends with a cadence in the tonic followed by a cadence in the dominant to prepare an entry in that key. After this new pair of entries (with keys reversed), and another sequence, Vallotti again sounds two cadences, but this time they are both in the tonic. Compare mm. 10–14 with mm. 25–28. How does Vallotti redistribute the motivic material so that the two passages sound similar? Handel's anthem in example 11.6 has a cadential pattern six quarter notes long, starting at m. 15, third beat, which is repeated in a varied form, so it resembles a sequence. In mm. 34–36 of the D-sharp minor fugue from *WTC I*, we find two cadences to G-sharp minor. We do not know why they are both there, except to get the bass out of the basement: the inverted thematic statement that begins in m. 36 in the alto could perfectly well have begun a measure earlier.

MODULATING BY MEANS OF SUCCESSIVE ENTRIES

As we know, thematic presentations in the beginning of a piece alternate between tonic and dominant keys. Later on in the piece, however, there may be reasons to use entries to move about between other keys. Loeillet (example 8.4) first presents one pair of entries with the second up a fifth (F to C in mm. 1–3); he alters the second one to return to the tonic, going up a fourth (m. 4 to m. 5). Later, after the cadence in D minor (m. 9), he has an entry in D minor, but immediately uses the second, altered version of the tune to lead to an entry up a fourth, in G minor (m. 11). In example 7.5, Vallotti's second pair of entries is also in the reverse relationship from the first.

In the course of a long piece, once there is no need to "close the circle," we might want thematic presentations to enter in a succession of different keys brought about by the use of the *same* theme form. Thus a series of subject forms of the tune or a series of answer forms can move us up or down the circle of fifths. This is like any other sequence, except that the *whole theme* is sounded, not just a fragment of it. This could be mighty boring. Look up the score of the Gloria of Bach's *G Minor Mass*, BWV 235. The following diagram (example 13.8) summarizes the succession of thematic entries in mm. 46–91. In general, the *subject* form modulates down a *fifth*. The *answer* form modulates down a *fourth*. The harmonic arrival in the new key occurs in the middle of the theme. The first note is always the root of the first harmony, but in some cases that harmony is already the dominant of the new key. Bach sounds the subject of the theme twice in a row in mm. 52 and 55, moving down a fifth twice, from D minor to G minor to C minor, as bracketed. Similarly, the two entries of the subject in mm. 63 and 66 move from V of B-flat major (F major harmony) to B-flat major to E-flat major.

The two entries of the answer form in mm. 78 and 81, on the other hand, move down a fourth twice, from G minor to D minor to A major.

Measure	46	49	52	55	58	60	61-2	63	66
Materials	S	A	S	S	False Entry	False entry reharm.	Cad. in B♭	S	S
1st note/last harmony of theme	D/G	G/D	D/G	G/C	C/B♭	F/B♭		F/B♭	B♭/E♭

Measure	70	73	77-78	78	81	83	86
Materials	S	A	Cad. in G	A	A	S	Cad. in D
1st note/last harmony of theme	G/C	C/G		G/D	D/A	A/D	

Example 13.8. (Bach, Mass in G minor, BWV 235, Gloria, mm. 46–91 schematized)

FRAGMENTARY ENTRIES

Fragmentary entries are also called *false entries* because they are incomplete. We have seen how a thematic entry might be begun and then diverted into a sequence (C major fugue, *WTC II*, mm. 55–60). Another way to surprise the listener (so important to Mattheson) is to introduce only the head of the subject, then move to some other element. In example 13.9, Handel starts a thematic entry in the viola and cello (m. 9), then simply breaks off and restarts it in the cello and bass (m. 11), this time making a complete statement. After that (m. 15), the viola and cello sound the second half of the subject, completing their statement, as begun in m. 9. This completion is cute but by no means necessary. After that, Handel sounds just the head of the subject before the dominant entry in the bass. Mattheson would have liked this—it's full of surprises!

Example 13.9. (Handel, op. 6, no. 4, ii, mm. 9–18, solo parts omitted) *For other examples of fragmentary entries see the B minor fugue from WTC I, m. 19, where the entry pops up in an inner voice ("I would not have looked for you here!") during a sequence.*

MOTIVIC UNITY

The best way to maintain smooth continuity from one section to another is to keep the surface similar. Of course, using motives from the theme or countermelody in the episodes assures forward momentum, but even in modulations, remodulations, and unnecessary transitions, it is a good idea to continue using motives. A good example is Bach's F major invention (example 13.11), mm. 15 and 19–20, where the sixteenth-note motives can be traced back to earlier material. If this cannot be done, and a new motive must be used, at least try to maintain the rhythmic shape of the motive. In mm. 13–14 of the C-sharp minor fugue, *WTC II*, Bach introduces a new syncopated motive without disturbing the rhythmic flow.

CASE STUDIES OF MODELING

Bach is known to have taken fugues by other composers (e.g., Vivaldi) and arranged them or substantially recomposed them.[5] In the previous chapter we saw some examples of harmonizations of the suspension chain that were taken from a fugue by Reincken that Bach reworked. What exactly did the young Bach do to his model, and what can we learn from it?

Reincken's is a three-voice permutation fugue, with entries every four measures (except for one transition two beats long in the exact middle and a cadence two beats long at the end). There are twelve entries in all. As you know, if one of the subjects contains fifths of chords, it may not appear in the bass unless (1) the offending note is changed or (2) a free instrumental bass is added. Example 13.10 shows the first thirteen measures of Reincken's fugal trio sonata. (Reincken keeps on rotating the themes and countermelodies for the remainder of this fugue, fifty measures long!) Label the subject, answer, countermelodies (CS1, CS2, CA1, and CA2), and all splices. Which countermelody cannot be used as a bass? What about the first note of countermelody 2?

Example 13.10. (Reincken, *Hortus Musicus*, Sonata 1, fugue of first movement, mm. 1–13)

Example 13.10. *(Concluded)*

Look up the score of the fugue from Bach's A minor keyboard sonata BWV 965. In the first fifty-seven measures Bach changes the countersubject of Reincken's fugue. Comment on the changes: Which notes are the same? What has Bach added? How does this added material grow out of the original? How does the added material contrast with it? Bach adds a fourth entry (the number of voices in this fugue is, as so often with keyboard fugues, very flexible, going from two to five). How much of the countermelody in mm. 5–8 does Bach reuse in mm. 13–16?

Most important, Bach has inserted episodes into Reincken's fugue. The first one begins in m. 17, and it is a pedal. This is surprising because we normally expect the pedal to occur at the end of a fugue (although the A minor fugue from *WTC I* has a pedal in the middle, m. 60). Note that in mm. 48–49 the first harmony lasts two eighths, while all the other harmonies last only a single eighth each. This irregularity allows Bach to fit the complete cycle of seven fifths into eight eighth notes so each measure begins with the same harmony.

For another interesting study, we propose three related fugues. Bach modeled his E major fugue from *WTC II* on J. K. F. Fischer's E major fugue from *Ariadne Musica*, and then Clara Schumann modeled on Bach's.[6] Look up the scores of the Fischer and the Schumann. You can learn a lot from a comparative study of these three pieces. Do all three fugues have the same number of entries? What did Bach add to Fischer? What did Schumann add to Bach?

EXERCISE 13-B

The following exercises may be used as final composition projects in a one-semester course. The student is to model on the complete pieces used as examples in this book or others chosen by the teacher.

1. *Analysis:* Analyze the sequences in the episodes Bach added to Reincken's fugue in different ways: (a) harmonically, (b) in terms of harmonic rhythm, (c) in terms of register, (d) in terms of texture, and (e) in terms of the position of themes and cadences.

2. *Composing:* Compose a two-part invention based on the structure of Bach's F major Invention (you saw mm. 1–12 in example 12.27—the rest is shown in example 13.11). Use a subject from earlier in this book (or, if you have studied chapter 17, you may use your own theme). Make sure the order of all the elements is the same, as marked in the score, and that the cadences fall in the same places, the reprise moves from IV to I the same way, and so on. Even though your model is not in vocal style, you can "fill" Bach's abstract form with more vocal themes.

Example 13.11. (Bach, F major Invention, mm. 12–34)

3. *Composing:* Compose a trio sonata. This can be based on Loeillet (example 8.4 and 13.7) or Vallotti (example 7.5). The second pair of thematic entries should be in the opposite order (and thus opposite key relationships) from that of the first pair, as they are in these examples.

4. *Analysis:* Example 13.12 shows the continuation of Predieri's example 9.12. Label harmonies, themes, and cadences.

5. *Composing:* Compose a totally thematic fugue. This can be based on Predieri (examples 9.12 and 13.12) or J. K. F. Fischer (example 11.1). Whichever one you choose, make sure you have the same number of entries all appearing in the same voices as in the original. Thus you will have to know in advance whether your theme/countermelody combination must be invertible.

Example 13.12. (Predieri)

Example 13.12. *(Concluded)*

6. *Composing:* Insert episodes and cadences into the fugue you wrote for question no. 5 above.

7. *Composing:* Write a fugue in a major key in three or four parts using one of the given subject/answer pairs (example 13.13, or an original subject if your teacher agrees, in which case you may want to consult chapter 17). If it is to be in four parts, arrange it according to the scheme given in example 13.14; if in three parts, base it on the arrangement of a three-part fugue that you like. If you are writing a vocal fugue, you may use a text. Be sure to show your teacher some of the basic building blocks (S/CS combination, sequence, etc.) before getting too far along.

Example 13.13a. *Takes tonal answer.*

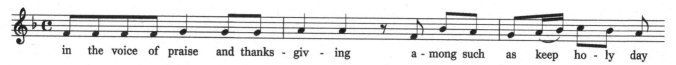

in the voice of praise   and thanks - giv - ing   a - mong such   as   keep ho - ly day

Example 13.13b. *Takes real answer.*

One ge - ne - ra - tion shall praise thy works un - to an - o - - - - - - - ther

Example 13.13c. *Takes tonal answer (splice shown).*

cum sanc - to   spi - ri - tu   in   glo - ria___ (De - o)

Example 13.13d. *Takes tonal answer.*

	theme group 1			ep.	th.grp. 2		ep. 2	th. grp. 3*		ep. 3	
	A	CS	---	seq.	S^V	CA^V	seq.			seq.	CS^I
S	CA	---	---	to	---	A^V	to	---	A^m	back	---
		A		V	---		minor	S^m	CA^m	to	---
	S	CA		(NB)			key*			tonic	S^I

Example 13.14. *Scheme*

These subjects are all in 4/4, and thematic entries in later sections may begin on the third beat of the measure. The CS and CA must contain some sixteenth-note motion. Note that the S/CS combo (and A/CA) must be invertible at the octave. The episodes must contain at least three voices, must be made out of subject or answer material, and may consist of sequences with applied dominants. (Note: If the answer ends in the dominant, the A/CA combo will already have reached the dominant key, and the sequence may merely confirm that key.) You must use at least two different types of sequence. Free material in the schema in example 13.14 is indicated by "---" and it must appear when indicated (thus there are only two mandatory four-part sections). The third theme group may be in any of the three closely related minor keys: ii, iii, vi with respect to the tonic (see asterisks). You will need to add a final cadence, and you may add "unnecessary" transitions and formal cadences. All sections must be smoothly connected, cadences elided with thematic and/or episodic sections.

If you have studied stretto, melodic inversion, mirror inversion, invertible counterpoint at other intervals than the octave, augmentation, diminution, and/or pedal (discussed at length in chapters 14–20), you may incorporate these into your composition project in consultation with your teacher. Be sure to show these to your teacher before getting too far along.

NOTES

1. Marpurg, *Abhandlung von der Fuge*, IV, 2, §§2–3, pp. 110–112.
2. Mattheson, *Der vollkommene Capellmeister*, III, 20, §15.
3. Mattheson, §16.
4. Sabbatini, *Trattato sopra le fughe musicali*, p. 26.
5. For much of the material in this section, we are indebted to Ulrich Siegele (1989).
6. Glickman and Schleifer, *Women Composers*, vol. 6, pp. 61–68. Clara Schumann also took two other fugues of Bach's to model on, printed in this same volume.

Part II

FREE STYLE AND ADVANCED TECHNIQUES

14

ADVANCED EMBELLISHMENT— FREE STYLE

Accented Dissonance; Sense of Direction; Suspensions that Resolve Upward; Leaps to or from Dissonance; Expanding a Harmony (Voice Exchange); Transferred Resolutions; Layers of Dissonance; The Benefits of Free Style

We have seen how embellishments make for rhythmic and melodic variety. In free style, dissonance is used more flexibly with respect to harmony, permitting lines to arrive at chord tones at different moments in different voices. There are basically five new possibilities in free style:

1. Accented dissonance

2. Suspensions that resolve upward

3. Leaps to and from unprepared dissonances (sometimes called *appoggiaturas* and *incomplete neighbors*)

4. Transferred resolutions of dissonant parts or tendency tones of chords (sevenths and leading tones)

5. Descending chromaticism

All but the last will be discussed in this chapter (descending chromaticism is covered in chapter 15). Once you have learned to control dissonance in strict style, you can handle it more confidently in free style because dissonance in free style is an extension of dissonance in strict style.

ACCENTED DISSONANCE

Accented dissonances (other than suspensions) can be found in five situations:

1. *Single accented passing tone (ap).* The passing tone occurs on the strong part of the beat or, in Kirnberger's terms, at the beginning of the "step." Single accented passing tones fall on the beat that carries the harmony then resolve to a chord tone. If we think of them as regular unaccented passing tones that have been shifted in time, we can reduce them to the types of embellishments that occur in strict style.

In example 14.1a, the circled C-sharp in the bass is an accented passing tone. Examples 14.1b and 14.1c show how the same idea might occur in strict style. This formula, IV–vii⁶–I, with scale degrees 1–2–3 on top, occurs frequently. Put it in your commonplace book!

Example 14.1. (Bach, "O Welt, sieh hier dein Leben")

Like weak passing tones, accented passing tones span a third; whenever your line falls a third between chord tones, instead of passing on a weak beat, you can insert an *ap*. Here are three more examples, two from Kirnberger and one from Bach.

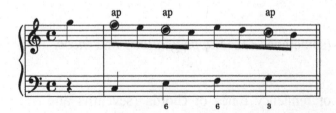

Example 14.2a. (Kirnberger) *The skip to the dissonant E is an appoggiatura, discussed below.*

Example 14.2b. (Kirnberger) *Reduction of example 14.2a.*

Example 14.2c. (Bach, *WTC I*, B-flat minor fugue)

Matteson tells us that the *descending* accented passing tone is far more common than the ascending one. An example of an ascending passing tone is shown in example 14.3.

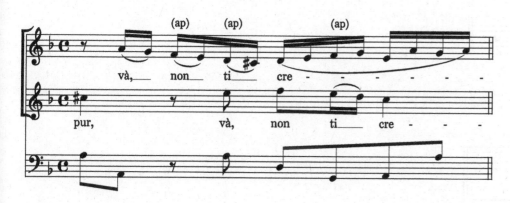

Example 14.3. (Handel, Duetto VII)

The cadential 6/4 may now occur as a pair of accented passing tones (see example 14.4).

Example 14.4. (Bach, *WTC II*, B-flat minor fugue, mm. 100–101)

The best accented passing tones are truly dissonant (like the fourth or the ninth with respect to the root; the sixth is less dissonant—it might sound like forming a new chord). Sometimes, in two-part writing the elements of the chord that make the dissonance are not present. This is like example 4.4 (*WTC II*, F-sharp major fugue, mm. 1–10), where a suspension created an interval that looked like it belonged to one harmony but the suspension was actually a nonharmonic tone (in a different harmony) that sounds consonant in only two parts. Example 14.5a is in strict style; if we move the F over to the right, we might hear a V–IV progression, as suggested in example 14.5b; the situation can be clarified by the addition of a third voice sounding a G (example 14.5c).

Example 14.5a.

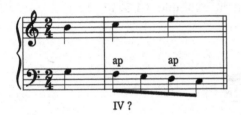

Example 14.5b.

Example 14.5c.

Example 14.6.

Accented passing tones can also occur in several parts simultaneously (see example 14.6).

All the passing tones illustrated above are *submetric*—they last only a part of the step unit, the accented passing tone resolving on the second half of the step. However, it is possible to have full-length accented passing tones, where the dissonance lasts for the whole step, as in this example from "Komm, Jesu, komm." Arnold Schoenberg uses this example to show how Bach liked thoroughly dissonant "chords";[1] the chord at the first asterisk contains E, F, G, A, B-flat, and C. The accented passing tone at the second asterisk also lasts a whole step.

Example 14.7. (Bach, "Komm, Jesu, komm," BWV 229, mm. 41–43)

2. *"Two in a row" (unaccented and accented passing tones).* In the preceding type, the accented dissonance was alone, surrounded by consonance, but it is possible to have two dissonances in a row. Kirnberger recommends alternating between unaccented and accented passing tones. By "alternation," he means sounding one right after the other: "Although the regular [unaccented] passing tone is the more agreeable, the alternation of both types makes the melody more charming. Initially, it is certainly not as comprehensible as the melody that contains only regular passing tones, but for this very reason it also becomes pleasing upon repeated hearings." He also reminds us: "But one needs to have a thorough knowledge of harmony in order to be able to distinguish both types of passing tones when they constantly alternate in a piece, or always to recognize the main note in the constant alternation; but without this, one is not able to figure the bass for the use of thoroughbass."[2] Multiple

accented passing tones can obscure the harmony, but clear sense of direction, stepwise motion, and clear harmonic departure and arrival all contribute to make the ambiguity acceptable (and "pleasing upon repeated hearings").

When a weak descending passing tone precedes the accented passing tone, the line spans a fourth between chord tones. In other words, the first dissonance must be a weak passing tone, and both dissonances are embedded in a line moving in a single direction. For instance, one often finds I⁶–V⁶ connected as in example 14.8a, with scale degrees 5–4–3 on top. We say the dissonant note "stands for" the chord factor and have labeled the harmonies on the step where they occur (even though one member hasn't gotten there yet). Make simplified versions of these examples, as we did in example 14.1. In example 14.8e, it is difficult to say what the harmonies are at the asterisk: if the D-flat in the tenor is an accented passing tone, the harmony is V and the pair of eighths in the soprano are passing and neighbor; if the soprano and alto on the downbeat are dissonant suspensions above the bass, it's a cadential 6/4. Either way, the sense of direction is clear and the very last eighth, V⁷, moves to i. What do you think about the last two eighth notes in m. 24 of example 14.8f?

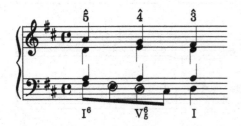

Example 14.8a. (Bach, "O Gott, du frommer Gott")

Example 14.8b. (Bach, "Jesu, nun sei gepreiset")

Example 14.8c. (Bach, "Mit Fried' und Freud")

Example 14.8d. (Bach, *WTC I*, B-flat minor fugue, m. 53)

Example 14.8e. (Bach, *WTC I*, B-flat minor fugue, mm. 10–12)

Example 14.8f. (Bach, *WTC I*, A minor fugue, mm. 24–25)

3. *"Two in a row" (both accented)*. Example 14.9a has two accented passing tones in a row, the harmonic rhythm moving in eighths. The possible reductions are shown in examples 14.9b–c. We never get the actual vii⁶ chord in Bach's example; it is simply implied, because when the A appears in the bass, the other voices have moved on to the next chord.

Example 14.9a. (Bach, "Aus meines Herzens Grunde")

Example 14.9b.

Example 14.9c.

4. *Anticipations in free style*. In strict style, anticipations anticipate consonant chord factors, but in free style they may anticipate accented dissonances. We take all of m. 20 (example 14.10) as dominant harmony.

Example 14.10. (Bach, *WTC II*, B-flat major fugue, mm. 20–21)

5. *Accented neighbors*. These are very rare, perhaps because they do not offer a sense of direction that compensates for the dissonance. There are a few in this chorale prelude by Bach (consult the complete prelude for many more).

Example 14.11. (Bach, "Gott durch deine Güte," mm. 11–12)

SENSE OF DIRECTION

With accented dissonance, we usually start off with a clearly defined harmony, go through a mysterious area, and come out the other side into a clear harmony. One of the ways we can evaluate whether the middle is acceptable is to see if it has a clear sense of direction. The contrary motion in example 14.10 above is a good example: we aren't quite sure what the chord on the second beat is, but we accept it because we come out of the woods at the next downbeat.

EXERCISE 14-A

1. *Writing:* Harmonize a chorale melody from examples 3.7a–d or 3.14a–d, using accented passing notes in the bass. Figure the bass and analyze with Roman numerals. Use ascending passing tones only if the same harmony is heard at both ends as in example 14.6. If the accented passing tone is not dissonant with the soprano, or if the harmony is not clear from the two outer voices alone, it will be necessary to fill in the inner voices.

2. *Writing:* First, compose an eight-measure melody over a figured bass in simple counterpoint (all consonance). The melody should contain many skips of descending thirds, as in example 14.2b. Second, add accented passing tones, as in example 14.2a. Be sure to analyze with Roman numerals. Use ascending passing tones only if the same harmony is heard at both ends, as in example 14.6. (If your accented passing tones are not dissonant with the bass, or the harmony is not clear from the two voices alone, it will be necessary to fill in the inner voices.)

3. *Composing (short):* Using a subject you have used earlier, compose a countersubject that contains accented passing dissonance.

4. *Composing (short):* Using a subject and tonal answer that you have used before, compose a countersubject and counteranswer that contain accented passing dissonance.

5. *Composing (long):* Using the combination from question 3 or 4, compose an exposition in three parts (subject–answer–subject) and a sequential episode in three parts, using the part of the countermelody that contains the accented passing tones.

SUSPENSIONS THAT RESOLVE UPWARD

These occur mostly in final cadences, where the 7–8 is delayed as well as the 4–3. See example 14.7, last measure, at the dagger. For another suspension that resolves upward see example 5.31, downbeat of m. 9 (G in first violin and voice).

LEAPS TO OR FROM DISSONANCE

Abstractly speaking, there are eight ways to arrange a leap and a step around a dissonant note (dissonance is never surrounded by skips on both sides in Baroque style, except in compound melody): the leap can be ascending or descending, the dissonance can be preceded or followed by a step, and the step can be either ascending or descending. Furthermore, the dissonance can occur on the strong or weak beat. From the sixteen abstract possibilities, only nine occur in the repertoire with some regularity. These are shown in example 14.12. Memorize them.

When the dissonance is on a weak beat and resolves by step, we often call it an *incomplete neighbor* (*in*). See nos. 3a, 4a, and 5a in example 14.12. Sometimes a skip into a dissonance can be considered a skip into a passing or neighbor tone in a compound melody (hence the term "incomplete neighbor"). When the dissonance is on a strong beat and resolves by step, we often call it an *appoggiatura* (*apg*). See nos. 3b, 4b, 5b, and 6. Repertoire examples of the nine types are illustrated in example 14.13.

Example 14.12.

Example 14.13a. (Handel, Messiah)

Example 14.13b. (Handel, Giulio Cesare, Act III)

Example 14.13c part 1. (Bach, *WTC II*, F-sharp minor fugue, mm. 25–26)

Example 14.13c part 2.

Example 14.13d. (Handel, Israel in Egypt, "The enemy said")

Example 14.13e. (Bach, organ fugue BWV 539, mm. 91–92)

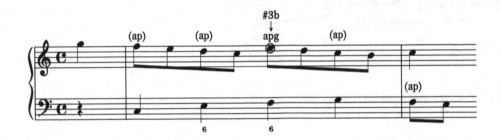

Example 14.13f part 1. (Kirnberger)

Example 14.13f part 2. (Bach, *WTC I*, D minor fugue, m. 6)

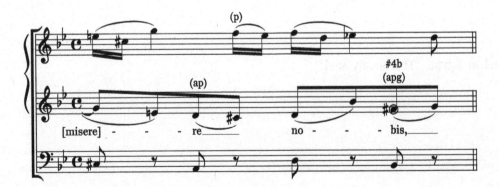

Example 14.13g. (Bach, B Minor Mass, Agnus Dei)

Example 14.13h. (Bach, French Suite I, Sarabande)

Example 14.13i. (Bach, Cantata BWV 201, "Geschwinde ihr wirbelnden Winde")

In two parts, dissonance in free style can create bewildering harmonic implications. For instance, in example 14.14 (B minor fugue, *WTC I*), can we really believe that the A–E fifth on the downbeat of m. 5 stands for an A-major harmony (VII of B minor)? One way to check is to look ahead at the same combination used in a three-voice context: in m. 10 (not shown here) we see that the corresponding downbeat note (E in the bass) is intended as an appoggiatura, making a 4–3 with respect to the root, B. So the A in m. 5 can now be read and played as an appoggiatura.

Example 14.14. (Bach, *WTC I*, B minor fugue, mm. 1–6)

EXERCISE 14-B

1. *Analysis:* In this section of a Mass movement, identify the harmonic progression, label all dissonances, and explain how the dissonances relate to the chord factors.

Example 14.15. (Bach, Mass in G minor, Gloria, "Et in terra," mm. 45–60)

2. *Analysis:* In the following aria ritornello, analyze the harmonic progression, label all dissonances, and explain how the dissonances relate to the chord factors. Sometimes we have to suppose an *imaginary* compound melody to explain some skips into dissonances.

Example 14.16. (Bach, Cantata 21, iii)

3. *Analysis:* In the following excerpt, analyze the harmonic progression, label all dissonances, and explain how the dissonances relate to the chord factors. Note that the figures are incomplete. Identify the sequences. How many chords does the model of each sequence contain?

Example 14.17. (Pergolesi, Stabat Mater, i, mm. 12–23, violin and viola parts omitted)

4. *Composing (short):* Choose a dance meter and write a melody with figured bass using five of the nine kinds of skip + dissonance shown above in examples 14.12 and 14.13. Label all embellishments and show harmonic analysis.

5. *Composing (short):* Choose a dance meter and write a melody with figured bass using the other four of the nine kinds of skip + dissonance shown above in examples 14.12 and 14.13. Label all embellishments and show harmonic analysis.

EXPANDING A HARMONY (VOICE EXCHANGE)

A good way of expanding a single harmony is to use different inversions of the same chord. The bass can skip about between chord members (usually exchanging with one or more of the upper parts). Heinichen illustrates the principle as follows.

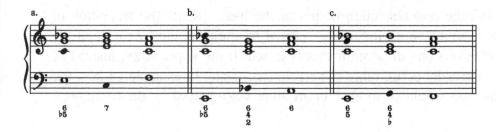

Example 14.18. (Heinichen)

In examples 14.18a and c the two moving voices literally exchange their notes. The bass in example 14.18a moves from E to C while the tenor moves from C to E. Similarly, in example 14.18c the bass moves from E to G and the alto from G to E. In example 14.18b, the members of the C^7 chord are rotated so that both chords are complete, but there is no direct exchange between two voices. Heinichen indicates a voice exchange by a large X (table 14.1).

Table 14.1

E   C

X

C   E

In strict style the correct voice leading must be observed at the change of harmony (i.e., leading tones and sevenths must resolve directly), and transferred resolutions do not occur. Voice exchanges involving leaps by a third are very common. The third is often filled in with a passing tone (which then can carry its own little harmony), as in the fugue by J. K. F. Fischer shown in example 20.2a (see m. 4, the third through the fifth eighth notes, and corresponding places later).

TRANSFERRED RESOLUTIONS

Kirnberger describes transferred resolution as follows:

> First, it happens sometimes that the resolution does not occur in the voice that has the dissonance, but in another voice. For instance, this progression [example 14.19a], which is written according to the strict rules, can be treated freely as follows [example 14.19b]. By means of an exchange in the other half of the measure the bass takes over the dissonance and resolves it down stepwise so that the resolution proceeds from the upper voice to the lower. The same also happens with the inversions of the seventh chord, as can be seen in the following example [example 14.20]. Instead of the seventh chord of the preceding example, its first inversion is used at (a), in spite of which the resolution can still happen in the bass as before. At (b) the same resolution happens in the bass, but in the upper voice occurs the third above the bass, so that it looks to some extent as if the earlier seventh had

been resolved upward; but the real resolution occurs in the bass. (Note: The resolution of the B in the bass would be to a C in an inner voice played by the continuo.) At (c) and (d) there are several cases of inversions of seventh chords in which the upper voice, instead of the bass where it should normally occur, takes the resolution. (Note: In example 14.20e, the resolution of the F in the bass would be to an E in an inner voice played by the continuo.)[3]

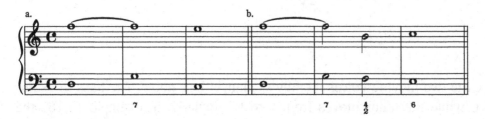

Example 14.19. (Kirnberger)

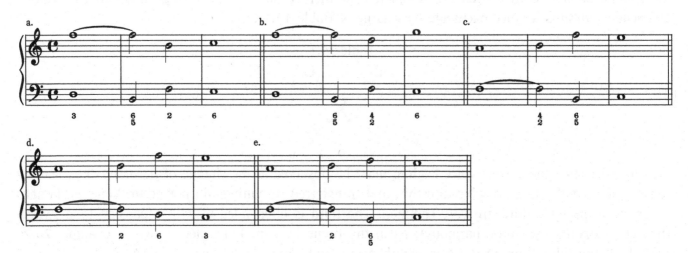

Example 14.20. (Kirnberger)

Examples 14.20b, d, and e need an inner voice that resolves the leading tone or the seventh, respectively. Kirnberger continues: "Second, instead of the seventh chord one can take all its inversions one after another during the time in which the seventh chord should be held. Thus the progression at [example 14.20a] above can be taken as the one shown at [example 14.21a] below, and instead of the progression at [example 14.21a], one can take the one shown at [14.21b]."[4]

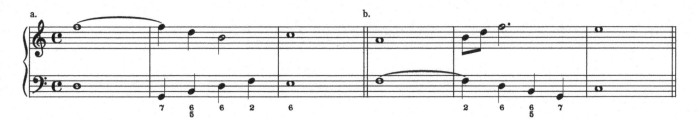

Example 14.21. (Kirnberger)

Kirnberger says the technique only applies to chord sevenths. Note that in all of these examples the last chord seventh to sound resolves directly; most often the last leading tone to sound also resolves (except in example 14.21b, where the arpeggiation in the bass concludes with the root).

Here are further examples by Heinichen that show how a harmony can be expanded by using different inversions of the same chord in a row and how resolutions can be transferred. It is important that embellishments never obscure the basic voice-leading. A good way of showing that the underlying voice-leading is correct is to do a voice-leading reduction. As we have seen, in a voice-leading reduction we simply remove all the embellishing notes until we arrive at a first-species, note-against-note texture. In each of the following examples, the embellished version is shown first, followed by Heinichen's own voice-leading reduction. How do you think Heinichen made his choices? Does he follow Kirnberger's rules?

Example 14.22a. (Heinichen)

Example 14.22b. (Reduction)

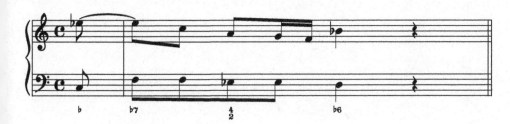

Example 14.23a. (Heinichen)

Example 14.23b. (Reduction)

Example 14.24a. (Heinichen)

Example 14.24b. (Reduction)

LAYERS OF DISSONANCE

Sometimes embellishments take place at different rates and in different rhythmic levels, as in example 14.7. Study this excerpt from a Bach chorale prelude (example 14.25) for interaction between dissonance at the half-note level, the quarter-note level, and the eighth-note level. Analyze the harmonies and label dissonances and transferred resolutions.

Example 14.25. (Bach, "Gott, durch deine Güte," mm. 1–12)

THE BENEFITS OF FREE STYLE

Some of the peculiarities of example 14.25 are the consequence of the basic compositional device that underlies the whole prelude: the canon between the soprano and bass. The bass imitates the soprano a measure later and an octave lower. Play just these two voices. Because the tune was not designed for canonic treatment, you notice that awkward crunches occur, like the dissonance on the downbeat of m. 5. Bach "justifies" the C–D ninth as part of a seventh chord—the addition of F-sharp gives strong harmonic direction that makes us more willing to accept the crunch (likewise the C–B-flat dissonance in m. 9). The canon, even justified as it is, would not be possible in strict style.

An amazing feature of this setting is the number of times Bach reuses measure-long motives in both the eighth-note line and the quarter-note line (these have been bracketed). These motive placements would not be possible in strict style. Note the transferred resolution of the alto F at the end of m. 3 and the transferred resolutions marked (with arrows) in m. 10.

Another benefit can be felt when composing a countersubject. The availability of accented dissonance can make it unnecessary to adjust the countermelody to accommodate the difference between the subject and answer; that is, there is no need for a tonal counteranswer. In example 16.18 (C minor fugue, *WTC I*), the sixth (asterisk in m. 3) becomes a ninth (asterisk in m. 7).

As you will see in the following chapters, many operations (stretto, invertible counterpoint at the twelfth) create peculiar successions of vertical intervals that can be made acceptable through the licenses afforded by the freer use of dissonance discussed in this chapter.

EXERCISE 14-C

1. *Keyboard harmony and improvisation:* Use these materials from Heinichen (bass line, given rhythm, examples 14.26a–c), and add embellished lines in the suggested rhythm, in which transfers are clearly resolved. Circle accented dissonance. Make an effort to cover enough ground (i.e., use many chord factors) so that the harmonies are clear. Be daring! Continue the first example until the double bar line.

Example 14.26a.

Example 14.26b.

Example 14.26c.

2. *Keyboard harmony and improvisation:* Use the Heinichen reductions in example 14.27 as the basis for improvisation in mixed values in free style (you may want to move the lower line down an octave).

Example 14.27a. (Heinichen)

Example 14.27b. (Heinichen)

3. *Writing:* Harmonize the melody shown in example 14.28. Accented dissonances are circled.

Example 14.28.

4. *Composing (long):* Using the combination from Exercise 14-A nos. 3 or 4, compose a three-part fugue exposition.

5. *Composing (short):* Compose a subject/countersubject combination that is invertible at the octave containing accented passing dissonance and voice exchange including transferred resolution.

NOTES

1. Schoenberg, *Theory of Harmony*, p. 327.
2. Kirnberger, *Die Kunst des reinen Satzes in der Musik*, I, 11, p. 215.
3. Kirnberger, 5, pp. 82–84.
4. Kirnberger, p. 84.

15

CHROMATICISM AND SEQUENCES

Ascending and Descending Chromaticism; The Diminished Seventh Chord; Two Types of Descending Chromaticism; Isolated Applied Dominants; Applied Dominants in Sequences; Sequences with Irregular Harmonic Rhythm; Sequences with Embedded Progressions; Applied Dominants in Compound Melody; More Harmonic Smudges; Chromatic Scales in Fugue Subjects; Chromaticism and Tonal Answer; A Famous Difficult Example; Partimento

ASCENDING AND DESCENDING CHROMATICISM

Ascending chromaticism is allowed in strict style because all the applied leading tones are resolved. We saw in chapter 12 how ascending chromaticism works in a sequence. In example 15.1 Kirnberger shows how it is used to embellish simple progressions in a different context.

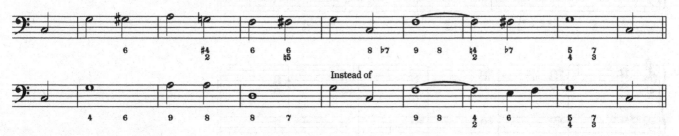

Example 15.1. (Kirnberger)

Descending chromaticism is not allowed in strict style because applied leading tones are not resolved. They are followed by notes a chromatic semitone lower, which most often appear as unprepared sevenths. Speaking of unprepared sevenths in general, Kirnberger explains, "In free style there are various cases where the seventh occurs without the preparation common in strict style. . . . The first case [a] can be justified by the fact that the root is reached by a fifth; the second and third cases [b and c] can be excused by the fact that the seventh and fifth [above the bass] respectively are allowed as passing tones of this kind in free style." His example (15.2) shows cases in which the seventh cannot be prepared because the previous chord does not contain that note (F). In b and c, he considers the sevenths not as dissonant upper neighbors but as passing tones from an imaginary G, as shown in d and e. (He could have done likewise for the first case.)

Example 15.2. (Kirnberger)

He says: "From here arise progressions of two successive dissonant chords which would appear too harsh in strict style. Thus the following progressions, written in strict style [example 15.3a], can occur in free style as follows [example 15.3b]."[1] Here we see that the descending chromaticism results from leaving out the resolution of the applied leading tone, moving instead directly to the seventh of the next chord.

Example 15.3. (Kirnberger)

THE DIMINISHED SEVENTH CHORD

It should be noted that whether this chord is analyzed as vii[7] or V[9] without the root, it normally has a dominant function. Kimberger says: "The diminished seventh chord, which arises from the first inversion of the seventh chord with suspended minor ninth (since one can take the chord in example 15.4b instead of the one in example 15.4a), can be sounded everywhere and freely in all its inversions. It has something special because of the three stacked minor thirds."[2] When we address in the next section the chord factors involved in chromaticism, we will refer to the "root" of the vii[7] chord as "T," the third of the imaginary (applied) dominant. The diminished seventh chord with scale degree 2 in the bass can be used to replace a clumsy V[6/4] chord.

Example 15.4. (Kirnberger)

TWO TYPES OF DESCENDING CHROMATICISM

In examples from Bach's *Musical Offering* (examples 15.8a and b), each type of descending chromaticism has been labeled. "C5" stands for the use of applied dominants and applied diminished seventh chords in a circle of fifths progression; "O" stands for other motions, as when the second note of a chromatic semitone pair is the fifth of the chord.

1. A. In the first type of descending chromaticism, just described, the applied leading tone in the first chord (T) is canceled, and instead of resolving, it is followed by a note a chromatic semitone lower, which is the seventh (S) of the next chord. The root of each chord is a fifth below that of the preceding, so a segment of the circle of fifths results, and we label it "C5." It is possible to interlock these functions so *every* chord is an applied dominant that doesn't resolve, as shown in example 15.3b.

Remember that you should not build an applied dominant on IV in a major key (and one rarely finds VII as V/iii in major, but it does occur) nor on VI in a minor key (you may build one on II as V/V because you often need to approach the dominant this way). In these places you may use natural diatonic seventh chords instead, and the roots will skip an augmented fourth or diminished fifth. This is the reason Kirnberger's example of "C5" chromaticism (example 15.3b) breaks off just at the point where he got to IV.

Baroque composers almost never use the circle of *perfect* fifths. Repeatedly pairing notes of the chromatic scale using applied dominants (in each pair the second note is part of an applied dominant), whether ascending or descending, divides the octave into whole tones and takes you too far out of the key (examples 15.5a and b). Consequently, we repeat a note instead of chromaticizing it (examples 15.6a and b at the asterisks). This can happen once or twice, in order to keep the key regions close. Of course, switching to another type of chromaticism ("O") can help (examples 15.6c and d; see section 2 below).

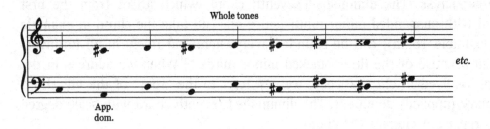

Example 15.5a.

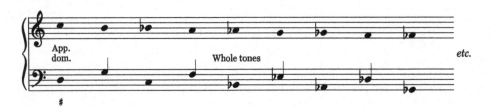

Example 15.5b.

Example 15.6a.

Example 15.6b.

Example 15.6c.

Example 15.6d.

1. B. This kind of chromaticism involves applied dominants in the form of *diminished seventh chords* instead of dominant sevenths. These can be read as incomplete V^9 chords, and the lowered version of the note is the ninth (N) of the applied dominant function. (Remember that if you prefer to think of diminished seventh chords as "vii of," then the lowered note is the seventh. We will continue to refer consistently to these chords in terms of their applied function, however.) In example 15.7a we see ninths resolving to fifths in a circle-of-fifths progression where the chromatic scale fills the upper tetrachord of the key. We can think of the ninth chords as substitutes for seventh chords. Thus while example 15.7b would not be possible in C major (E-flat is too far out), we could substitute V^9 of I under the A-flat, as shown in example 15.7c.

Example 15.7.

In the second type of descending chromaticism (generically labeled "O" for "other"), chromaticism involves either the same chord factor or two different chord factors. It is often used when the C5 type would take us too far out of the key (see examples 15.6c and d).

2. A. Descending chromaticism involving two versions of the *same chord factor*: the most common example is a minor chord following a major chord with the same root. The chromaticism occurs between the two different "versions" of the third (T) of the chord and it is labeled "O–T/T" (for "other, third-third") (see example 15.8a, m. 5). The chromaticism in m. 6 of example 15.8a between D and D-flat is "O–R/R," in other words both D and D-flat are the roots of the respective chords. Another interesting example of this type of chromaticism appears in m. 117 of example 15.8b, where we have labeled "O–F/F"; find other instances of the same chord factors chromaticized.

2. B. Descending chromaticism involving *different chord factors*: In example 15.8a, m. 14, the applied leading tone C-sharp to D (T = third of a chord) moves by chromatic semitone to C-natural, a stable tone (F = fifth) in the following F major chord. This pattern is repeated in the next measure.

Example 15.8a. (Bach, Musical Offering, 4, mm. 1–15)

Example 15.8b. (Bach, Musical Offering, 1, mm. 115–129) *Note the melody from the D minor fugue in* WTC II.

The safest segments to use for descending chromatic lines are the upper tetrachord (from 1 down to 5, example 15.7c) and the upper part of the lower pentachord (from 5 to 2). The chromatic upper tetrachord is often used as the bass in sad pieces in the seventeenth and eighteenth centuries, where it is called the *lament bass*. The upper tetrachord is easy to spell because the scale degrees pair up nicely and are easy to harmonize using the two types of chromaticism in three pairs of notes: 8–7, ♭7–6, ♭6–5 (example 15.9a). A common substitution in the lower pentachord (5–1) is the Neapolitan sixth (♭II in first inversion). It is often preceded by ♮ii⁶, as shown in example 15.9b (see also examples 15.6d and 15.8a, m. 6).

Example 15.9.

ISOLATED APPLIED DOMINANTS

We sometimes find applied dominants within the fugue subject. In the following fugal gigue by Bach, the subject contains a V⁷/IV harmony in m. 2. When the real answer enters, what seems like a return to the region of D major (m. 8) is actually a momentary move to IV of A.

Example 15.10. (Bach, Partita IV, gigue, mm. 1–19)

In the next example, the splice falls between the third and fourth notes. The subject appears to continue in C-sharp major after the splice but in fact the F-sharp in the bass is the flat seventh degree of the scale of the dominant, G-sharp, functioning as part of V/IV. That this is so is proved by the answer, which has a corresponding B-natural as part of V/IV in C-sharp on the second beat of m. 2.

Example 15.11. (Bach, *WTC II*, C-sharp major fugue, mm. 1–3)

APPLIED DOMINANTS IN SEQUENCES

Applied dominants are often found in sequences, which are a good means with which to prolong a subject as shown in example 15.12.

Example 15.12. (Handel, Sonata 6, iv, mm. 1–15)

Example 15.13 is another Handel trio sonata excerpt with a cut-and-paste progression when the second violin enters in the tonic (with one change of chord inversion). In m. 3, we assume that the F-sharp downbeat resolves to an imaginary G on the second beat, and that the F-natural that follows is a seventh introduced as a passing tone. However, when the second violin sounds the theme, the first violin proves us wrong in m. 9 by sounding an F-natural in the same register immediately on the second beat (these transfers are shown with circled notes in m. 9). In these cases, two dominant seventh chords succeed each other directly in circle-of-fifths fashion, with lines moving in "parallel" descending diatonic and chromatic semitones, alternating vertical diminished fifths and augmented fourths, as you'll see if you make a three-voice chorale-style reduction of mm. 9 and 10. Note that Handel abandons chromaticism when he reaches III[7] in m. 4 and in m. 10—he could have made it V[7]/VI, but then he would have had to restore the A-natural two beats later. He avoids the cross-relation by using diatonic sevenths.

Example 15.13. (Handel, Sonata 8, i, mm. 1–12)

The harmonies in the next example (example 15.14) are a bit harder to hear right off, especially in the fourth measure of the subject. Is the low note a pedal or part of a harmony? Analyze these harmonies; note the passing 6/4 chords and Neapolitan harmonies. In the countersubject, all the applied leading tones in the compound melody resolve correctly. (We'll look at the B section, where the subject is inverted, in example 20.4b.)

Example 15.14. (Bach, English Suite 5, gigue, mm. 1–14)

SEQUENCES WITH IRREGULAR HARMONIC RHYTHM

Some sequences use an irregular rhythm throughout the model. In example 15.15, Bach uses a three-chord model in which the first harmony lasts a full measure, then the other two harmonies last a half measure each. The result is a sequence of ascending thirds.

Example 15.15. (Bach, *WTC II*, F major fugue, mm. 38–46)

SEQUENCES WITH EMBEDDED PROGRESSIONS

We saw a small circle-of-fifths sequence within each measure in mm. 30–32 of Handel's concerto grosso in example 12.9, where the downbeats of each measure also made a large circle-of-fifths sequence. We say the smaller sequence is embedded in the larger one. Likewise, the descending-thirds sequence we saw in the D major fugue of *WTC I* (example 12.4) is actually stated three times in a larger sequence of descending steps whose model is a full measure, as shown with a bracket in example 15.16, m. 17 (ii substitutes for vi at the beginning).

Example 15.16. (Bach, D major fugue, *WTC I*, mm. 15–19)

The following sequence from Bach's Brandenburg Concerto No. 4 uses as its model the last two measures of the bracketed fugue subject. The last chord of the model represents a local tonic arrival, except that its third is raised, with the chord now functioning as the dominant of the following progression. As a result, the key areas move up a fourth every two measures. On the downbeat of m. 143 Bach deviates from the sequence pattern by replacing the expected D in the bass by G-sharp (vii⁶/ii). G-sharp then moves to C-sharp on the second beat (V⁷/ii). Had the sequence continued as expected, it would have reached D in m. 143 (V⁷/III), continuing the overall motion up by fourths. Instead, the sequence now continues a semitone lower (in F-sharp minor instead of G major). Bach then repeats the model one more time without further changes, moving to B minor in mm. 145ff. The sequence pattern breaks off at the end of m. 146. The overall effect of the harmonic shift in m. 143 can be schematized as follows:

Table 15.1

Measures:	135–138	139–140	141–142	143-144	145–146
Bach's key areas with the shift:	E⁻	A⁻	D⁺	F♯⁻	B⁻
Hypothetical key areas without the shift:	E⁻	A⁻	D⁺	G⁺	C⁺

There are a few more subtleties worth noticing in Bach's sequence: the model uses a cadential pattern in the bass. At the moment when you expect the dominant, for the first time on the third quarter of m. 138, Bach flattens the third of that dominant harmony. (It turns into ii of the ensuing A minor key.) This surprise is repeated two measures later (third beat of m. 140). Bach does not replicate the surprise again after a further two measures, however, but instead brings in the regular dominant harmony in m. 142. That in itself is now experienced as a surprise and is followed by the changed bass in m. 143. The third of the dominant in m. 144 is again lowered as in the earlier statements of the model. The last repetition of the model in mm. 145–146 uses the expected dominant harmony with A-sharp.

Example 15.17. (Bach, Brandenburg Concerto 4, last movement, mm. 134–152, violin and viola parts omitted)

APPLIED DOMINANTS IN COMPOUND MELODY

Example 15.18 is called the "Cat" fugue because it was said that the bizarre subject was made by Domenico Scarlatti's cat walking across the keys. Measures 2–3 of the subject use three augmented or diminished melodic intervals in a row. These are the result of compound melody. Deduce a harmonization from Scarlatti's counteranswer against the real answer in mm. 6–10 and make a chorale-style reduction in four voices.

Example 15.18. (Domenico Scarlatti, "Cat" fugue K. 30, mm. 1–19) *Scarlatti adds and subtracts voices freely.*

MORE HARMONIC SMUDGES

As we saw in chapter 12, one often eases into a sequence with a chord that is ambiguous. In example 15.10, a diatonic circle-of-fifths sequence (mm. 3–5) follows the V^7/IV chord we discussed. While we all agree the C resolves to the B, is that B part of a G major harmony? It sounds as if it should be, given what came before, but it's all alone; in principle it could belong to an E minor or even B minor harmony. To seek clarification, we can look at the corresponding two-part presentation of the same material (now in the dominant) in m. 9. Unfortunately, we still can't be sure what the harmony is on the downbeat because two pitch classes alone can belong to at least two different harmonies. The F-sharp and the A could be part of triads on D or F-sharp. We expect D major because of the V^7/IV that precedes, but we get a different idea if we consider the harmonies that we are sure of in mm. 9–11. They seem to be B, E, A, and D in irregular dotted quarter- and dotted eighth-note harmonic rhythm. Reading backward, we now hear the F-sharp and A in m. 9 as a vi chord, the normal precursor of ii in the circle of fifths in A. But when we got there, we thought it "should" have been a D major chord. The ambiguity disappears completely when we look ahead at m. 18. There we learn that the dominant seventh on D resolves irregularly to B minor (making a harmonic smudge).

EXERCISE 15-A

1. *Analysis:* Analyze the descending chromaticism we have not labeled in example 15.8b, using the appropriate labels.

2. *Analysis:* Make a diatonic reduction of mm. 117–122 in example 15.8b. Find the model and sequence. Add a voice to create a four-voice texture.

3. *Composing (short):* Compose descending chromatic countersubjects to diatonic subjects you have used in earlier chapters. Provide a harmonic analysis. Experiment, starting on different notes and making the chromatic line unfold at different speeds, before you assign harmonies. You may even have to change your idea of what key you're in!

Sample: Given F–G–A–B-flat as subject (example 15.19), you could write countermelodies a, b, or c and then harmonize each to make the interval succession convincing. You may reject some solutions at the harmonization stage because the interval successions simply can't be made to fit into a convincing harmonic progression.

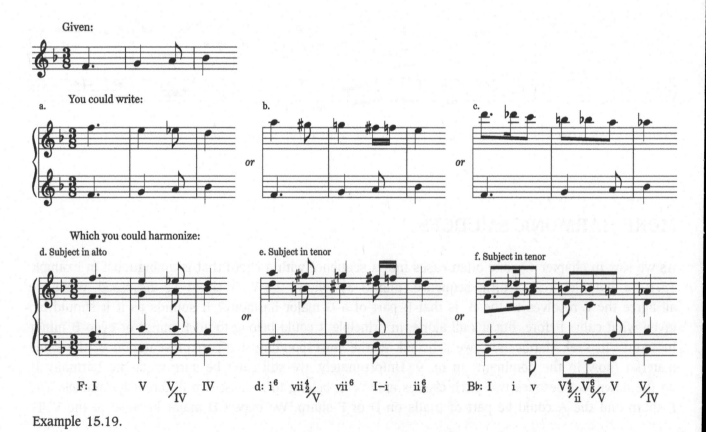

Example 15.19.

CHROMATIC SCALES IN FUGUE SUBJECTS

Marpurg writes the following about chromatic fugue subjects:

> Chromaticism does not take place only in the minor key, as a certain famous teacher of music [Marpurg probably means Rameau] wants to assert, (although it is true that it is used mostly there), but also in the major key. While in diatonic fugue subjects one moves only within the key of the tonic or dominant at all times, in chromatic fugue subjects different keys appear one after another, and hence one tends to choose a chromatic subject if one wants to give an example of one's knowledge of harmony.[3]

(Marpurg does not suggest that text affect might play a role, nor does he tell us how to compose a chromatic fugue subject.)

The following fugue subject by Johann Ernst Eberlin makes use of two types of chromaticism (C5, O–T/T). Consider the third entry where the harmonic implications of the subject are clearly recognizable in the three-part realization. Label the harmonies in m. 7.

Example 15.20. (Johann Ernst Eberlin, Versus secundus contrarius, mm. 1–10)

CHROMATICISM AND TONAL ANSWER

Marpurg proposes the following strategy for finding the tonal answer to a chromatic fugue subject (his terminology substitutes *dux* for leading voice, or subject, and *comes* for consequent, or answer). He says:

> In order to find the *comes* to a chromatic subject, one first needs to turn it into a diatonic one by removing the accidentals. Then one looks for the *comes* that uses a similar diatonic progression following the instructions given [for finding the tonal answer]. Once this is done,

one returns the accidentals to the *dux* and imitates these accidentals in the scale of the *comes* in similar fashion. For example let us give the following chromatic subject in A minor.

A | C–C#–D–D# | E

There are two semitones here which are not part of the A minor scale, C-sharp against C and D-sharp against D. If we discard these two semitones, the following basic diatonic melody remains:

A | C–D | E

This would be answered . . . by . . .

E | F–G | A

One then aligns the two subjects as follows:

A | C–D | E

E | F–G | A

Since the first chromatic semitone appears on scale degree C and the other one on scale degree D of the *dux*, one imitates in a similar way these two semitones in the *comes* on those scale degrees which correspond to C and D. These scale degrees are F and G in the *comes,* and consequently the two subjects correspond in the following way:

Table 15.2

Dux	A |	C	–	C-sharp	– D –	D-sharp	|	E
Comes	E |	F	–	F-sharp	– G –	G-sharp	|	A

One has to proceed in this way with all chromatic subjects, whatever their key and regardless of whether the intervals ascend or descend. Besides this, one notices in this example that if the second note C in the *dux,* which forms a third against the *incipit* note A, were transposed down an octave, thus forming a lower sixth against the A, then one would find that similarly transposing down an octave the second note F of the *comes* would transform the sixth C–A into a seventh, namely into F–E, such as is done in an example by Capellmeister Handel where the seventh F–E is turned into the sixth C–A. [The chromaticism itself does not affect the splice that Marpurg is now talking about.][4]

Example 15.21. (Handel, fugue 5 in A minor, mm. 1–7)

EXERCISE 15-B

1. *Composing (short):* Find the answers to these chromatic subjects (example 15.22a–c).

2. *Composing (short):* Compose countersubjects and counteranswers to the above. Provide a harmonic analysis.

Example 15.22a.

Example 15.22b.

Example 15.22c.

A FAMOUS DIFFICULT EXAMPLE

Probably the most famous example of nonharmonic tones coupled with extreme chromaticism is the B minor fugue from *WTC I*. Kirnberger had some trouble analyzing the subject. Joel Lester compares Kirnberger's analysis (example 15.23a) with his own (example 15.23b), showing how differently modern writers think about eighteenth-century music.[5] Kirnberger was concerned with anything that appeared to be a chord, while many analysts today tend to think in broader terms, on a larger scale, identifying some chords as merely "embellishing" and eliminating them from a reduction. These examples will repay close examination and discussion.

Example 15.23a. (Kirnberger's analysis of the subject)

Example 15.23b. (Lester's analysis of the subject)

PARTIMENTO

The following little partimento by Pasquini has only three thematic entries. See if you can reuse the countermelody over the third entry.

Example 15.24. (Pasquini)

This fugue from the Langloz Manuscript (example 15.25) features clever interrelationships between the ascending and descending chromatic scale segments. The descending chromatic line in the second half of the subject, for instance, is the retrograde of the first six notes of the answer. Try to find places to reuse the countermelody or place the theme in an upper voice. The countermelody inexplicably clashes with the figures in mm. 10, 13, 22, and 41: you'll have to choose whether to stick to the figures or maintain the countermelody.

Example 15.25. (Langloz Manuscript, #25)

Example 15.25. *(Concluded)*

Example 15.26. (Fenaroli, Partimenti, Gj 1402)

Example 15.26. *(Continued)*

Example 15.26. *(Continued)*

Example 15.26. *(Concluded)*

This partially figured fugue by Fenaroli (example 15.26) is a double fugue of the second and third type. Maybe mm. 9–16 are still in two voices to give you a chance to memorize the voice pair before you jump into more voices and have to figure out where the thematic statements are. Sometimes the figures are not spaced exactly below the measure: you'll have to decide where to put the natural third in m. 52 for instance. It is a good idea to mix fast- and slow-moving lines in the same measure.

NOTES

1. Kirnberger, *Die Kunst des reinen Satzes in der Musik*, I, 5, pp. 88–90.
2. Kirnberger, p. 90.
3. Marpurg, *Abhandlung von der Fuge*, III, 10, §3, pp. 74–75.
4. Marpurg, §4, pp. 75–76.
5. Lester, *Compositional Theory in the Eighteenth Century*, pp. 248–49.

16

MULTIPLE COUNTERPOINT

Why Use Invertible Counterpoint? Invertible Counterpoint at the Tenth (IC10); Parallel Tenths; IC10 and Harmony; IC12; IC12 and Harmony; A Bach Story; Invertible Double Counterpoint in Three Parts; Invertible Counterpoint at the Octave and Tenth; Invertible Counterpoint at the Tenth and Twelfth; Invertible Double Counterpoint in Four Parts: IC8, 10, and 12; Triple and Quadruple Counterpoint; Composing Boxes of Artful Devices First . . . ; . . . And Then Unpacking the Boxes; Uninverted Double Counterpoint

Multiple counterpoint (e.g., double, triple) deals in general with recombinations of the same melodic lines in different relationships. Double counterpoint involves moving two melodies around; triple involves three melodies, and so on. We assume one combination to be the "original" and later ones to be transformations of the original. Sometimes these transformations involve switching the relative locations of the melodies (an upper one goes below and a lower one appears above). If there are two melodies, we refer to the transformation as *invertible double counterpoint*. Other times the melodies retain their relative positions but the distance between them is changed; this we call *uninverted double counterpoint*. We will abbreviate invertible double counterpoint simply as "IC" because we always analyze the transformations in terms of pairs of voices. Not all counterpoint books make this distinction or use these terms the same way.

WHY USE INVERTIBLE COUNTERPOINT?

We use invertible counterpoint primarily to vary thematic presentation. In chapter 9 we showed how IC8 was used to present a theme and countermelody in a different relationship, allowing for various orders of entries (you may want to review that discussion). IC8 keeps all pitch classes the same (unless the entire combination is transposed), so the harmonic progression is unchanged in the inversion (i.e., all the names of the notes are the same, and they represent the same chord factors, but because their register is changed, the chord voicing and maybe inversion are changed).

All other intervals of inversion produce new pitch classes (i.e., new notes). Even though the melodies are the same, the intervals between the parts are changed beyond just a change in register. There are new notes because one of the melodies is transposed by an interval other than an octave. That means that some consonant vertical intervals in the original combination may turn into dissonances in the inverted combination, and it means the original harmonic progression might not work.

Why would anybody do this? The best reason is given by Mattheson, who says: "An assiduous organist no less than an ingenious composer or Capellmeister can draw materials and inventions from these artifices for the rest of his life."[1] In other words, you might come up with things you would never have thought of on your own without the application of invertible counterpoint.

Another reason is economy of material. Invertible counterpoint allows you to reuse the same combination(s) over and over in varied manifestations. As we will see, it is often sufficient to compose a "box" of invertible counterpoint to generate many measures of fugal texture. Invertible counterpoint, at other intervals than the octave, gives you ways of varying the presentation of the same two melodies. Usually, these presentations are not heard right in a row in the piece; rather, the original may be heard at the beginning and the inverted combination later. The effect on harmony can be great, as we will see, and some surprising and delightful new dissonances may occur as well.

INVERTIBLE COUNTERPOINT AT THE TENTH (IC10)

Marpurg shows the following example of IC10 in example 16.1. Instead of showing the two combinations side by side, he puts them both together—that is, the melody that starts with a whole note appears both above and below the one that starts with a rest, to save space. Marpurg explains that either combination could be considered the original, and either could be considered the inverted combination:

> The upper and middle voices contain the main composition [the original—example 16.1a], and the middle and lowest voices contain the inversion. One could also consider the middle and lowest voices as the main composition [Example 16.lb]; then this middle voice and the upper voice make up the inversion [Example 16.la]. It is the same thing. In both cases the countermelody stays in its place and the other part is inverted at the tenth. This is the first type of inversion of the main composition, in which . . . the upper part is moved down a tenth. In [Example 16.lc], the upper part becomes the lower part and the lower part becomes the upper part via inversion at the tenth, and this is the second type of inversion or rather a transposition of the former [type of inversion].[2]

In other words, the inverted combination and the original are reciprocals of each other.

Example 16.1. (Two-voice combinations from Marpurg) *Combination b is the inversion of a, just as combination a is the inversion of b. Combination c is the inversion of a in a different way: the lower line of a has been moved up a tenth, and the upper line dropped an octave (strictly speaking, this is inverted at the seventeenth; i.e., a tenth plus an octave).*

The vertical intervals in each combination have been labeled. The following chart shows how the vertical intervals in the original combination are changed in the inverted combination.

Table 16.1

Original:	1	2	3	4	5	6	7	8	9	10
Inverted at 10:	10	9	8	7	6	5	4	3	2	1

The corresponding intervals sum to 11. All dissonances map onto each other, as do all consonances, so this seems easier even than IC8 (where a fifth in the original becomes a fourth). However, the problem is with imperfect consonances: thirds, sixths, and tenths become octaves, fifths, and unisons, respectively, so parallel motion in imperfect consonances is not available in the original, as this would result in parallel perfect intervals in the inverted combination. The simple thing to remember is that your original combination, to be invertible at the tenth, must consist of only oblique and/or contrary motion. If you hear a duo that uses no parallel motion, you can be sure it will invert at the tenth (see "A Bach Story" below).

The dissonant fourth, second, and seventh can always be used as nonharmonic passing or neighbor tones (example 16.1, mm. 6 and 7). However, fourths can appear under other circumstances as well. Marpurg says of the original combination shown in example 16.2a, that the fourths require a subordinate voice. In order to "justify" the fourths on the strong steps, he has added a middle voice that clarifies the harmonies of the progression. In example 16.2b, the fourths are between the sevenths and the thirds of the chords, and the progression is a descending circle of fifths.

When the original combination is inverted at the tenth, the fourths become sevenths, and the harmonic progression is altered. It's still a descending-step sequence with a two-chord model, but the root of every other chord is now a third lower (so the roots rise by step and fall by a third instead of by a fourth and fifth—example 16.2c).

Example 16.2a.

Example 16.2b.

Example 16.2c.

In the rare instances where parallel fourths occur in the original, parallel sevenths will result (available only in free style). Marpurg shows us an example (16.3): the original combination appears in example 16.3a with parallel fourths; example 16.3b shows the combination inverted at the tenth, with parallel sevenths. The harshness of two sevenths in a row on the "steps" is softened by the second one being diminished. Example 16.3c shows these combinations, with voices added by Marpurg to clarify the harmonies.

C: I⁶   vii⁶   I

d: V⁷   vii⁷/V   V

Example 16.3.

In general, we avoid dissonant suspensions in writing IC10 because the resolutions of 4–3 and 7–6 suspensions result in resolutions to perfect intervals when inverted. However, Marpurg says that a 9–8 suspension will invert successfully at the tenth: "The most convenient resolution of the ninth is into the octave with a stationary bass, as in [example 16.4a], or into the fifth if the bass ascends by a fourth, as in [example 16.4b]."[3]

Example 16.4a. (Marpurg, Table LVIII, Fig. 4) *Each example shows both the original and inverted combinations.*

Example 16.4b. (Marpurg, Table LVIII, Fig. 5)

PARALLEL TENTHS

One of the most important features of invertible counterpoint at the tenth is the possibility of playing the original and the inversion simultaneously, which yields parallel tenths. In example 16.1, we know the original soprano–alto combination is good, and we know parallel tenths are good between the bass and soprano, but how can we know if the bass (the voice doubling in tenths) will fit with the alto? If the rules for invertible counterpoint at the tenth are followed, we can be sure the whole three-voice combination will work. You can experience this by playing all three voices of example 16.1 and 16.2c simultaneously.

IC10 AND HARMONY

Invertible counterpoint at intervals other than the octave often implies new harmonies, as for instance when it produces triads whose roots are a third away from those in the original. In example 16.1a by Marpurg, the original contains a 5–6 progression in mm. 1–4 with apparent roots G–C–A–D–B, and so on (otherwise known as an ascending stepwise sequence—see chapter 12). In the inverted combination we have the same type of sequence a third lower (roots E–C–F–D–G, etc.). When all three parts are played together, the chord factors we ascribed to the original duo must be reinterpreted. Note the cross-relation in m. 3. Finally, because of the "third lower syndrome," the final cadence of the inverted combination (mm. 7–8) is deceptive, while in the original it was authentic. The third lower syndrome only changes harmony when IC10 makes a new bass line; if the new interval combination occurs in the middle parts, it may or may not have new harmonic meaning.

Invertible counterpoint often sounds better when we use accidentals, implying new keys. In example 16.1, the original combination seems to be in G major, but the inverted combination uses F-natural to avoid the tritone skip, implying C major. This depends on which voices are transposed and how far. In example 16.1c, Marpurg has created a different combination from the original in example 16.1a, moving the upper voice down an octave and the lower one up a tenth. This one definitely starts as if in G major, but the C-sharp in the upper voice (required for the skip to F-sharp) implies D major.

The next two examples show how the two subjects from Contrapunctus 10 of Bach's *The Art of the Fugue* are combined (example 16.5a) and later inverted at the tenth. In example 16.5b, subject 2 is moved up a tenth; subject 1 appears an octave lower. As 10 + 8 = 18, the interval of inversion is actually a seventeenth (a tenth with an octave added). The vertical intervals sum to 18 as well. You will notice that the bare two-voice combinations don't necessarily sound so good without a third voice to enrich the sound with other chord factors that add a sense of harmonic direction and yet more rhythmic variety.

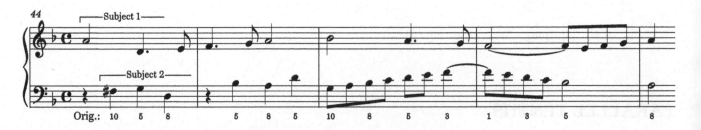

Example 16.5a. (Bach, The Art of Fugue, Contrapunctus 10, mm. 44–48)

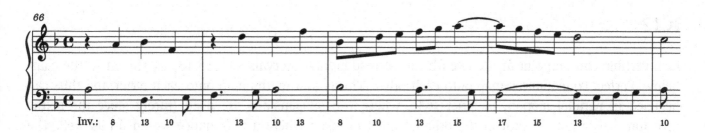

Example 16.5b. (Bach, The Art of Fugue, Contrapunctus 10, mm. 66–70)

Example 16.6a shows the answer and counteranswer pair from Bach's G minor fugue (*WTC II*). This pair is inverted at the tenth in example 16.6b.

Example 16.6a. (Bach, G minor fugue, *WTC II*, mm. 5–8)

Example 16.6b. (Bach, G minor fugue, *WTC II*, mm. 36–39) *Note in example 16.6a Bach's free use of 6/4 chords changing to root positions on the weak beats. Also note that Bach does not sound the fourth above the bass in these 6/4 chords.*

EXERCISE 16-A

1. *Writing (short):* Add a third voice to example 16.5a. How do you decide whether the added voice is to be above, below, or in between the two given voices? Compare your solution to Bach's. Add a third voice to example 16.5b and proceed in the same way.

2. *Writing (short):* Add a fourth voice to your trio from question 1. Compare your solution to Bach's.

3. *Composing (short):* Take a subject from anywhere in this book (except this chapter) and write a countersubject invertible at the tenth. Add a third voice to the original and the inverted combination and provide harmonic analysis for both.

IC12

In invertible counterpoint at the twelfth the corresponding intervals sum to 13, as shown in the chart below. Perfect consonances map onto each other. Thirds and tenths map onto each other and thus can be used in parallel motion. In strict style, where 7–6 suspensions are used (rarely since the sixths turn into sevenths), a sixth in the original must be used where a dissonance would do as well. The only suspension that can be used successfully in two parts over a stationary bass is the 4–3 in the original, which becomes a 9–10.

Chart for the inversion:

Table 16.2.

Original:	1	2	3	4	5	6	7	8	9	10	11	12
Inverted at 10:	12	11	10	9	8	7	6	5	4	3	2	1

The following examples by Marpurg show how sixths may be used in the original, with sevenths resolving correctly.[4] (You may find others that may work when a third voice is added.) Most of these examples are presented as above, with the two combinations shown on top of each other to save space. However, all three voices in these examples cannot be played at the same time as in IC10. Why not?

a.

b.

c.

d.

Example 16.7. (Marpurg, Table LX, Fig. 7–13) *Note that the inverted combination in example d is a case of legal ap; examples e–g can only be used in free style.*

Example 16.7. *(Concluded)*

Example 16.8. (Marpurg, Table LXI, Fig. 1) *Note the delayed resolutions in example a. Notice also that the roles of agent, dissonance, and resolution are exchanged in the inverted version.*

The next example from Bach's G minor fugue (*WTC II*) uses IC12 and contains delayed resolutions like those we just saw. Compare this example with the original combination shown earlier in example 16.6a (note the splices in the subject and countersubject). In example 16.9 the subject in the dominant is in the lower voice. The countersubject in the upper voice is the counteranswer from example 16.6a transposed up a twelfth.

Example 16.9. (Bach, G minor fugue, *WTC II*, mm. 28–31)

IC12 AND HARMONY

Because tenths above become thirds below in IC12, it is possible to maintain some of the same harmonies, as for instance if the voice transposing down a twelfth is the fifth chord factor in the original, becoming the root in the inverted combination. On the other hand, if it is the root that is moved down a twelfth, it may become the root of a chord a fifth below. Again, accidentals are often used to wrestle the new interval succession into a sensible progression.

Look back at Handel's anthem in example 11.7. A third subject, in half notes, enters in the first violin at m. 11, sounding the fifth chord factor above C, and then, rising a step, sounds the third chord factor above F, and so on. When this combination is inverted at the twelfth in m. 16 (shifted by a half measure), the first note of this subject is the root, and so is the second note (the second chord is a substitute, vi for I). Note that in the original, in the second half of m. 11, the first chord, made by the three subjects, is complete and the second incomplete, while in m. 16 the first chord is incomplete and the second complete (the simple counterpoint notes have been circled in the example).

In the following example from Bach's A minor fugue from *WTC I*, the E at the beginning of the answer is the fifth of the chord; in the inverted combination (m. 8), it appears as the root. At the end of the original combination (m. 5), the D-sharp is the third of the chord, accompanied by the

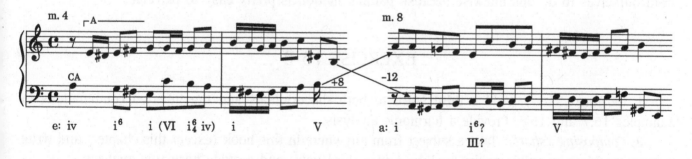

Example 16.10a. (Bach, A minor fugue, *WTC I*) *Example 16.10a has been slightly adapted, as you will see if you compare Bach's voice leading in the beginning of m. 9. Note how sixths in the original become accented passing sevenths in the inverted combination—free style makes many combinations possible that strict style would preclude.*

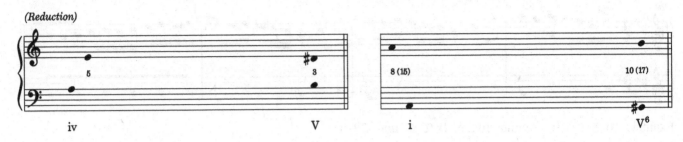

Example 16.10b. (Reduction)

root, B; in the inverted combination (m. 9), the corresponding G-sharp is also the third of the chord, but it is accompanied by the fifth chord factor, B. The reduction in example 16.10b may clarify these transformations. Note Bach's use of accidentals in the counteranswer: in the inverted combination the G-sharp is introduced on the downbeat of the second measure to clarify the key and harmony.

A BACH STORY

In a letter to Bach's first biographer, Johann Nikolaus Forkel, C. P. E. Bach wrote of his father: "When he listened to a rich and many-voiced fugue, he could soon say, after the first entries of the subject, what contrapuntal devices it would be possible to apply, and on such occasions, when I was standing next to him, and he had voiced his surmises to me, he would joyfully nudge me when his expectations were fulfilled."[5]

We can imagine a concrete instance of this. If "after the first entries of the subject" Bach had heard that the theme/countermelody pair contained no parallel motion and no dissonant suspensions, he would have known immediately that the pair could be presented in invertible counterpoint at the tenth, and that either the theme or the countermelody might be doubled in thirds or tenths. We can train ourselves to do this likewise because parallel motion is pretty easy to perceive.

EXERCISE 16-B

1. *Writing (short):* Add a third voice to both the originals and the inverted combinations in examples 16.7 and 16.8. Provide a harmonic analysis.

2. *Composing (short):* Take a subject from anywhere in this book (except this chapter) and write a countersubject invertible at the twelfth. Add a third voice and provide harmonic analysis.

3. *Listening (short):* (1) The teacher plays a theme/countermelody combination; students say what interval(s) it is invertible. (2) The teacher plays a combination and its inversion; students say at what interval it has been inverted.

INVERTIBLE DOUBLE COUNTERPOINT IN THREE PARTS

It is possible to use two intervals of inversion at the same time; when the two intervals are a third or a sixth apart one line is doubled in parallel thirds or sixths. We call it *double counterpoint* in three parts because there are still only two different melodies. The most common ways are to combine IC8 and IC10 or to combine IC10 with IC12.

INVERTIBLE COUNTERPOINT AT THE OCTAVE AND TENTH

We can schematize this in two ways. In example 16.11a, voice A stays in the same place and voice B moves up an octave and also up a tenth. This means that voice B is now doubled in thirds. Or voice B could stay in the same place and voice A could be moved down an octave and down a tenth. In example 16.11b, voice A is moved down a sixth and an octave, and voice B is moved up a third, so the intervals sum to 9 (IC8) and 11 (IC10). (Remember, as we said in chapter 9, the sum of the absolute values of the intervals of transposition equals one more than the interval of inversion.)

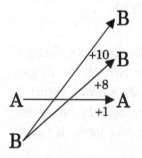

Example 16.11a.

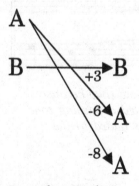

Example 16.11b.

Here is an example from a fugue by J. K. F. Fischer (example 16.12). The lower voice splits in two as in example 16.11a, and although the intervals are different, they sum to the same numbers (after we subtract the extra octave that has been added for spacing reasons). The upper voice (A) is moved down a twelfth, and the lower voice (B) is moved up a sixth, making ICl7 (which is IC10 when we subtract the octave), and also a fourth, making IC15 (which is IC8 when we subtract the octave). Both excerpts have the same harmonic progression ii–V–I (a fifth apart). This is because of the use of IC8 and the fact that the added thirds are above: since the countermelody had only roots and thirds of chords, these chord factors become thirds and fifths.

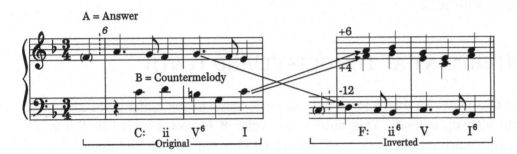

Example 16.12. (J. K. F. Fischer) *In chapter 20 we will examine the whole fugue from which this excerpt is taken.*

INVERTIBLE COUNTERPOINT AT THE TENTH AND TWELFTH

The combination of IC10 and IC12 can be schematized as in example 16.11, with the numbers changed appropriately. In the following example from Bach's Contrapunctus 10 from *The Art of the Fugue*, the bass has subject 1 (answer form) while the alto and soprano sound subject 2 (answer form) in parallel thirds. Compare this example with the original combination shown in example 16.5a above; with respect to that example, the alto and bass here form IC10, and the soprano and bass, IC12.

Example 16.13. (Bach, The Art of Fugue, Contrapunctus 10, mm. 85–88, IC10 and 12) *Note that because the first two notes of the answer form of the second subject rise a third, Bach has inserted a passing tone C-sharp in the soprano, confirming the key of D minor. Note also that an extra octave is added to the inverted combination, as in example 16.6b.*

INVERTIBLE DOUBLE COUNTERPOINT IN FOUR PARTS: IC8, 10, AND 12

In the following inverted combination (example 16.14a), both the subject and countersubject are played in parallel thirds. A brief fragment of the original combination (the alto and tenor in example 16.6a) is reprinted here in example 16.14b, with arrows and labels showing how the original combination has been inverted: the soprano and bass are in IC12 (6 + 7 = 13), the alto and bass are in IC10 (4 + 7 = 11), the soprano and tenor are in IC10 (6 + 5 = 11), and the alto and tenor are in IC8 (4 + 5 = 9).

Example 16.14a. (Bach, G minor fugue, *WTC II*, mm. 59–62, IC8, 10, and 12)

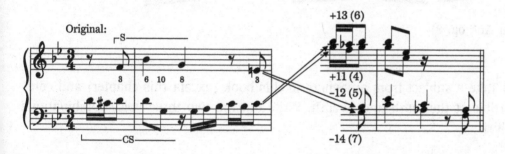

Example 16.14b.

You can think of these operations in terms of a first stage and a second stage. When the first transformation is IC8 (alto and tenor), adding a second statement of the countersubject a third *above* the alto produces IC10 between soprano and tenor. Similarly, if the first transformation is IC10 (soprano and tenor), adding a second statement of the subject a third *below* the tenor produces IC12 between soprano and bass. Here is an example from J. K. F. Fischer's D minor fugue.

Example 16.15. (J. K. F. Fischer, D minor fugue, mm. 1–3, m. 13) *Only the bracketed fragments are inverted (the bracketed fragments don't begin until after the splice). Note that Fischer has removed the repeated notes in dotted rhythm in the inverted combination. We will look closely at the entire fugue in chapter 20.*

EXERCISE 16-C

1. *Analysis:* Break down the combinations of invertible counterpoint in J. K. F. Fischer's little block of double counterpoint in four parts (example 16.15) as we did in example 16.14b. Draw arrows and label each with the interval that the voice has moved, and then identify the interval of inversion.

2. *Analysis:* Do the same for mm. 11–12 of the A minor fugue from *WTC I*. Why does the soprano interrupt its melody in m. 12?

3. *Analysis:* How is the counterpoint in mm. 9–13 of the gigue by Galuppi shown in example 12.35 invertible?

4. *Analysis:* How is the counterpoint in example 16.16 invertible?

Example 16.16. (Strozzi, from Arie op. 8)

5. *Composing (short):* Take a subject from anywhere in this book (except this chapter) and compose a countersubject invertible at the tenth and twelfth. Write out the two three-voice combinations and provide harmonic analysis.

TRIPLE AND QUADRUPLE COUNTERPOINT

In triple counterpoint three melodies are recombined in different ways, and in quadruple counterpoint, four. It has been noted that of the six possible ways of combining three melodies, Bach seems never to use more than five in a given piece. No one knows why. The six ways are schematized below in example 16.17.

1.	2.	3.	4.	5.	6.
A	A	B	B	C	C
B	C	A	C	A	B
C	B	C	A	B	A

Example 16.17.

A celebrated example of triple counterpoint appears in Bach's C minor fugue in *WTC I*, shown in example 16.18. There, the inversions are all at the octave.

Example 16.18. (Bach, C minor fugue, *WTC I*, complete) *The three melodies, labeled A, B, and C starting in m. 7, are the subject and two countersubjects. The Xs in mm. 12, 16, and 21 refer to alterations in melody C. As we saw in chapter 14, the descending scalar countersubject B is not altered to accommodate the answer at the astrisk in m. 7. How does Bach handle fifth chord factors? We will discuss this fugue in its entirety in chapter 20.*

Example 16.18. (*Concluded*)

You have already seen permutation fugues and you now recognize them as examples of quadruple counterpoint. The ones we saw in chapter 11 involved IC8 only. The following excerpt is from a permutation fugue from one of Marcello's famous psalm paraphrases that uses IC8 and IC12. The subject and three countersubjects are labeled in example 16.19a.

Example 16.19a. (Marcello, permutation fugue, mm. 10–14) *Note that the subject, in F major, begins on "scale degree" 6 (on unusual places to start, see chapter 17).*

In mm. 11–12, the second countersubject (in the soprano) has the fifth of each chord. It is thus not usable as a bass line; a string of 6/4 chords would result. What will Marcello do to avoid this when the second countermelody appears in the bass, as it must in a permutation fugue? In example 16.19b, the answer form of the subject is now in the alto, the first counteranswer is now in the tenor, and so on. The second counteranswer is now in the bass but no longer sounds the fifths of the harmonies. This is because each of the three upper voices now forms IC12 with the bass, which now sounds the roots of the chords.

Example 16.19b. (Marcello, mm. 14–18) *A nice feature of this use of IC12 is that the answer and CAs 1 and 3 are in the dominant, all transposed up a fifth, but CA2 is at its original pitch level. This pitch-class invariance can be used compositionally to great advantage.*

COMPOSING BOXES OF ARTFUL DEVICES FIRST . . .

Marpurg suggests that the composer have these complicated contrapuntal devices planned in advance:

> All the melodic materials that need to be connected with each other must first be assembled according to the rules of double counterpoint so that they can be inverted this way and before one takes up the working-out. Second, each [bit of] thematic material must be examined separately, as in the single fugue, [to see] whether it could follow itself in this or that way, below or above, between two, three, or more voices, and at the same time in [parallel] thirds, in stretto periodically or in canon, and how one or more melodic materials [i.e., themes and countermelodies] can likewise be connected. Third, one has to examine whether, among the melodic materials, any are capable of augmentation, diminution, metric displacement, interrupted imitation, or mixed melodic motions.[6]

Marpurg is concerned not only with making combinations first but with testing out which melodic elements of the combinations will succeed each other smoothly. Like Marpurg, Mattheson seems to think that you start with combinations of the melodic materials in different double counterpoints before arranging them in the "working-out" stage of composition. He thinks the composer has to master these combinations first:

> Now how will a person who does not know how to write counterpoint at the twelfth grapple with the double [i.e., multiple] fugue, especially if three or more subjects are to appear? For then they cannot possibly always all form correct and proper restatements upon inversion.[7]

Mattheson's treatise contains some combinations that he has culled from some of his favorite fugues. In Example 16.20, he presents a "box" (a combination "with three subjects") and its inversion by Johann Krieger, which he assumes we will know how to "unpack."

Example 16.20a. (Johann Krieger, printed in Mattheson) *Note that the subject is in D Dorian. When the melody labeled "2" appears in the soprano in the inverted combination, it supplies the fifths of chords, making richer sonorities.*

Example 16.20b. *Note that the little figure at the end of melody "3" in a. is given to the end of melody "2" in the inverted combination at b.*

Of another example "with four subjects" (example 16.21, also by Krieger), Mattheson applauds the rhythmic independence of the parts in the "box." He says the example has "the greatest strength in the differentiation of so many themes, and is accomplished through the various note values and their intelligent mixture. . . . We should also note how the themes follow one another at different time intervals. The first begins on the downbeat; the second after an eighth rest; the third after a dotted quarter; and the fourth after three quarter rests."[8]

Example 16.21. (Krieger, printed in Mattheson) *Show how the voices are inverted by drawing lines labeled with numbers, as we did in example 16.14b. Note the deviation at the end of melody "3" in the inverted version.*

To make the permutation fugues in chapter 11, you only needed two boxes: the subject box and the answer box. Now, for the exercise below, you will need four: the original subject box, the inverted subject box, the original answer box, and the inverted answer box.

. . . AND THEN UNPACKING THE BOXES

EXERCISE 16-D

1. *Writing (long):* Using Marcello's material in examples 16.19a and b as two of the "boxes" of a permutation fugue, string out the melodies as you did in chapter 11, tacking CA1 onto the end of the subject, CS2 onto that, and so on. Note that it will be necessary for you to create an original (i.e., inverted) box for the answer and to adapt Marcello's inverted combination, as presented in the answer box in example 16.19b, to the subject when CS2 appears in the bass. Check to see if there is any other melody that cannot appear in the bass. Make at least six entries, starting with TASB; the last two may be in any order.

2. *Writing (long):* Likewise, string out the three tunes in example 16.20, treating melodies labeled 1, 2, and 3 as the theme and the first and second countermelodies, respectively. Note that you are given subject boxes *only* so that to make an exposition, you will have to make two "answer boxes" first (an original one and an inverted one). You should use a tonal answer. Make an exposition for four voices, with four entries: ATBS (you must compose free material for the alto at the end). You may start with the subject or the answer, you may enter themes on the second or the fourth beat of the 4/4 measure, and you will want to fill the space between themes (indicated by rests in the boxes) with free material.

3. *Writing (long):* Likewise, string out the materials in example 16.21.

4. *Composing (long):* Compose a box of three voices that can be rotated like the three tunes in Example 16.18. Be careful that 6/4 chords appear in plausible places.

5. *Composing (short):* Go back to exercise 16-B no. 2, but this time add the *same* voice to both your original and your inverted combinations; in other words, create a block of triple counterpoint.

UNINVERTED DOUBLE COUNTERPOINT

If the subject (and/or the countersubject) is transposed without inverting the original subject-countersubject positions, we speak of *uninverted double counterpoint* (simply abbreviated as UC). Usually, this is used to produce parallel motion (in thirds, sixths, tenths), which is a fundamental part of the "sound" of Baroque music.

Marpurg generalizes the conditions necessary for adding parts in parallel motion to an existing combination:

> If, in the original of a contrapuntal combination of this kind (inverted at the octave), a) only thirds, octaves, and sixths are used, b) two consonances of the same kind are avoided in parallel motion, c) passing notes are the only dissonances used, and finally, if one is careful with oblique and contrary motion, then one can easily turn such a composition into a three- or four-part texture. Three-part, if one adds an upper third to either the upper or lower voice. Four-part, if one adds an upper third to both the upper and lower voice.[9]

Example 16.22. (Marpurg)

He begins by showing an example in which the upper and middle parts are inverted at the octave, an essential feature for this kind of thing.

He continues: "This example [example 16.22] is now turned into four parts in [example 16.23a] by adding upper thirds to each voice. If one wishes to turn it into only three parts one can simply leave out one of these added voices. This four-part example can be inverted as in example 16.23i. In the main example as well as in its inversion, one can turn the thirds into sixths and tenths, in order to give the harmony a different shape."[10]

Example 16.23. (Marpurg)

In summary, we can think of the generation of example 16.23a from the original combination in example 16.22 as occurring in two stages.

1. Original two-voice combination: subject in the soprano, countersubject in the alto of example 16.22 (knowing the combination is invertible at the octave).

2. Add a line above each line: subject in parallel thirds in the soprano and alto of example 16.23a, countersubject in parallel thirds in the tenor and bass.

In example 16.23a, the alto and bass are the original combination in example 16.22. The soprano and tenor of example 16.23a have the same combination a third higher. The soprano and bass thus invert the inverted combination of example 16.22 at the tenth (the bass of example 16.22 is transposed up a tenth plus an octave). As a result, the alto and tenor are inverted at the sixth. (Take the inverted combination of example 16.22 and transpose the alto down a sixth.)

Examples 16.23b–h show how different spacings can be used in the four-part version. Several of the examples we have seen so far have produced pairs of voices in thirds quite far from each other. More "even" chord voicing is better for vocal music and has a very different sound. Spacing, to be discussed in chapter 20, is an essential part of Baroque composition, and an important structural device in fugue. Examples 16.23b, d, and h have brief 6/4 chords making cameo appearances as arpeggiations. Example 16.23i shows how example 16.23a can have its pairs of voices inverted. Note that in this example it is not possible to reverse the positions of the lower two voices—6/4 chords would result all over!

In the following example (16.24) the subject (soprano) is combined with its inversion (tenor) in canon. (The inversion is around D-flat/E-flat.) Bach then adds parallel motion in sixths and thirds in the alto and bass. The bass has the inversion of the subject at UC3 (which is the same as the tenor inverted at the octave followed by IC10). The alto sounds the subject at UC6 (which is the same as the soprano inverted at the octave—actually the double octave—followed by IC10). However, the resulting contrapuntal combination does not work throughout and Bach has to make an adjustment. Starting with the pick-up to m. 98 he changes the alto part from parallel lower sixths to parallel lower thirds to the soprano. UC6 is replaced by UC3. Example 16.24b illustrates what would have happened had Bach used UC6 throughout. Problematic moments are marked with an asterisk.

Example 16.24a. (Bach, B-flat minor fugue, *WTC II*, mm. 96–101)

Example 16.24b. (Hypothetical mm. 96–99 with alto UC6 throughout)

EXERCISE 16-E

1. *Analysis:* Analyze the double counterpoint in the following passages: Bach, *The Art of the Fugue*, Contrapunctus 10, mm. 75–79; Bach, G minor fugue, *WTC II*, mm. 45–48; also mm. 51–54.

2. *Writing (short):* Using the given subject and answer in example 16.25 (by Kirnberger himself!), harmonize each note. Compose a countersubject and counteranswer based on this harmonization that are both invertible at the twelfth. You may use accented dissonances, appoggiaturas, incomplete neighbors, and transferred resolutions in the countermelody. Supply harmonic analysis and label NHTs. Write out the four two-voice combinations (original S/CS, inverted S/CS, original A/CA, and inverted A/CA) and add a third part to each. What effect does inversion have on the harmony? On the splice?

Example 16.25. (Kirnberger)

3. *Writing (short):* For the same subject and answer, compose a new CS and CA that are both invertible at the tenth. Proceed as above.

4. *Composing (long):* Compose a three-voice sequential episode based on the above material, containing two parts that are invertible at the tenth; write out the inversion. Compose another that contains two voices invertible at the twelfth; write out the inversion.

5. *Composing (short):* Take any three fugue subjects we have discussed in part II of this book (except for those from the fugues in G minor [*WTC II*], B-flat minor [*WTC II*], *The Art of the Fugue*, and those by Fischer) and for each: (1) write a countersubject invertible at the twelfth, (2) write a countersubject invertible at the tenth, and (3) write a countersubject invertible at the octave. This gives you six combinations.

6. *Composing (short):* Then add a third line to each of the combinations you made in question no. 5 (above or below, whichever strikes you as more appropriate for some reason you can articulate). You should use parallel thirds or sixths in the combination that's invertible at the tenth. If legal passing accented dissonance happens, so much the better.

NOTES

1. Mattheson, *Der vollkommene Capellmeister*, III, 22, §47.
2. Marpurg, *Abhandlung von der Fuge*, VIII, 3, §1, pp. 177–78.
3. Marpurg, §2, p. 179.
4. Marpurg, 5, §2, p. 186.

5. David, Mendel, and Wolff, *The New Bach Reader*, p. 397.
6. Marpurg, *Abhandlung von der Fuge*, IV, 3, p. 132.
7. Mattheson, *Der vollkommene Capellmeister*, III, 23, §70.
8. Mattheson, §74, §77.
9. Marpurg, *Abhandlung von der Fuge*, VIII, 1, §5, p. 168.
10. Marpurg, pp. 168–69.

17

WRITING AN ORIGINAL SUBJECT

Types of Subject; Harmonic Rhythm; Borrowing and Assembly; Melody; Rhythm; Length of Subject; Head and Tail—Beginning, Middle, and End; Overall Shape; Unpacking the Box to Make a Subject; Real or Tonal Answer?; Multiple Splices; Hybrid Themes; Starting on Unusual Scale Degrees; Unusual Scale Degrees after the Splice; Unusual Subjects; Partimento

Virtually all eighteenth-century authors agree that what one needs first, to write any kind of piece, is a good subject. Yet apart from Mattheson, few authors illustrate how one writes a good melody or what a good melody "contains." Rather, most of them focus on what will happen to the tune in the course of a fugue, explaining what the composer does with it.

Rameau, who said that melody sprang from harmony, maintains that "you should never invent melodies to use in a fugue for which you have not imagined at the same time the bass and the answer."[1] In other words, you cannot write a good countersubject, much less add other parts, unless you have a clear idea of what harmony is implied by the subject.

When we write a fugue subject and its countermelodies, the planning of harmonic and surface rhythm often go hand in hand. Marpurg says:

> The melody of the subject has to be made such that all kinds of harmonic figures and movements can be set against it. In order to accomplish this sooner than later, it is a good idea to imagine at once the bass and the countermelodies when inventing the subject. This has the advantage that one can examine simultaneously whether the invented subject is easy to handle or not at all. Not all melodies allow for manly [sic] and beautiful harmony. One has to look for them.[2]

In addition to harmony, subjects are determined by other aspects as well, such as melodic range, overall shape, rhythm, and momentum. We will discuss each of these in turn further below. But before writing our own subjects we will first familiarize ourselves with the various types of subjects, then learn the fastest way to construct a subject by reassembling little bits from existing subjects. This was common practice in the Baroque era. Baroque composers were not worried about plagiarizing each other's (or their own) materials because they added and rearranged freely. In Mattheson's words: "Borrowing is permitted; but one has to pay back the borrowed material with interest; that is, one must arrange and work out the borrowed materials such that they look more beautiful and better than the pieces from which they are taken."[3]

TYPES OF SUBJECT

Each subject has its own distinct character. We can distinguish various types of subjects based on specific stylistic features. Sing and/or play the following examples and familiarize yourself with their character. Do a harmonic analysis of each example. The following subject-type classifications, except for "Concerto," are based on Kunze, 1969.

> *Ricercar.* Ricercar-type subjects move in a slow, alla breve meter and usually use mainly half notes and quarters, with 4/4 meters occurring as well. Ricercar-type subjects represent the "old" style (*stile antico*). They are vocal and severe in nature. The fugues that they occur in tend to be more "recherché" and complex, using more fancy tricks.

Example 17.1. (Pachelbel, Ricercar in C minor, mm. 1–16) *For more examples see* WTC I, *fugues in C-sharp minor and B-flat minor and* WTC II, *fugues in E major, B-flat minor, and B major. See also example 15.8a, from Bach's Musical Offering.*

Canzona. Some authors say that canzona subjects distinguish themselves from Ricercar-type subjects in that they are faster and lighter in mood. Canzonas are a descendant of the French chanson, which starts whole, half, half. In the Baroque, this rhythm appears diminished to quarter, eighth, eighth (or eighth rest + three eighths), often with repeated notes. For an example, see the subject from Bach's C major Overture (example 10.14).

Pathetic. Expresses a passionate character, filled with emotional pain. Subjects of this type are always in minor and make ample use of chromaticism. For examples of this type see *WTC I*, fugues in F minor, F-sharp minor, G-sharp minor, B minor and *WTC II*, fugue in A minor, as well as the theme from the *Musical Offering* (example 15.8a).

French overture. The subject has the character of the festive opening of a French overture, usually in duple meter and with dotted rhythms. A famous example is Bach's D major fugue from *WTC I*. For other examples of a subject in the style of a French overture, see Contrapunctus 6 from *The Art of the Fugue* ("in Stile Francese") and the gigue in 4/4 from the French Suite 1.

Concerto. These subjects borrow the virtuosic figurations from string concerti: repeated notes, arpeggios, fast repeating skips (string crossings), and fast scales. See examples 17.36, 17.38, and 17.39.

Fugue subjects are frequently written in the style of a dance. The most common types are gigue and minuet.

Gigue. Gigue subjects are usually in triple and compound triple meters, but simple and compound duple meters occur as well. (The gigues from J. S. Bach's first French Suite and first Partita are in 4/4, for instance.) The following subject is of the gigue type.

Example 17.2. (J. K. F. Fischer, Ariadne Musica, fugue no. 7 in E Dorian, mm. 1–4) *For further gigue-type subjects see* WTC I, *fugues in G major and A major, and* WTC II, *fugues in C-sharp minor, F major, and G-sharp minor.*

Minuet. The subject is in 3/4 or 3/8 and moves mainly in quarters and/or eighths. The following subject and counteranswer by Bach in example 17.3a assemble three typical minuet rhythms (X, Y, and Z), as illustrated by the excerpt from a minuet by Handel in example 17.3b.

Example 17.3a. (Bach, B minor fugue, *WTC II*, mm. 1–17)

Example 17.3b. (Handel, minuet 2 from Trois Leçons, mm. 17–24) *For two other fugue subjects in minuet style see* WTC I, *fugue in F major, and* WTC II, *fugue in B-flat major. Compare the former subject with the gigue-type subject from J. K. F. Fischer's fugue 10 in F major, example 20.3a.*

Stile antico versus galant style. We can also classify fugue subjects depending on whether they are written in the "old" (*stile antico*) or new style. Old-style fugue subjects include the ricercar, canzona, and pathetic subject types. A good example of *stile antico* is the "Sicut locutus" subject (example 12.16a) from Bach's *Magnificat.* Bach uses this style to represent the text, which speaks of promises made "to our fathers." Fugue subjects in the new, galant style—which is characterized by light texture, ornamented melody, and free style dissonance treatment—include the various dance types. For an example of a fugue in galant style, see the D major fugue, *WTC II.* The galant style sometimes combines into a single subject melodic types with contrasting affects, as in the D minor fugue from *WTC II* that starts as a gigue and suddenly turns pathetic.

HARMONIC RHYTHM

Whereas fugue subjects can start with a variety of harmonies (depending on the scale degree with which the subject opens), all authors agree that there needs to be a harmonic arrival toward the end of the subject (see "Head and Tail—Beginning, Middle, and End" later in this chapter). The harmonic arrival takes place either on the tonic or dominant (if it is a modulating subject) and occurs either just before or with the entry of the answer. In Marpurg's words, "The answer has to enter either at the moment of harmonic arrival, or else this point of arrival must be hidden by means of melodic artifice through the addition of some notes quickly moving away from the one that occurs on the harmonic arrival."[4] The following example (17.4) illustrates Marpurg's point nicely: the free style dissonance on the downbeat of m. 124 (an appoggiatura), plus the sudden motion, plus the fact that the pattern rises by steps, draws our attention so much that we are surprised to note the entrance of the real answer in the tenor. Imagine if the bass voice had sounded a dotted-quarter G on the downbeat of m. 124.

Example 17.4. (Bach, Christmas Oratorio, "Herr, wenn die stolzen Feinde schnauben," mm. 120–126)

Rameau places the harmonic arrival on a strong beat: "The subject begins on any beat you want, but it must naturally finish on the first beat; the third beat of a four-beat measure can stand for this first beat."[5]

Mattheson also explains that the harmonic rhythm has to make a good fit with the metric subdivision of the measure. "The division [of the measure] always falls on the first and third beat, if the meter is even, never on the second and fourth beat. In triple meter the division happens nowhere else than on the downbeat."[6] He compares bad harmonic rhythm to a situation in which a poet puts an unaccented syllable on an accented beat. The following example (17.5) shows what he had in mind. The melody at example 17.5a arrives on the dominant on the fourth beat of the first measure and the final tonic arrival occurs on the fourth beat of the second measure. Mattheson's corrected version in example 17.5b "shows how easily such mistakes can be avoided, and that is right at the beginning: otherwise they keep dragging on further, and start to snowball."[7]

Example 17.5a. (Mattheson)

Example 17.5b.

However, he adds, "A small exception needs to be made here, namely, that in choral and melismatic matters, sometimes in triple meter the last beat has to serve as the ending: if . . . one continues it throughout. But such happens purposefully, and not out of imprecision or out of ignorance of the rule."[8] The following melody in D Dorian consists of two phrases. The first ends on the third beat of m. 4, the second on the third beat of m. 8.

Example 17.6. (Mattheson)

Regarding cadences at harmonic arrivals, Marpurg warns us that "One has to make sure, however, that the end of the subject is not accompanied by a formal cadence, in that the points of rest do not happen until the end of the fugue."[9] Mattheson says, "The fewer formal endings a melody has, the more fluent it is for sure. . . . The cadences must be chosen and the voice led around well before one proceeds to the point of rest. In the course of the melody the few points of rest which appear along the way must have some connection to what follows."[10]

Mattheson further explains: "The best way is not to end the theme on the same note as the one with which it began, and with a formal cadence in the tonic. However, it does happen sometimes with good effect in the hands of a good master of polyphony who, so to speak, can make something out of nothing. But nevertheless, this procedure does not include as much diversity or variation as when the closing and opening notes are different."[11] For examples of fugue subjects that end with the 2–1 members of a formal cadence on a strong beat, see example 11.7 and "He trusted in God" from Handel's *Messiah*.

BORROWING AND ASSEMBLY

CHORALE TUNES

Mattheson tells us that "in all melodies there has to be something that is known to almost everybody."[12] In other words, any melody we write should use some commonplace material, or even use bits from other preexisting tunes. This is the best way to write idiomatically in Baroque style.

Mattheson proposes two ways in which one can produce a new melody (fugal or otherwise) from preexisting tunes.

1. Extract parts from a chorale tune. We have already seen an instance in example 10.1.

2. Embellish a chorale tune. The subject and answer in example 17.7a are embellished diminutions of the opening of the chorale tune shown at example 17.7b. Check the notes of the chorale in the answer, as we have done for the subject, and label the embellishments.

Example 17.7a. (Pachelbel, chorale prelude, "Allein Gott in der Höh' sei Ehr," mm. 1–5)

Example 17.7b. (The simple chorale tune)

Bach embellishes the same tune in 6/8 as shown in example 17.7c. Find the notes of the chorale (check as in example 17.7a), do a harmonic analysis, and label the embellishments.

Example 17.7e shows how Bach embellishes the tune "Ein' feste Burg" given in Example 17.7d. The descending fourth from the third to fourth note of the tune is filled in stepwise. In the tonal answer that fourth becomes a fifth (example 17.7e, m. 7), which is also filled in stepwise, making the answer sound even more similar to the subject than in the unembellished version. Note also that the countermelody is based on the second chorale phrase.

Example 17.7c. (Bach, "Allein Gott in der Höh' sei Ehr," mm. 1–8)

Example 17.7d. ("Ein' feste Burg," chorale tune)

Example 17.7e. (Bach, Cantata 80, "Ein' feste Burg," mm. 1–10)

BORROWING FROM OTHER TUNES

Another way of producing a new melody is to assemble memorized bits of other tunes. Mattheson explains this as follows:

> For the theme or subject . . . there must be a repertory of special formulae which can be applied in general narration. That is to say: through much experience and attentive listening to good works the composer must occasionally have assembled some modulations, little turns, skillful descents, pleasant stepwise progressions and leaps, which, although they consist only of single things can nevertheless produce something general and complete when assembled well. If, for instance, I had in mind the following three different and incomplete progressions:

Example 17.8a. (Mattheson)

and wanted to make from them a coherent melody, it could look something like this:

Example 17.8b. (Mattheson, assembled melody)

For, even though one or the other of these instances and turns might have been used already by different masters, and had come to my mind just so, without thinking of the earlier authors or without knowing them, the assemblage gives the entire melody a new guise and character, such that it can count as an original invention. It is also unnecessary to do this deliberately; it can happen unintentionally.[13]

Note that Mattheson has altered the original fragments in the assembled subject. The first fragment is transformed from 6/8 into 4/4, the third from 3/8 to 4/4. All three fragments are transposed within the diatonic scale. The first fragment appears one scale degree higher, the second fragment a third higher, and the third a fourth lower. In other words, all three fragments are moved to different scale degrees with the result that some of the interval qualities are changed (e.g., the descending minor third at the beginning of fragment 1 turns into a descending major third in the last measure of the assembled subject). Note also that Mattheson has added linking material in the new subject. How do you like his subject?

Mattheson suggests subjecting the remembered or stolen tunes to changes in note value, to inversion or permutation, to repetition, and to canonic treatment. While he does not recommend that one strictly write down fragments academically and make a commonplace book out of them, he admits that the *loci topici* "can provide quite good resources for the invention in the art of melodic composition." He admits they may be useful for "minds not especially inclined to independent thinking" and concludes that "whoever does not need them does therefore not have any reason to prohibit them to others."[14]

It is very much in the spirit of the Baroque era to model a fugue subject after a particular style, character, or theme type. A common strategy is to take rhythms from dance movements and integrate them into a new subject (gigue rhythms are often used in this way). One often even models on another composer's fugue (compare examples 10.9a and b—it might be that Bach modeled on J. K. F. Fischer).

Compare the two fugue subjects below. Do you think Kirnberger rearranged the bracketed materials from the Bach subject?

Example 17.9a. (Bach, *WTC I*, F minor fugue subject, mm. 1–4)

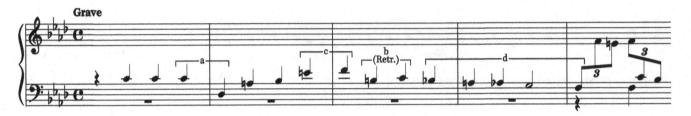

Example 17.9b. (Kirnberger, Huit Fugues 4, mm. 1–5)

Sometimes a composer models a subject on one of his or her own subjects. Two subjects by Bach that use the same melodic framework are the "little" organ fugue in G minor (BWV 578) and *The Art of the Fugue*. The former is like an embellished version of the latter. We suggest you look up the scores and mark the corresponding pitches in each. See also the discussion of examples 17.22 and 17.23.

FRANKENSTEIN SUBJECTS

An application of Mattheson's method is to take bits from Bach's (or anyone else's) subjects and make them into the beginning, the middle, and/or the end of a new subject. Here is an example (17.10) of such a Frankenstein subject by a student who assembled bits from the subject of Bach's C major Overture and two subjects from *WTC II*. The brackets indicate the sources, all transposed to A minor. The opening segment from the C major Overture is transformed from the major into the minor mode.

Example 17.10a. (Frankenstein subject)

Another student assembled bits of two subjects from *WTC I*.

Example 17.10b. (Frankenstein subject)

In the two examples above, each borrowed segment appears in the same metric position as in the original. This need not always be the case. You can shift the borrowed segments metrically and also translate them into a different meter as long as the result produces good harmonic rhythm. For example, m. 2 of the following Frankenstein subject has poor harmonic rhythm because the dominant resolves to the tonic on a strong beat before the subject is over. The tonic then lasts for two beats, producing a harmonic arrival that is too strong for the middle of a subject.

Example 17.10c. (Frankenstein subject with poor harmonic rhythm)

MELODY

RANGE

Mattheson says that composing is easier if one

> sets certain boundaries which every average voice can reach comfortably . . . but I would advise a budding composer that for the beginning he choose a range of a sixth or octave. . . . For what does it serve me that only this or that person is able to sing an aria that for instance extends over two octaves? I would like to sing along, even though only mentally, which causes the greatest pleasure. But I will not be allowed to do so; the melody is too wide-ranging for me.[15]

Marpurg thinks it is good to observe the general rule of staying within an octave and points out that there are fugue subjects that "do not even exceed the range of a third or fourth."[16] For examples of the latter see the subjects of the C-sharp minor fugue from *WTC I* and the E major fugue from *WTC II*. Here is an example by Mattheson of a subject and answer whose range is only a third.

Example 17.11. (Mattheson)

The importance of subjects with small ranges is that they are easier to work with in thicker textures, in fugues with more voices, where a large range may entail voice crossing. Of course there are exceptions (see the B-flat minor fugue from *WTC I*).

MELODIC INTERVALS

Mattheson recommends switching back and forth intelligently between using steps and skips and emphasizes that one should never use too many of the same intervals in a row.[17] For instance, he considers the following succession of three melodic fourths unsingable.

Example 17.12a. (Mattheson)

On the other hand, two melodic fourths in a row are fine if followed by a step in the opposite direction, as in the following instance.

Example 17.12b. (Mattheson) *See also Handel "Thou art the glory of their strength" (example 11.6).*

Mattheson also tells us to avoid diminished or augmented intervals between strong beats as in example 17.13a. He fixes the problem as shown in example 17.13b, where the B on a strong beat is followed by the E-flat on a weak beat. He recommends filling in the diminished fourth with ornamental passing tones, as shown by the small stemless noteheads.

Example 17.13. (Mattheson)

Mattheson provides the following guidelines for combining melodic steps and skips:

1. In an ascending melody, use skips first then steps. In a descending melody, use steps first, then skips. (We call this the *pyramid rule*.) For example, he tells us to avoid the following melody in example 17.14a, where two steps are followed by a third and another step in ascending order. Mattheson recommends either filling in the third with a passing tone or, even better, changing melodic direction by replacing the ascending third B-flat–D with a descending minor third B-flat–G, followed by an ascending minor sixth, as in example 17.14b.

Example 17.14a. (Mattheson)

Example 17.14b.

The following descending melody also violates the pyramid rule. Mattheson suggests filling in the third with a passing tone.

Example 17.14c.

2. It is better to have leaps (in either direction) preceded by steps in the opposite direction. In both of the following examples each leap is preceded and/or followed by motion in the opposite direction.

Example 17.15. (Mattheson)

COMPOSING A MELODY

Mattheson also admits that the composer goes back and forth between melody and bass:

> Although it would seem contrary if somebody were to put down the bass line of a song first in order to compose a charming singable melody over it afterwards, such is not only useful as an exercise but . . . often absolutely necessary . . . especially in so-called obbligato basses [bass parts that are fully written-out independent lines, not just thoroughbass parts], fugal movements, and in other circumstances. Whoever diligently practices to be at ease adding upper parts to a previously chosen bass, will soon understand what advantages there are to it, and how by means of this exercise one will master harmony much more easily than otherwise. The beginning must be made as stated above [by putting down the bass]. But one needs to compose the upper parts in such a way that not everybody recognizes which part has seen the light of day first or last. This the composer keeps to himself, and leaves the listener always in doubt about it.[18]

RHYTHM

METRIC POSITION OF THE FIRST NOTE OF THE SUBJECT

You will have noticed that many of the subjects we have seen start with a rest. Rameau says that the fugue may begin on any beat of the measure. In 2/2 or 4/4, themes often appear shifted by half a measure. This is common practice because the metric shift does not alter the distribution of strong and weak beats.

METRIC POSITIONS OF IMPORTANT NOTES LATER IN THE SUBJECT

We have noticed that in good subjects that use a lot of the same scale degrees, one has to make sure that the recurring notes appear in different metric positions. Analyze the metric positions of the pitches A, B, C, D, and E in the subject of Bach's A minor fugue in *WTC I*.

LENGTH OF SUBJECT

As we have seen throughout this book, subjects can be of vastly differing lengths. Here is what advice Marpurg and Mattheson have to offer:

Marpurg says: "Meanwhile one can not determine how many measures a fugue subject should have. This much is sure, however, that a fugue subject is long enough if it contains a distinct and complete thought."[19] Mattheson: "It is rather arbitrary how long the so-called leader [subject] of a fugue might be."[20]

HEAD AND TAIL—BEGINNING, MIDDLE, AND END

Many fugue subjects can be analyzed in terms of their beginning, middle, and end. For instance, the subject from Bach's C major fugue, *WTC I* (example 9.15), starts with an ascent from scale degree 1 through 4 (beginning), followed by a melodic sequence (middle), and a sixteenth-note run closing the subject with a D–T progression (end). Many fugue subjects take this tripartite form.

Some fugue subjects consist of a beginning and end only, as is the case with the subject from Bach's C major Overture (example 10.14). It starts with the descending third G–E, followed by a cadential progression (IV, ii, V, I). The subject from the D major fugue, *WTC I*, is also best analyzed in terms of its beginning (thirty-second runs) and end (dotted rhythms with cadential progression). The following is an example whose head (m. 1–2, downbeat) and tail (m. 2–3, downbeat) have the same rhythm. This subject begins like a classical sentence.[21]

Example 17.16. (Bach, English Suite 5, prelude, mm. 1–5)

Fugue subjects are often developmental, as in the case of the C minor fugue from *WTC I* (example 16.18). It starts with the rhythm ♪♪♪♪♪♪ in the first half of the first measure. This rhythm is repeated in the second half of the measure. The rhythm is then expanded and developed in the second measure, ending with a cadential progression leading to the downbeat of m. 3. This subject follows the classical form type of a sentence.

A good way to write a fugue subject is to start with a splice (1–5, 5–1, or 5–3, etc.) and add a sequence followed by a cadence. The cadence may come directly out of the sequence, as in the vii⁶ cadence in this example (see mm. 3–4):

Example 17.17. (Pachelbel, fugue in C major)

Rameau says that "you hardly ever begin and end fugues [subjects] other than on the tonic note, its dominant, or its mediant."[22] (As we shall see, however, it is actually rare that a fugue subject starts on the third scale degree!) By "end" Rameau and other writers mean the point of harmonic arrival, which occurs just before or together with the entry of the answer.

The following subject seems to end on the fourth scale degree at the asterisk. This degree is set against the tonic note with which the answer enters, forming a 4-3 suspension. Ultimately, the fourth scale degree at the end of the subject thus "stands for'" the third scale degree. The subject is also unusual in that it tonicizes iv for a considerable amount of time.

Example 17.18. (Mattheson) *For another subject that emphasizes iv, see Handel example 17.25.*

The first phrases of some chorale tunes end on the fourth scale degree and, if used as fugue subjects, will lead to 4-3 and 7-6 suspensions against the first note of the answer, as in the example above. This ties in well with Mattheson's more general recommendation to make ample use of suspensions when writing a fugue.

Again, the fourth scale degree at the end of the following subject ultimately stands for the third scale degree. This subject is based on the fifth phrase of the chorale tune "Durch Adams Fall," but the first note, A, has been replaced by the tonic, D.

Example 17.19. (Mattheson)

As we will see shortly, subjects can, in principle, start on any scale degree, although some possibilities occur only rarely.

OVERALL SHAPE

One of the particularly memorable elements of a subject is its overall melodic shape. We can analyze this aspect of the melody by reducing its contour to the most significant pitches. For example, the most prominent pitches of the subject shown in example 17.20a are the ones circled. These are the pitches that define the outer limits of the melody as we move through it. The circled pitches are shown again in example 17.20b, this time with all the remaining pitches omitted. We now have a clear picture of how the overall melodic contour evolves.

How exactly did we produce the contour reduction? The connecting lines in example 17.20b indicate that there is an implied upper and a lower "part." More specifically, every pitch in the upper "part" is a local high point and every pitch in the lower "part" is a local low point of the subject. This means that on every circled note in example 17.20a (except for the first and last note) the melodic contour changes direction and hence marks the local extreme point of the melody. We always circle the first and last notes of the subject as well. The highest note of the contour reduction appears twice and is particularly notable, so we have marked it with an asterisk. Note that all circled notes in example 17.20a are chord factors.

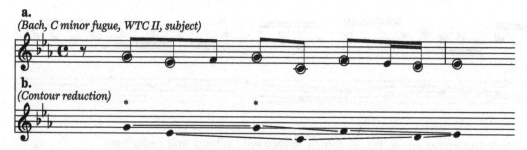

Example 17.20. (Bach, C minor fugue, *WTC II*, subject and contour reduction)

You will have noted that the reduction in example 17.20b looks like a reduction of a compound melody. This is generally true for contour reductions as they extract the highest and lowest parts of the implied multipart texture of a melody.

In the example above, the upper and lower lines of the contour reduction converge on a single pitch, the third scale degree in m. 2. This property of convergence is a common feature of most fugue subjects, as we shall see.

The highpoint of Bach's subject occurs early. By contrast, the following subject works its way up to the high point toward the end (at the asterisk in example 17.21b).

Example 17.21. (Bach, D-sharp minor fugue, *WTC II*, subject and contour reduction)

The upper and lower lines of the contour reduction in example 17.20b above move mainly in contrary motion, and the ones in example 17.21b in similar motion. The reduction of the following long subject (example 17.22) reveals both types of motion. (The neighbor notes labeled "n" in m. 2 are local low points, but we do not circle them because they are not chord factors.)

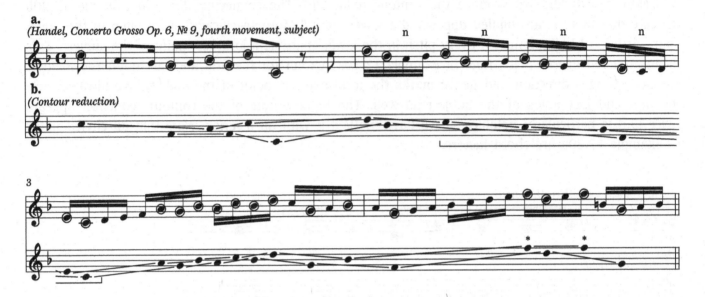

Example 17.22. (Handel, Concerto Grosso op. 6, no. 9, fourth movement, subject and reduction)

The purpose of the contour reduction is not to account for all the important chord factors represented in the melody. For instance, in m. 3 of example 17.22a, the F on the second quarter represents the arrival on the tonic harmony, but that F does not appear in the reduction (because it is not a local turning point). The purpose of the contour reduction is to account for the overall shape and not for all harmonic progressions within it. The highest point in this subject appears at the end (at the asterisk).

Note that the bracketed section in the reduction of the following subject uses the same sequential pattern as the one found in the reduction of m. 2 of the example above. In other words, starting on the second quarter of m. 2, the subject above embellishes the interval pattern of m. 3 (third quarter) to m. 4 (second quarter) of the subject below.

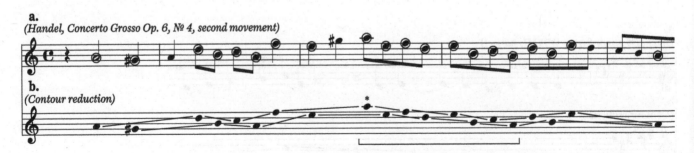

Example 17.23. (Handel, Concerto Grosso op. 6, no. 4, second movement and reduction)

UNPACKING THE BOX TO MAKE A SUBJECT

A good way to write an original subject and countersubject pair is to pick a harmonic progression, choose from it chord factors that make a good melodic framework, and embellish it to turn it into a good subject. We then produce a countersubject from the same harmonic progression. More specifically, the strategy involves the following five steps:

1. *Step 1:* Make a box by choosing a good harmonic progression. If you want a tonal answer, be sure the progression starts I–V or V–I.

2. *Step 2:* Pull out roots and thirds from this harmonic progression to make the framework for a subject. This requires careful consideration.

3. *Step 3:* Pull out the complementary chord factors from the harmonic progression to make the framework of the countersubject. (As we showed in example 3.13, thirds and roots are complementary; if you extracted the root of a particular chord in step 2, you take the third in step 3 and vice versa).

4. *Step 4:* Combine the two frameworks by notating one above the other.

5. *Step 5:* Embellish the frameworks using commonplace motives from chapter 5.

Any subject/countersubject pair obtained following steps 1–5 above will be invertible at the octave. Example 17.24 illustrates the entire procedure.

Example 17.24a and b. (Steps 1 and 2)

Example 17.24c. (Step 3)

Example 17.24d. (Step 4)

Example 17.24e. (Step 5)

Example 17.24e can be used as a "box" to unpack: play the box from memory, play the box in invertible counterpoint at the octave, make up the "answer box" and play it in IC8, and make a little exposition out of these materials.

REAL OR TONAL ANSWER?

As we have seen, some fugue subject types typically take tonal answer and some take real answer. There are no strict rules as to which fugue subjects take real answer, as in fact every subject can, in principle, be followed by real answer. Subjects that start and end on a scale degree of the same scale commonly either take real answer or possibly tonal answer with multiple splices, to be discussed shortly.

SUBDOMINANT EMPHASIS

Fugue subjects that open with a move from 1 to 4 take real answer. For instance, the subject of the C major fugue from *WTC I* ascends stepwise from 1 to 4, taking real answer (see example 9.15). Some subjects start with a skip from 1 to 4, as in the following example.

Example 17.25. (Handel, B minor fugue 4, mm. 1–12) *See also Bach, D major fugue*, WTC II.

Marpurg says that earlier theorists prohibited such leaps to the lower fifth of the tonics because they "render the key uncertain," but in the light of the two examples mentioned, he rejects the prohibition as "mere prejudice."[23] The subject starts and ends on the same harmony. The same holds for the answer as well. It starts on V and ends in m. 10 on v.

MULTIPLE SPLICES

A subject that moves from the tonic to the dominant can have a real answer as long as it has a retransition or is in a two-part fugue, like the E minor fugue from *WTC I*, which needs no third entry and just goes on to an episode and entry in a foreign key. Subjects like the one in the D-sharp minor fugue from *WTC I* that take tonal answer can have more than one splice. This means that the subject and answer change between the tonic and dominant scale more than once. The following subject and answer pair from Bach's *Musical Offering* (example 17.26) has two splices, one before and one after the third note. In other words, the subject starts with the first two notes in the tonic scale, moves to the dominant scale for the third note, and returns to the tonic scale on the fourth note. There is a short modulation before the entry of the answer. The answer then exchanges the two scales as labeled.

Example 17.26. (Bach, Musical Offering, Ricercar à 3, mm. 1–12) *The rest of the answer is a transposition of the subject a fourth below.*

As a rule of thumb, we can state that a subject that starts and ends in the same scale has either no splices or an *even number* of splices. On the other hand, a subject that starts and ends in different scales has an *odd number* of splices.

Bach's subject in example 17.26 starts and ends in the tonic scale. Its tonal answer thus has an even number of splices. The following subject by Vivaldi starts in the tonic scale and ends in the dominant scale. Hence, it has an odd number of splices, namely three. Note that the countersubject has only two, in other words an even number of splices, because it starts and ends in the dominant scale. This is so because the countersubject enters *after* the first splice in the subject has already taken place. At first hearing, many observers believe the answer form of the subject in example 17.27b by Bach is far inferior to the subject form because the arpeggiation is lost (see discussion of reciprocity in chapter 10).

Example 17.27a. (Vivaldi, Gloria, mm. 1–11) *This is a type 2 double fugue.*

Example 17.27b. (Bach, Cantata 21, xi) *For another example, see Bach,* WTC I, *fugue in E-flat major, mm. 1–6.*

HYBRID THEMES

Sometimes, a thematic entry in the course of a fugue presents neither the subject nor the answer but a version that is a combination of both. We call such themes hybrid because they take their splices from both the subject and the answer. The subject/answer pair in example 17.28a has two splices as marked. The three themes used in the stretto combination shown in example 17.28b are hybrids because they take their first splice from the answer and the second from the subject.

Example 17.28a. (Bach, D-sharp minor fugue, *WTC I*, mm. 1–4)

Example 17.28b. (Stretto in mm. 52–53)

The subject of Bach's B minor fugue, *WTC I*, has two splices. The subject starts and ends on the fifth scale degree; the answer starts and ends on the first scale degree. The subject is used later in the fugue in its hybrid form (in mm. 38–41). The hybrid functions to move from E minor to F-sharp minor. The step after the opening E is like the answer, but the step after the G is like the subject.

STARTING ON UNUSUAL SCALE DEGREES

All of the subjects we have discussed so far start on the first scale degree of either the tonic or dominant scale. In tonal answer, the note after the (first) splice would be the first, third, or sixth scale degree of the opposite scale. These possibilities cover the most common situations. For example, forty-seven of the forty-eight fugues in the two volumes of Bach's *Well-Tempered Clavier* use either real answer or tonal answer following the above principles (the exception is the B-flat major fugue, *WTC II*).

However, there are subject/answer pairs that work differently. In principle, a subject can start on any scale degree. At first, we might not know how to interpret the scale degree in terms of the scales that we use to reckon the answer. Now we will discuss the various possibilities, listing them according to scale degree in the tonic scale and classifying them into those that take real and those that take tonal answer. We begin with subjects that start on scale degrees 3 and 6 and then discuss subjects starting on the remaining degrees (2, 4, 5, 7).

1. *Subjects starting on 3/T.* The answer starts with 3/D (exceptions to this are discussed further below). If the subject is nonmodulating, the answer is usually real. Transition and/or retransition may be needed. The following example by Johann Daniel Leuthard (quoted by Marpurg) has a three-measure retransition.

Example 17.29. (Johann Daniel Leuthard)

Subjects that move from the tonic to the dominant often take a tonal answer so that there is no need for a retransition or remodulation. In the following example, the splice does not occur right at the beginning of subject and answer but somewhat later. We have labeled the scale degrees on both sides of the splices.

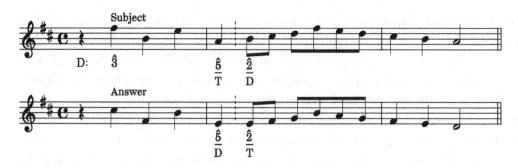

Example 17.30. (Johann Adolph Scheibe, after Marpurg)

Occasionally, subjects starting with 3/T are answered with 2/D (real or tonal answer). There are no hard and fast rules as to when this takes place. Rather, the decision depends on how to get the most satisfying melodic solution.

2. *Subjects starting on 6/T.* These almost always take real answers starting on 6/D.

3. *Subjects starting on 2/T.* The subject has to be considered as starting either on 2/T or on 5/D. (1) If the subject moves to V and the answer starts on 2/D, it must be tonal (example 17.31a). (2) If the subject moves to V and the answer starts on 5/T, the answer will be real (example 17.31b). The overall effect is the same as if the answer were tonal starting on 2/D.

Example 17.31a. (Marpurg)

Example 17.31b. (Marpurg)

The subject of Bach's B-flat major fugue from *WTC II* also starts on 2/T, which is heard here as an upper neighbor to the tonic (and is often harmonized as such in the course of the fugue). One can think of this subject as starting with an incomplete upper neighbor, with the tonic scale degree on the downbeat of the first measure being replaced by an eighth rest. In this interpretation, the answer starts with a suppressed fifth scale degree F. The F harmonizes perfectly with the last note of the subject on the downbeat of m. 5. Note how the third entry in m. 13 starts with 2/T as a neighbor note. The answer is tonal. Because the number of splices is even, the overall effect is like real answer: the subject ends on 3/T (on the downbeat of m. 5) and the answer ends on 3/D (on the downbeat of m. 9), followed by four measures of retransition. Note how (as expected) the tonal answer allows Bach to stay longer in the tonic key but destroys the triadic arpeggiation from the fourth through the sixth note. Is the answer form of the theme inferior to the subject form?

4. *Subjects starting on 4/T*. The answer is always real and always starts on 4/D, that is, the tonic scale degree.

5. *Subjects starting on 7/T*. The subject can be considered as starting on either 7/T or 3/D. (1) If the subject stays in T and the answer starts on 7/D, the answer will usually be real (example 17.32a). (2) If the subject moves to V and the answer starts on 7/D, the answer will be tonal (example 17.32b, the splice occurs here between the sixth and seventh note). Analyze example 17.32c.

Example 17.32a. (Marpurg)

Example 17.32b. (Marpurg)

Example 17.32c. Compare the opening of this subject with the one from Bach's F-sharp major fugue, *WTC II*.

6. *Subjects starting on 5/T.* Such subjects are rare and always take real answer. Remember that subjects starting on the fifth scale degree as 1/D almost always take tonal answer.

Example 17.33. (Vallotti, quoted in Sabbatini) *This is a type 2 double fugue.*

UNUSUAL SCALE DEGREES AFTER THE SPLICE

Just as we could have any scale degree before the splice, any scale degree could, in principle, appear right after the splice. Above is an example by Vallotti (example 17.33) that uses the seventh scale degree after the splice; 1/D–7/T in the opening of the subject is imitated by 1/T–7/D in the answer.

The subject of the "Sicut locutus est" from Bach's *Magnificat*, shown in example 12.16a, uses the fifth scale degree after the splice: 1/T–5/D is answered with 1/D–5/T. For an example that uses the fourth scale degree after the splice, see example 10.8, where 1/D–4/T is answered by 1/T–4/D.

UNUSUAL SUBJECTS

Despite the guidelines for good melodic writing mentioned here, and other basic voice-leading rules, we should keep in mind that composers sometimes decide not to obey them, especially in cases where a subject is intended to produce some special effect. Here are some examples. The following subject (example 17.34) has a melodic leap of a diminished fourth from G to D-sharp. Handel obeys Mattheson's rule about diminished melodic intervals, given above, in the sense that G occurs on a strong beat and D-sharp on a weak beat. However, the compound melody of Handel's theme is "incorrect" in that the leading tone D-sharp never resolves to E (unless you think it is transferred to the second violin and resolved in m. 2). Do a harmonic analysis.

Example 17.34. (Handel, Concerto Grosso op. 6, no. 3, Andante, mm. 1–4)

A subject that is famous for its exorbitant range and melodic leaps is the one from Scarlatti's "Cat" fugue already discussed in example 15.18. The (applied) leading-tones are again not resolved properly in this compound melody.

The following subject (example 17.35) translates the year of composition into melodic intervals. The first note is considered to represent a unison (1); the remaining numbers 7, 4, 8 are read as a melodic seventh, fourth, and octave, ascending or descending as the case may be. The result is a succession of leaps with no counterweight of stepwise motion (except for the inserted grace notes):

Example 17.35. (Gregor Joseph Werner, "Musical Instrumental Calendar," 1748 fugue, mm. 33–41)

Some subjects take a particular idea to an extreme. The following subject (example 17.36) starts with a repeated note that accelerates in each of the first three of the subject's four measures. The repeated note is followed by the splice (at the bar line between mm. 3 and 4) and a sequence (in m. 4). Between mm. 4 and 5 the tonic harmony is repeated across the bar line. It's fine here because the entry of the answer marks the beginning of a new phrase.

Example 17.36. (Handel, Concerto Grosso op. 6, no. 7, Allegro, mm. 1–16) *The answer of mm. 5–8 is followed by what seems like an unnecessary transition in mm. 9–11. In other words, the third entry could come in at the beginning of m. 9 if the second violin line were altered. Handel uses the transition to modulate back to the tonic so that the third entry sounds like a dominant pedal in the tonic key rather than the tonic of the dominant key. Likewise, the answer in the bass sounds like a dominant pedal in the subdominant key. The first measure of the "unnecessary" transition (m. 9) continues the sequence from the end of the answer and leads to an avoided cadence in m. 11: the E-flat, in the first violin of m. 11, comes as a surprise, as we would expect E-natural instead (7–6 suspension to the leading tone of F major).*

EXERCISE 17-A

1. *Analysis:* Look over examples in this chapter beginning with example 17.9 and determine the subject types. Do a harmonic analysis for examples 17.9 and 17.27a.

2. *Composing:* Write fugue subjects of approximately two to four measures that contain all of the given rhythms in any order.

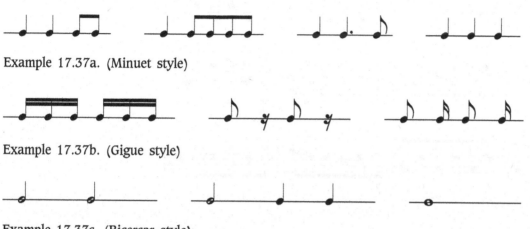

Example 17.37a. (Minuet style)

Example 17.37b. (Gigue style)

Example 17.37c. (Ricercar style)

3. *Writing:* Turn some chorale tunes into themes. Show both the subject and the answer form.

4. *Analysis:* Analyze the overall shape of some fugue subjects (including the "Sicut locutus" subject in example 12.16a) using the reductive contour method outlined in this chapter.

5. *Composing:* Write Frankenstein subjects using bits from different Baroque fugue subjects. Bracket the segments and label their origin. Make sure that your Frankenstein subjects have good harmonic rhythm. Identify the styles of your Frankenstein subjects, keeping in mind that you may mix the types to produce galant style.

6. *Writing (unpacking the box):* Use Nadia Boulanger's cadential progression from example 2.3a and arrange thirds and roots into a subject and countersubject, as shown in example 17.24.

7. *Composing:* Go back to example 17.27b (from Bach's Cantata 21) and add the third entry in the alto starting in the eighth measure. Add the countersubject in the tenor and compose a second countermelody in the bass. Compare your solution with Bach's.

PARTIMENTO

The themes in these fugues from the Langloz Manuscript (examples 17.38 and 17.39) are in a style that reminds us of string concertos, with their repeated wide leaps. Some continuo figures are redundant and others are missing. The answers are real and the entries at the beginning are periodic because of the use of modulation/remodulation.

Example 17.38. (Langloz Manuscript, no. 8)

Example 17.38. (*Concluded*)

Example 17.39. (Langloz Manuscript, no. 18)

Example 17.39. *(Concluded)*

NOTES

1. Rameau, *Traité de l'harmonie réduite à ses principes naturels*, III, 44, p. 336.
2. Marpurg, *Abhandlung von der Fuge*, II, §5, p. 29.
3. Mattheson, *Der vollkommene Capellmeister*, II, 4, §81.
4. Marpurg, *Abhandlung von der Fuge*, II, §6, p. 30.
5. Rameau, *Traité de l'harmonie*, III, 44, p. 338.
6. Mattheson, *Der vollkommene Capellmeister*, II, 5, §89.
7. Mattheson, §92.
8. Mattheson, §93.
9. Marpurg, *Abhandlung von der Fuge*, II, §6, p. 30.
10. Mattheson, *Der vollkommene Capellmeister*, II, 5, §51.
11. Mattheson, III, 20, §14.
12. Mattheson, II, 5, §48.
13. Mattheson, 4, §§15–16.
14. Mattheson, §§20–22.
15. Mattheson, 5, §§65–66.
16. Marpurg, *Abhandlung von der Fuge*, II, §4, p. 29.
17. Mattheson, *Der vollkommene Capellmeister*, II, 5, §124.
18. Mattheson, III, 16, §§16–17.
19. Marpurg, *Abhandlung von der Fuge*, II, §2, p. 28.
20. Mattheson, *Der vollkommene Capellmeister*, III, 20, §20.
21. Caplin, *Classical Form*, p. 37.
22. Rameau, *Traité de l'harmonie*, III, 44, p. 337.
23. Marpurg, *Abhandlung von der Fuge*, III, 1, p. 41.

18

STRETTO

There are two basic elements in fugues, *thematic entries* and *episodes*. Totally thematic fugues contain only imitative entries, while most fugues contain episodes for contrast. Composers add variety to those two basic elements and show off their technique by adding the fancy tricks that you will learn in this chapter and in chapter 19. Most of these devices create new interval successions between two or more parts (just as invertible counterpoint does), and consequently they may have new harmonic implications. If you are using chapters 18 and 19 while still limited to strict style, you have to be careful that the harmonic progression is clear.

You should probably not think that composers first write the subject and then "discover" whether it will be suitable to sound against its own inversion, or whether it will work in stretto. Rather, you have to plan from the outset what devices you want to use down the road. One of our students wrote a very nice subject that he wanted to use later in a stretto. When it wouldn't work, we suggested a change, cautioning him that he might not like the new melody. Frustrated by that time, he said, "I don't care if I like it, I just want it to work!" Thus we must negotiate between the melodic material itself and the use to which we want to put that material. You have already experienced this in composing a countersubject: if it is to be invertible, it may not end up as the tune you first had in mind.

Marpurg solved this problem by telling us that we are first to compose the most complicated contrapuntal item, then go back and let the fugue work up to it, the way a shaggy-dog story sets up a punch line:

Once one has investigated the subject (or subjects if there are several) in the manner shown here, then the fugue is, so-to-speak, already made. One simply needs to connect the different passages that arise from close imitation [stretto] and shortening and dismemberment of the subject with good episodes. . . . The disposition [of the fugue] must be done in such a way that the devices of greatest artistry are saved for last and that the weaker ones always precede, so that . . . though the beginning is good, the middle is even better and the end is excellent.[1]

If you are using a given subject, you will mostly have to see, on an ad hoc basis, which fancy devices you can use, trying and rejecting different possibilities, although we will give you some hints for spotting solutions. If composing from scratch, you should try Marpurg's suggestion, composing the fancy presentation first, perhaps creating the subject as you go along. The resulting possibilities can be used as "spare parts" in an actual fugue.

STRETTO

Stretto means "squeezed" in Italian. In a stretto the imitative entries are squeezed together in time, each one seeming to enter before the previous one has ended. The effect is of greater intensity, as if the voices were rushing in to interrupt each other. Composers often save it for the end of the piece, although there exists a category of fugues called *stretto fugues*, where the entries are in close time intervals from the very beginning (e.g., *WTC II*, fugue in C-sharp major).

If a subject is given, finding the stretto possibilities is like solving a puzzle canon (see chapter 2). You need to check all possible combinations of the subject with itself at every possible time interval and pitch level. To do this, pretend the subject is notated on a transparent sheet of plastic, with the staff lines, clefs, and key signature hidden. Imagine the transparency to be put over a piece of paper that shows the subject with a second blank staff below. Sliding the transparency freely in both the horizontal and vertical dimensions over the second staff will produce all possible stretto combinations.

Example 18.1 summarizes this process for a subject found in Mattheson. We are to find all combinations of the subject with imitations at the unison (octave), fourth, and fifth entering after one whole note, two whole notes, and so on. We limit the possibilities by requiring that the time interval of imitation be no more than two measures. (Note that the example is in 4/2 and that the "step" is the half note.) Under these conditions, there are four metric positions where the second voice may enter and three different pitch levels, resulting in a total of twelve possible combinations.

Combinations marked with an X produce illegal voice-leading in strict style. Note that we allow an entry on a dissonance after a rest only if the voice entering has the agent in the suspension. The remaining combinations work either as shown (as two-part combinations) or with the help of at least one more voice added below (fourths between the two parts need to be accommodated by a third voice below unless they produce legal suspensions).

Example 18.1. *The interested reader will wish to compare this subject with the subject of the "judicabit in nationibus" section of Handel's "Dixit Dominus."*

Example 18.1. (*Concluded*)

EXERCISE 18-A

1. *Analysis:* For each combination marked with an X in example 18.1, indicate how the voice-leading is illegal in strict style.

2. *Writing:* Sketch possible harmonies for the remaining (legal) combinations. Perhaps not every succession of vertical intervals that is legal will produce good harmonic progressions.

3. *Writing:* Add a third voice above each of the legal combinations. The result need not be invertible at the octave. Be careful with any of the legal combinations in example 18.1 that have vertical fourths. They may not be usable in this exercise.

4. *Writing:* Add a third voice below each of the legal combinations. The result need not be invertible at the octave.

5. *Writing (long):* For the subject shown in example 18.1, find all possible stretti after one, two, three, or four whole notes at the pitch intervals of second, third, sixth, and seventh. For these new possibilities, repeat questions 2, 3, and 4.

6. *Writing (long):* For the subject shown in example 18.1, find all possible stretti after one, three, five, or seven *half* notes at the second through seventh. For these new possibilities, repeat questions 2, 3, and 4.

In example 18.2a, Mattheson follows the same subject with its answer a fourth below. The answer enters after the tonic arrival of the subject (tonic arrival on F after the whole note G). The opening ascending second C–D of the answer is harmonized as V–IV^6 with a 7–6 suspension in the counteranswer. Note that the first measure of the counteranswer (m. 4) contains the same motive as the second measure of the subject. This is the same as the second measure of the subject being combined with its first measure a fifth below, with vertical intervals 5–8–7–6 on the four half notes as in example 18.1f (inverted at the octave).

Example 18.2. (Mattheson)

In example 18.2b, the time interval between the entries of the subject and its answer a fourth below is shortened to two measures. The last measure of the subject (which Mattheson calls the cadence of the subject) now overlaps with the first measure of the answer. The answer's ascending second C–D is harmonized as V–vi.

The stretto combination between the bass and soprano in example 18.2c—imitation at the octave, six half notes apart—is marked with an X in example 18.1c. This is because parallel unisons/octaves would occur in the third measure. However, Mattheson alters the last note of the subject in the bass of example 18.2c. At the double dagger, D–C is changed to D–E, now "fleeing the cadence" (see chapter 13). As a general rule, we will allow such alterations as long as there is a minimum overlap of four steps between the two unaltered thematic statements (here: four half notes).

In example 18.2d, the time interval between the two entries is shortened to two half notes. The combination corresponds to the possibility shown in example 18.1i. In example 18.2d, the imitation's ascending second C–D is again harmonized as V–vi. The same two-part combination is used between the alto and tenor of example 18.2e. This example shows a stretto in three parts. Soprano and alto form a new combination, with the alto entering one measure after the soprano. (Note that Mattheson shortens the first note of the subject.) This is the combination we already predicted in example 18.2a above, where the first measure of the counteranswer uses the same motive as the second measure of the subject. This particular vertical alignment appears in the combination of example 18.1f, a stretto imitation at the lower fifth or upper fourth one measure apart. The harmonic progression in m. 2 of example 18.2e is I–V$^{4-3}$. The ascending second of the tenor entry is harmonized as V–vi.

STRETTO AND TONAL ANSWER

When looking for stretto possibilities, you may find more results by combining the subject form of the theme with the answer form.

In examples 18.3a–d, Marpurg makes several stretti out of a subject and answer by Bach. Marpurg numbers the "empty" measures in the consequent voice to draw attention to the variety of time intervals.

Example 18.3. (Marpurg) *Find two other stretti after three measures starting below and lasting at least two measures.*

As for the harmonies that these pairs of voices might represent, in example 18.3b the first vertical interval between the two parts is a fifth, followed by a tenth and octave. The harmonic progression might be V–ii–I⁶. In example 18.3c, the first three intervals between the two parts are a fifth followed by two sixths. The harmonic progression is vi–IV⁶–V⁶. Example 18.3d combines *three* entries in stretto. Note the accented passing tone figure ("legal ap") in the middle voice of m. 2, the top voice of m. 3 (together with another passing tone in the middle voice), and in the third voice in m. 4.

In the above examples, Marpurg retains the metric positions of all the notes. In this next one, however, he switches strong and weak beats in the lower part, a technique that is allowable in stretto.

The following stretto (example 18.5) combines two statements of the subject at the octave. (We have marked the splices. For the tonal answer of this theme, see example 17.28a.) This tune works well in stretto because the pitches on every quarter for the first seven beats are members of the tonic

Example 18.4. (Marpurg)

Example 18.5. (Bach, *WTC I*, D-sharp minor fugue, mm. 19–22)

triad. They thus combine well—as long as illegal 6/4 chords are avoided. Note that Bach slightly alters the rhythm by adding eighth rests in m. 21. Why do you think Bach made this alteration?

STRETTO AND HYBRID

In addition to combining subject form with answer form, you can also try combining hybrid forms of the theme, as seen in chapter 17. These have multiple splices and mix features of the subject and answer. In the next excerpt, the stretto combines two statements of the hybrid theme a fifth apart, again at the time interval of a half note.

Example 18.6. (Bach, *WTC I*, D-sharp minor fugue, mm. 27–30)

VARYING STRETTO COMBINATIONS BY INVERTIBLE AND UNINVERTED DOUBLE COUNTERPOINT

Stretto combinations can be used more flexibly (and repeated more often) if they can be varied by invertible and/or uninverted double counterpoint (you may have found such possibilities for example

18.3). Examples 18.7a–c show how the combination made out of entries one measure apart can be varied by transposition.

Example 18.7. (Marpurg) *The importance of "legal ap" cannot be overestimated. Which of these combinations are invertible?*

USING REDUCTION TO EXAMINE A SUBJECT FOR STRETTO POSSIBILITIES

Generally, reducing the subject and/or answer to first species allows us quickly to recognize stretto possibilities, whether in composing or analyzing. We can turn Bach's subject used in Marpurg's examples above into first species by eliminating weak quarters and halves and reducing it to the first notes of each measure: D–E–B–D–A–C. The resulting succession is sequential, starting with the second note of the reduction: An interval pattern of a descending fourth followed by an ascending third is repeated. The answer form of the theme reduces to G–B–F-sharp–A–E–G, which is sequential from the very beginning. The following list shows all legal combinations of subject and answer in their first-species reductions. Three of the six combinations are invertible at the octave.

Table 18.1.

S :	D – E – B – D – A – C	
S :	D – E – B – D – A – C	(Must be below in 2-part counterpoint)
S :	D – E – B – D – A – C	
A :	G – B – F♯– A – E – G	(Invertible at the octave)
S :	D – E – B – D – A – C	
A :	G – B – F♯– A – E – G	(Invertible at the octave)
S :	D – E – B – D – A – C	
A :	G – B – F♯– A – E – G	(Must be above in 2-part counterpoint)
A :	G – B – F♯– A – E – G	
A :	G – B – F♯– A – E – G	(Must be below in 2-part counterpoint)
A :	G – B – F♯– A – E – G	
A :	G – B – F♯– A – E – G	(Invertible at the octave)

HARMONY AND STRETTO

Stretto yields pairs or trios of voices that obey the rules of voice leading but that were not necessarily originally designed with a harmonic purpose in mind. Some combinations created by this process imply weird harmonies, as the exercises below will demonstrate. Nevertheless, there is usually *some* way to add voices to almost any combination.

However, if you compose the stretto first, as Marpurg suggests, you can make sure that the combination has a clear sense of harmonic direction. The advantage of this method is that when you unplug either voice from the stretto, you can be sure that it will work alone in the same progression.

TIME-SHIFTING THE COUNTERMELODY

A procedure that resembles stretto is sliding the countermelody back and forth in relation to the theme. Marpurg advocates this (see chapter 20), although it is rarely discussed. A nice example can be found in Bach's A-flat major fugue, *WTC II*. The subject is shown in example 18.8a, with a reduction in example 18.8b. Notes 4–7 in the reduction have a definite sequential implication. Knowing that Bach will use a chromatically descending line as a countersubject, where would you put it? The chances are you would put it as shown in example 18.8c, where it makes a clear circle-of-fifths sequence with applied dominants (see chapter 15) with vertical intervals of minor sevenths and major thirds. Bach does use this combination, but not until mm. 37–38 (reduced in example 18.8c), against the subject in the subdominant.

What does Bach do the rest of the time? At the beginning (mm. 3–4 and 6–7), he presents the countermelody with a slight deviation (mm. 6–7 are reduced in example 18.8d). The vertical intervals are now major sixths and minor thirds, and the progression is much more mysterious harmonically. The difference is the tied A-flat in m. 37 of example 18.8c versus the semitone in m. 6 of example 18.8d (compare at the asterisks). In m. 37, Bach has shifted the subject one quarter note to the left relative to the countersubject. The harmonies in mm. 6–7 may be unclear, but the tonic arrival in m. 8 is on a strong beat. In mm. 37–38 the harmonies are clear but the tonic arrival in m. 39 is on a weak beat, and the strong and weak beats in the chromatic line are still in the same places.

Example 18.8a. (Bach, A-flat major fugue, *WTC II*, mm. 1–3)

Example 18.8b. (Reduction of a)

Example 18.8c. (mm. 37–39, transposed up a fifth)

Example 18.8d. (Reduction of soprano and tenor, mm. 6–8)

With Bach's third voice, the reduction of which is shown in example 18.9a (see "CS2"), the combination in mm. 6–8 sounds clearer because the important chord factors are there. Example 18.9b, from later in the same fugue, is derived from example 18.9a through the use of invertible triple counterpoint. Compare the two examples—by what procedures is the second derived from the first? Analyze the harmonies in example 18.9b.

Example 18.9a. (Bach, A-flat major fugue, *WTC II*, mm. 6–8)

Example 18.9b. (Bach, A-flat major fugue, *WTC II*, mm. 22–23)

STRETTO FUGUE

There are two meanings for the term *stretto fugue*. Some fugues begin with a very short time interval of imitation right away from the outset, like the C-sharp major fugue in *WTC II* (example 15.11). In such fugues, stretto alone is not the climactic technique that it would be in a normal fugue, unless the composer makes even closer imitations or imitations at more unusual pitch intervals. Other techniques of intensification include texture, register, and modulation. Another meaning of the term *stretto fugue* applies to fugues that have no episodes and use various short time intervals of imitation instead. The C major fugue from *WTC I* has no countersubject (i.e., it's a simple fugue) and it contains no episodes at all but many different stretti.

EXERCISE 18-B

PART I

1. *Writing:* The subject and answer in example 18.10 are by Kirnberger and were used by Marpurg to illustrate various stretto possibilities. (a) Reduce these two melodies to first species (seven quarter notes). (b) Modeling on example 18.1, write out all stretto combinations at the fourth, fifth, or octave of your reductions of subject and answer. You may do this in music notation, in letters, as in table 18.1, or by playing at the keyboard. The minimum overlap is four "steps" (i.e., quarter notes). Thus, imitations can start on the second, third, or fourth notes. Remember that you can write all solutions above or all below, it makes no difference (you'll make a note to fix fourths with an added voice below). Make sure to try subject followed by subject, answer followed by answer, subject followed by answer, and answer followed by subject. Because there are three available metric positions, three pitch intervals, and four combinations of subject and answer, there are theoretically thirty-six solutions (3 × 3 × 4). Mark unusable ones with "X."

2. *Writing:* Add a third voice above or below each of the usable combinations and provide a harmonic analysis.

3. *Analysis and writing:* Which usable combinations are invertible at the tenth? The twelfth? Add a third voice to the inverted combinations. If you can add the same voice to both the original (in question 2) and inverted combination, you are writing invertible triple counterpoint!

Example 18.10. (Marpurg)

PART II

4. *Writing:* Add a third voice below Bach's stretto in example 18.11a (mm. 16–17). The added voice must move mainly in sixteenths notes. Continue the alto in m. 17. You can check your solution with Bach's.

5. *Writing:* Add a third voice that moves mainly in sixteenths below the stretto of example 18.11b (mm. 23–26).

6. *Writing:* Add a third voice *above* the stretto in example 18.12 that moves in eighths, quarters, and half notes. You may use rests as well.

Example 18.11a. (Bach, *WTC II*, C minor fugue, mm. 16–17)

Example 18.11b. (Bach, *WTC II*, C minor fugue, mm. 23–26)

Example 18.12. (Bach, *WTC II*, B-flat minor fugue, mm. 27–31)

PART III

7. *Writing:* Using the four pairs of subject and/or answer given in examples 18.13a–d, examine all thirty-six stretto possibilities after 1, 2, and 3 steps and at the three primary intervals (fourth, fifth, octave). Write out all successful combinations and add a third voice to each. For the purpose of this exercise, the minimum overlap is four "steps." After four steps, you may write a free continuation.

8. *Writing:* Proceed as in question 7 above, but use other pitch intervals (second, third, and sixth, above or below).

9. *Writing:* Proceed as in question 7 above, but use fractional time intervals.

Example 18.13.

PART IV

10. *Composing (short):* Compose a subject/answer pair that is four measures long and has at least two different stretto possibilities. You might want to start by sketching the melodic material in a single note value and combining the melodies in first species, as in the reductions in Table 18.1, adding embellishments later. Add a hypothetical third voice.

PARTIMENTO

In this double fugue of the second type (example 18.14), Handel thinks of the slower-moving line as the subject and the faster-moving line as the countermelody or "contrasubj." (You will recognize the subject as the chorale tune "Aus tiefer Not" in a major key.) In m. 8 we think the entrance on F-sharp should be part of a #6/4/3 chord. The countermelody cannot always be sounded in its entirety. Where is the invertible counterpoint? At what interval? Where are the stretti?

Example 18.14. (Handel)

Example 18.15. (Handel)

In this example from Handel (example 18.15), the entries fit closely together in stretto, as you can see from the voices and pitches he indicates below the bass.

NOTE

1. Marpurg, *Abhandlung von der Fuge*, IV, 3, p. 120.

19

OTHER TECHNIQUES

Augmentation and Diminution; Melodic Inversion; Mirror Inversion; Simultaneous Inversion; Pedal; Combined Techniques; Partimento

In this chapter, we continue to produce new combinations for which we will have to find suitable harmonic clothing, just as we have done in the chapters on invertible double counterpoint and stretto. The new combinations discussed in this chapter are the result of other operations that qualify as artful devices that the composer may save for late in the composition.

AUGMENTATION AND DIMINUTION

In augmentation the note values of a melody are multiplied by a constant factor. The following fugue is a stretto fugue, and the third voice enters with the inversion (example 19.1a). In example 19.1b, the answer's note values are doubled in the middle voice in m. 25.

Example 19.1a. (Bach, *WTC II*, C-sharp major fugue, mm. 1–3)

Example 19.1b. (Bach, *WTC II*, C-sharp major fugue, mm. 25–26)

In the C minor fugue from *WTC II*, the note values of the subject are doubled in the tenor of mm. 14–15. Note the similar motion to the F octave in m. 14; we would normally call this gauche in two parts, but composers have always permitted themselves some license when doing some difficult "trick," and the awkwardness may actually draw our attention to the subject combined with its augmentation.

Another good example of the augmentation of a theme combined with the original theme occurs in mm. 67–72 of the D-sharp minor fugue from *WTC I*. The augmented (hybrid) theme appears in the middle voice. The hybrid theme enters in its original rhythm in the third voice an octave below, two quarters earlier. It ends halfway through the middle voice's augmentation and is followed by another statement of the hybrid theme in the top voice (m. 69). You saw another example of augmentation, combined with melodic inversion, in Handel's anthem in example 11.7: the first five notes of the third subject (m. 11, in half notes) are the inversion of the first five notes of the answer in doubled values.

In diminution, the note values are divided by a constant factor. In the following example from the same fugue whose beginning is shown in example 19.la, the answer in the bass of m. 6 is followed by diminutions in soprano, alto, and bass (inversion).

Example 19.2. (Bach, *WTC II*, C-sharp major fugue, mm. 5–7) *For another example, see WTC II, E major fugue, mm. 30–31.*

AUGMENTATION OR DIMINUTION?

Augmentation and diminution are in a reciprocal relationship, and sometimes it is not possible to tell which one is the case. In the following fugal chorus from *Messiah* (example 19.3), the subject in the strings in mm. 4–5 unfolds at two different speeds. One serves as the countersubject to the other, but which is which? The second pair of entries in the chorus of mm. 5–6 is a fourth below, with the first interval in the alto altered. The second pair of entries thus combines tonal and real answer. Compare the S-A duo in mm. 5–6 with the S-B duo in mm. 7–8. How are they related?

Example 19.3. (Handel, Messiah, Chorus 35, mm. 1–8)

MELODIC INVERSION

Fugue subjects can be melodically inverted at various pitch levels. A common type is one in which chord factors of the tonic triad are mapped onto each other, with members of vii°7 likewise being mapped onto each other. The subject of the fourth fugue from *The Art of the Fugue* is the inversion of the subject from the first fugue. The inversion is around the third of the tonic triad.

Example 19.4a. (Bach, The Art of Fugue, Contrapunctus 1, mm. 1–3)

Example 19.4b. (Bach, The Art of Fugue, Contrapunctus 4, mm. 1–3)

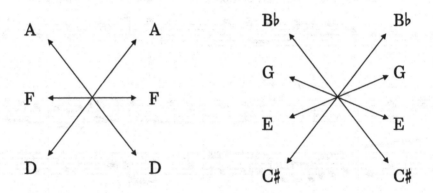

Example 19.5.

The same inversional axis (third of the tonic triad) is used when Bach inverts the subject of the A minor fugue from *WTC I*. Compare the subject in mm. 1–4 with its inversion in the soprano of mm. 14–17. Note that some interval sizes are changed in order to accommodate the key. For instance, the alterations of G (instead of G-sharp) in m. 15 and F-sharp (instead of F) in m. 16 serve to accommodate the tonal area. For another example of melodic inversion around the third of the tonic triad, see the B-flat minor fugue, *WTC II*, mm. 1–4 (subject) and mm. 67–70 (inversion of subject in the tenor).

But other inversions are possible as well. In the F-sharp minor fugue from *WTC I*, the subject (mm. 1–4) is inverted in the bass of mm. 32–35 around the tonic scale degree F-sharp.

MIRROR INVERSION

In mirror inversion, a melody and countermelody are each melodically inverted and their relative positions are exchanged as well. It combines melodic inversion with invertible counterpoint, and it is sure to succeed, because if the mirror combination begins with the same vertical interval, it will reproduce the entire interval succession of the original. In example 19.6, Marpurg shows more possibilities using the theme we saw in example 18.4. Example 19.6b is the mirror inversion of example 19.6a. The mirror starts when the second voice enters; the transposition makes the first vertical interval a third, as in the original, so you can be sure the rest will contain all the same vertical intervals.

   Another way to think about this is to consider the axes of inversion. The upper part of example 19.6a is inverted and transposed down a twelfth in example 19.6b (= inverted around E/F-sharp above middle C). The lower part of example 19.6a is inverted and transposed up a twelfth in example 19.6b (= inverted around E/F-sharp above middle C). Since both parts are inverted around the same axis of symmetry, the vertical intervals between the two parts are preserved.

Example 19.6. (Marpurg)

   There is an example of mirror inversion in Handel's example 11.7. In mm. 22–24, three subjects are melodically inverted and placed against each other in the same relationship as in mm. 15–17. Find them. In the G major fugue from *WTC I*, the answer/counteranswer pair from mm. 5–8 is used in mirror inversion with a third voice added in mm. 20–23.

SIMULTANEOUS INVERSION

Simultaneous inversion means playing the theme against its inversion starting at the same time. One way to ensure success in this is to use a subject whose pitch range is limited to the seventh between scale degrees 7 and 6; it can be combined with its inversion around the third of the tonic triad. Here is an example by Marpurg (example 19.7). The upper voice plays the subject from example 18.3. It is combined simultaneously with its inversion in the lower voice.

Example 19.7. (Marpurg) *For another example of simultaneous inversion, see the D-sharp minor fugue,* WTC II, *mm. 43–46. The range of the subject (in the soprano) is slightly smaller, from scale degrees 7 to 5. Its inversion is played simultaneously in the tenor. The inversion again maps the key's third scale degree F-sharp onto itself, exchanges the first and fifth scale degrees (D-sharp and A-sharp), and so on.*

PEDAL

TONIC PEDAL

Tonic pedals are most commonly found at the ends of fugues, following the final cadence (5–1 in the bass). The pedal serves as a prolongation of the tonic harmony, while the upper parts may use other harmonies as well, often in a texture based on material from the subject and/or countersubject.

A typical harmonic progression above a tonic pedal is tonic–subdominant–dominant–tonic with the subdominant tonicized as in the following example.

Example 19.8. (Bach, *WTC I*, C minor fugue, mm. 29–31)

In keyboard fugues, the number of voices often increases over the final tonic pedal, as here, making a textural climax. For another example, see the E-flat major fugue, *WTC I*, mm. 36–37.

DOMINANT PEDAL

The dominant is prolonged, usually as part of the final cadence. A common progression is simply to alternate tonic and dominant harmonies over the dominant pedal, as in example 13.12 (mm. 30–32). Neighboring 6/4 chords are typical, as for example in mm. 57–58 of the F minor fugue, *WTC I*. For a typical example of a statement of most of the subject over a dominant pedal, see mm. 74–76 from the B minor fugue, *WTC I*.

Pedals are often combined with other techniques discussed in this chapter. Examples of stretti over a pedal can be found in mm. 24–27 of the C major fugue, *WTC I*, and in mm. 83–87 of the A minor fugue, *WTC I* (the latter contains a stretto of fragments of the subject and its inversion over a tonic pedal).

In m. 17 of the Bach-Reincken fugue in A minor, BWV 965, mentioned briefly in chapter 13, a pedal is introduced on the dominant of E minor, but it gradually turns into the second degree of A minor because the harmonies above changed. This kind of diversion would not occur at the end of a fugue.

Measures 105–106 of the Ricercar à 3 from Bach's *Musical Offering* contain a chromatic harmonic progression over a dominant pedal. Note that vii°⁷/vi is not used over a tonic pedal, but its enharmonic equivalent, vii°⁷/I, is good. Avoid vii°⁷/ii because of the cross-relation with the tonic note.

In the following excerpt (example 19.9), Bach uses the tonal answer followed by the subject over a dominant pedal. (We saw this subject in example 18.3.) Note the embellished splice in the answer.

Example 19.9. (Bach, Sonata 3 for solo violin, second movement)

EXERCISE 19-A

1. *Composing (short):* Compose a subject that can be combined with its own diminution or augmentation. Add a hypothetical third voice.

2. *Composing (short):* Compose a subject, invert it, and supply both the original and the inversion with a figured bass.

3. *Composing (short):* Compose a subject/countersubject pair, mirror invert it, and add a hypothetical third voice to the original and the mirror inversion.

4. *Composing (short)*: Compose a subject that can be combined with itself in simultaneous inversion. Add a hypothetical third voice.

Note: You should think of the "hypothetical third voice" as a countersubject. It is there to fill in missing chord factors, clarify harmonic progression, and add rhythmic contrast and melodic direction.

Example 19.10. (Bach, *WTC I*, D-sharp minor fugue, mm. 77–83)

COMBINED TECHNIQUES

1. *Stretto with augmentation.* In example 19.10, the augmentation of the hybrid theme in the first voice is paired with an embellished version of the hybrid theme two octaves below in the third voice. (This combination is the same as the one in mm. 67–69, not shown here.) A hybrid theme a twelfth below follows in m. 80 in the middle voice. Starting in m. 77, the middle voice plays the hybrid theme in augmentation an octave below the first voice. It is slightly altered rhythmically and forms a stretto combination with the augmentation in the first voice.

2. *Stretto with diminution.* For an example see mm. 26–32 of the E major fugue, *WTC II*. Note that the subject appears in its original form in the alto of mm. 30–32.

3. *Stretto with inversion.* For an example see mm. 22–30 of the D minor fugue, *WTC I*. The subject in the middle voice of mm. 28–30 is preceded by various statements of its inversion in stretto. Some statements are fragmented. Note that this subject uses the range between sharp-7 and flat-6 and could thus be played simultaneously against its own inversion around the tonic's third scale degree. Bach uses this possibility in fragmented form at the end of the fugue over a pedal (see example 19.13). This particular inversion appears in the top voice of mm. 27–29 in stretto with the subject in the middle voice of mm. 28–30.

For another example of the subject and its inversion used in stretto, see mm. 80–84 of the B-flat minor fugue, *WTC II*. A voice-leading reduction of the subject and its inversion helps to understand how the stretto with inversion works. The reduction shows the structural pitches on every half note.

Since the subject moves mostly stepwise, the stretto of subject and inversion moves mostly step-wise in contrary motion. This means that the resulting combination contains blocks that work like simultaneous inversion. The blocks are bracketed below. The (simultaneous) inversion in these blocks is around B-flat, thus producing unisons (octaves), thirds, and fifths as vertical intervals.

Inversion (sop):	E♭	D♭	C	B♭–F	E♭	D♭	C–E♭	B♭–D♭	A♭–C	G–B♭
Subject (ten):		G	A♭	B♭	C–F	G	A♭	B♭–G	C–A♭	D♭–B♭

Example 19.11.

4. *Mirror inversion of stretto.* See mm. 14–18 of the D minor fugue, *WTC II.* Starting in m. 14, the subject (in the middle voice) is combined with its answer a fifth above (in the top voice) in stretto. In mm. 17–18, this combination is mirror inverted. The middle voice starts the inversion on A and the lowest voice enters with the inversion on D, one quarter later. The intervals between the two parts are preserved. The third part is free.

In the B-flat minor fugue, *WTC II,* the stretto of the subject and its inversion in mm. 89–93 is a mirror inversion of the combination in mm. 80–84. The remaining two parts are free.

5. *Stretto with inversion and parallel sixths/thirds.* We have already discussed this in example 16.24.

6. *Stretto over a pedal.* See mm. 24–27 of the C major fugue, *WTC I.* We also saw a stretto over a dominant pedal in example 11.6 (mm. 23–25). The arrival on the pedal tonicizes the dominant; the stretto is between two statements of the second subject.

7. *Simultaneous inversion with parallel thirds.* In example 19.12, the simultaneous inversion of soprano and bass (already discussed in example 19.7) is doubled in thirds. The voice pairs—sopra-no-bass and alto-tenor—invert around the same pitch axis E/F-sharp. The inversion preserves the third scale-degree B and thus guarantees chords made of thirds throughout (third, triad, seventh chord).

8. *Simultaneous inversion with parallel thirds over a pedal.* In example 19.13, following the final cadence from m. 42 to m. 43, the outer parts each hold the tonic pedal D. In the last two measures, the middle voice splits into four parts. These four parts play the first half of the subject in simultane-ous inversion with parallel thirds. Other examples you may wish to study: Bach, *Canon im Einklange,* BWV 1072; Bach, *Canon triplex à 6 vocibus,* BWV 1076.

Example 19.12. (Marpurg) *Note that at the circled D, Marpurg seems to have departed from his strict procedure. This may be a mistake, or he may prefer V$^{4/2}$ over vii$^{6/4/3}$.*

Example 19.13. (Bach, *WTC I*, D minor fugue, mm. 42–44)

PARTIMENTO

Here is a piece by Pasquini in partimento notation, in which the inversion of the theme is introduced, first in the bass (mm. 17–18), then later again in other voices (note that the instruction "entra la fuga al roverso" may not indicate the only entrance of the inverted subject in an upper voice). The tutti begins in m. 3 but the soli make another appearance in m. 15. As usual, the figures are incomplete, and when Pasquini indicates entries in the upper voices with little vertical lines, they may have to be altered or incomplete. You have to figure out on what note to start and whether the theme must be inverted—it's a puzzle. (In one case he gives you a hint, writing "re mi" in m. 28. This refers to hexachordal solmization, and in this case means the notes G–A.) Vertical fourths in m. 15 should be interpreted as parts of *implied* 6/4/2 chords.

Example 19.14. (Pasquini, fuga in basso continuo)

Example 19.14. (*Continued*)

Example 19.14. (*Continued*)

Example 19.14. (*Concluded*)

20

OVERALL DESIGN AND LAYOUT OF A FUGUE

Key; Contrapuntal Intensity; Register and Texture; Marpurg on Fugal Form; Fugue as Jewelry; Borrowed Form; J. K. F. Fischer Fuga 3 in D Minor; J. K. F. Fischer Fuga 10 in F Major; Binary Form; Ritornello Form in Fugue; Competing Analyses of the C Minor Fugue from *WTC I*; Varying the Presentation of the Theme(s); Melodic Inversion; Varying the Theme/Countermelody Pair; Introducing Episodes for Contrast; Means of Varying Intensity

In chapter 13, we discussed assembling thematic sections, episodes, cadences, transitions, and fragmentary thematic statements into inventions, trio sonatas, and fugues. In chapters 16, 18, and 19 we acquired more techniques that are used in fugues. How will we assemble the resulting material? What is the form of a fugue? This is a hotly debated question, and some people think fugues have no form in the sense of AAB, or exposition-development-recapitulation, and so on. Tovey's famous characterization of fugue as a "texture" doesn't tell us much.[1] And yet we need to know what principles *might* govern what happens when.

In this chapter, we will propose some different ways of thinking about large-scale form, considering criteria of key, contrapuntal intensity, and texture and register, as they contribute to various kinds of formal layouts: *binary form*, *arch form*, *parallel section form*, *exposition-development-recapitulation form*, and *climax form*. In addition, we will consider an alternative to constructing the form of a fugue from scratch: Marpurg, who does not name any of the form types mentioned, suggests borrowing a formal structure from an existing fugue by a "good author."

KEY

Marpurg says that distant keys should be saved for later in the piece and should be approached using episodes (see "Marpurg on Fugal Form" below). He also says one should return to the main key at the end. Many authors define exposition-development-recapitulation form in terms of keys, with the more distant keys in the central section.

CONTRAPUNTAL INTENSITY

Contrapuntal intensity depends on degree of challenge to the composer; it is in proportion to the difficulty of the constructive task being undertaken. Invertible counterpoint at the octave is relaxed, compared to three-voice stretto or triple counterpoint at the twelfth. On the other hand, complex combinations are often not heard as intense at all: double counterpoint in four parts is hard to work out but can sound remarkably smooth on the surface. As we have seen in chapter 18, Marpurg says that in making the outline ("disposition") of the fugue, we should make sure that complicated contrapuntal devices are saved for later.[2]

REGISTER AND TEXTURE

We discussed register and texture a bit in chapter 11. Think back to Handel's "And with His stripes" (example 11.2a), where the long sequential episode (mm. 71–78) takes place in the three lower voices so that the high soprano thematic entrance surprises us in a pleasant way. In this chapter we will describe the use of register and texture in a kind of ad hoc way and try to show how the other aspects of fugue interact with register and texture.

We believe that changes in register and texture are the secret form-giving elements in fugue, and that they "determine" where the artful devices are placed. The problem is in defining categories for these parameters. Music theory has never developed as precise a language for describing texture, register, and spacing as it has for other parameters such as key, motive, phrase structure, form, or contrapuntal artifice. It is easy to say that something special is happening in the central episode in the C minor fugue from *WTC I* (example 16.18, mm. 13–15), which contains the highest note in the piece and some unusual spacing, but does it have the same significance as the following striking moment from the A minor fugue from *WTC I* (see example 20.1)? All we can do now is draw your attention to these elements and encourage you to experiment with them.

MARPURG ON FUGAL FORM

Marpurg's general guidelines for what comes when are based entirely on key, choice of which voice gets the theme, and contrapuntal artfulness. He never bases his guidelines on texture or register. He divides his scheme into six parts:

Example 20.1. (Bach, A minor fugue, *WTC I*, mm. 63–64)

(1) Once the subject has been led through the various voices, one either continues the harmonic fabric for a number of measures according to the rules for episodes and then makes a cadence or one makes this cadence immediately after the completion of the first group of themes, in the case where the melody of the subject is inclined that way. This cadence can take place in the tonic or in the dominant, depending on what seems to be most natural for the preceding harmony.

Note: Since we have said throughout [this book] that points of rest do not belong in fugues, and since we seem to contradict this here through the advice of [using] a cadence, we need to explain ourselves. The prohibition of points of rest is to be understood with respect to all voices simultaneously, and [it is] not to be interpreted that some voices by themselves could not be permitted to form closure among themselves. It is not required that all voices rumble along constantly in one breath and that we would not find any sign of distinction among the parts anywhere. The close should just either not be formal (as one can avoid it in the three ways explained above [see chapter 13]) or, if it is formal, (1) the final note or one of the other final [goal] sounds must start the [next] subject or an episode or (2) one has to immediately get off one or the other note of the cadence and then take up the subject itself or an episode, as we have said. There will be examples of this.

(2) At this cadence, one lets either the subject version or the answer version of the theme enter in that voice in which it did not last appear, or if the cadence was not preceded by an episode, one sounds at this cadence an episode in order to produce an even stronger craving for the repetition of the subject, which can then enter on a convenient harmony, either with the subject or answer, as we said, that is in the voice that didn't have it last.

(3) Once the melody shows itself anew in a voice, one tries, if one so wishes and if the melody permits, many kinds of close imitation [stretto], introducing the subsequent answer in the following voice a little closer, otherwise the fugue will become rather too long. One does not expect the same distance at which it followed the other voice in the first group of themes. This answer can happen at the octave or fifth depending on how the subsequent voice can follow the preceding one most closely.

(4) One follows this second group of themes, based on the number of voices, with mixed episodes either in all parts or only in some because one can let the voice that will have the

subject first in the third group of themes be silent, by means of some rests beforehand. But one arranges these episodes so that one can cadence into a related key, for which the rule is: one has to reach the ordinary keys before one goes to the extraordinary ones. ["Ordinary keys" are V, vi, and iii in major and v, III, and VI in minor; "extraordinary keys" are IV and ii in major and iv and VII in minor.[3]] One can stick to this order in the interest of more security until one knows how to rise above these rules and to modulate with reasonable freedom.

(5) Now the theme appears at a totally different pitch, and perhaps at the same time in another key than was sounded at the beginning. If the theme has ended up moving from a major key to a minor key, then one makes the answer in a subordinate minor key in relation to the original tonic key. And the same applies if the theme moves from a minor key to a major key. The answer happens in a related major key.

(6) One steadily continues in this way to use the theme as often as possible in all related keys, sometimes complete, sometimes shortened and dismembered. One interweaves the themes with good episodes and finally approaches the tonic key again in a good manner going through the theme in various ways, now complete, now shortened, with all kinds of imitation, periodically and canonically, and one can finally conclude emphatically, if one so wishes, in a prolonged cadence or a so-called pedal point.[4]

EXERCISE 20-A

1. *Analysis:* Analyze a fugue of your or your teacher's choice to see if it behaves as Marpurg suggests.

FUGUE AS JEWELRY

Imagine that all the different parts of the fugue are beads or gemstones to be strung to make a necklace. The little gems must all exist prior to the actual composition of the fugue: they are all there, in their little cases, waiting to be strung together. The gems might include a theme/countermelody pair that is invertible, a "box" of invertible counterpoint, a stretto, a simultaneous inversion, a pedal, a sequential episode, and so on—all the artful devices you have learned. The jeweler looks in the many cases that contain the various precious and not-so-precious items to choose what goes next.

Marpurg says you should compose these "gems" before laying them out in the fugue. That is why we urge you to compose a theme in terms of some combinations that you could make with it, not just as a pretty tune, to provide you with the contents of all the little jewel cases from which to pick.

You should not think that the stringing out is random, one thing at a time, or that any gem just pops up from what immediately preceded. Indeed, the function of so-called unnecessary transitions is often to set up the next contrapuntal item. In a bad fugue, you have the impression that the composer is doing only one thing at a time, but in a good fugue you feel several things happening at once. These things can be a matter of changing harmonic goals, texture, register, and so on. These can often be described in terms of increasing and decreasing intensity, and even in terms of climaxes.

BORROWED FORM

One way to learn how to do this is to take apart somebody else's fugue and see how that composer has arranged the gems. Marpurg recommends that the schematic outline of the fugue be borrowed from another author and sketched in: "One can also, until one no longer needs it, make a disposition of the later entries following the example of good authors, and mark these roughly and only provisionally in the score, so as to work out the fugue completely later."[5] Following Marpurg's advice, we will analyze two little fugues that Bach knew by J. K. F. Fischer. These are tiny by Bachian standards, but they are completely satisfying and quite sophisticated. For both of these fugues we have provided schemas with the string of thematic entries and other elements labeled in bold in the middle, with the devices (the "gems") identified above and their probable intensity function below.

J. K. F. FISCHER FUGA 3 IN D MINOR

The only features bracketed in the score (example 20.2a) are those bits where a thematic statement (S or A) does not sound; these are a transition (T), unnecessary transitions (UT), an episode (Ep), and a pedal (Ped). Go through each voice and find all the thematic statements. The step is the eighth note.

An "exploded view" of the fugue appears in example 20.2b. A time line runs through the middle of the page, showing all elements, and the gems are broken out and shown above. Note that the part of the countermelody (motive Y) that is reused begins after the splice, so it requires no alteration. A nice feature of motive Y is that it begins with the same rhythm as the theme (three eighth notes); this is sounded when the theme has moved on to another rhythm, so the two rhythms complement each other.

Two answers can sound in a row (example 20.2a, mm. 2–4) because the end of the first answer (E–A) is made to sound more like 2–5 in D minor than 5–1 in A minor (the 5 in D minor is accompanied by 6 of v = 3 of i, that harmonic smudge often used by Pasquini; see example 8.19). The combination in mm. 3–4 is repeated in mm. 8–9, but with an added voice in free style and different harmony, illustrating repetition varied with increased intensity.

In example 20.2b, the intensity functions are shown below the time line. The gems may or may not be directly related to the intensity functions. That is, some gems add contrapuntal intensity but they may or may not occur at the same time as registral extremes, which can happen anytime.

Example 20.2a. (J. K. F. Fischer, Fuga 3 in D minor) *Note Dorian key signature.*

J. K. F. FISCHER FUGA 10 IN F MAJOR

As above, the only features bracketed in the score (example 20.3a) are those where a thematic statement does not sound; these are a transition (T), an unnecessary transition (UT), and an episode (Ep). As above, go through each voice and find the thematic statements.

> *Gems.* The countermelody (CM) begins after the splice, so it requires no alteration. Only five notes of the countermelody are reused (motive Y), and the continuation is varied, often moving the harmony to the flat side. A nice feature of the first statement of the countermelody is that it begins with the same two notes as the subject, creating a strong continuity between subject and countermelody. A second countermelody (Z) sounds in the tenor in mm. 10–11 and in the bass in mm. 31–32, making a three-voice combination that repeats. The first time it happens, the harmony on

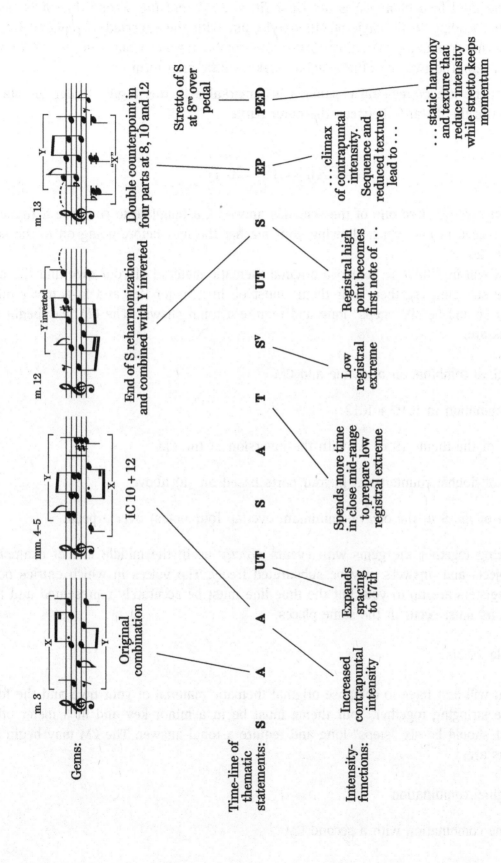

Example 20.2b. ("Exploded" view of Fischer's Fuga 3)

the third beat of m. 10 is not clear (ii or vii⁶?), but the second time it is clearly vii⁶, leading to iii, circle-of-fifths-style, but with the expected vi replaced by I, a harmonic smudge. Another three-voice combo repeats from mm. 16–17 to mm. 27–28. The two repeating combos make a little arch form.

Intensity. The use of registral expansion is remarkable in this fugue. Under the staves, write the distance between the outer parts.

EXERCISE 20-B

1. *Composing (long):* Use one of the schemas above as a template to compose a fugue of your own. You will proceed in two steps, showing your teacher the first before going on to the second.

For example 20.2b:

Step 1: You will first have to compose original thematic material of your own and the five gems that you will be stringing together. Your theme must be in a major key and in a meter other than 4/4. The subject should be six "steps" long and require a tonal answer. The CM may begin after the splice. The gems are:

a. The original combination of theme and CM

b. The combination in IC10 + IC12

c. The end of the theme (S or A) with the inversion of the CM

d. A lump of double counterpoint in four parts based on (b) above

e. A canon of the S at the octave (minimum overlap four notes) over a pedal

Step 2: String together the gems with events *exactly* as in the middle line of example 20.2b, except that subjects and answers may be substituted freely. The voices in which entries occur, and the keys and registers are up to you, but the time line must be accurately represented and the same intensity functions must occur in the same places.

For example 20.3b:

Step 1: You will first have to compose original thematic material of your own and the four gems that you will be stringing together. Your theme must be in a minor key and in a meter other than 3/4. The subject should be six "steps" long and require a tonal answer. The CM may begin after the splice. The gems are:

a. The original combination

b. The same combination with a second CM

c. The S (or A) with the first CM inverted at the 8 and 10

d. A stretto of the CM

Step 2: String together the gems with events *exactly* as in the middle line of example 20.3b, except that subjects and answers may be substituted freely. The voices in which entries occur, and the keys and registers, are up to you, but the time line must be accurately represented and the same intensity functions must occur in the same places. Remember that the gem from mm. 16–17 recurs in expanded range in mm. 27–28, and later the gem from mm. 10–11 recurs in mm. 31–32, also in expanded range, making a sort of arch form.

Example 20.3a. (J. K. F. Fischer, Fuga 10 in F major)

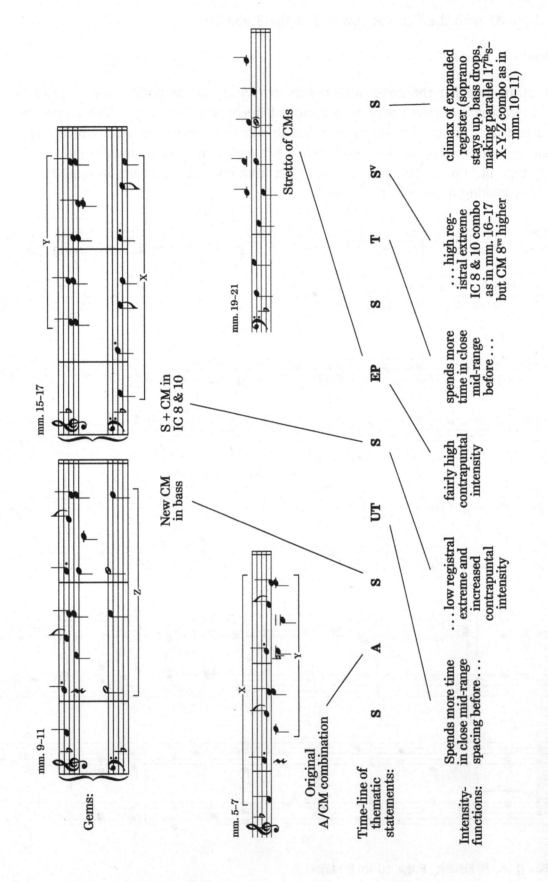

Example 20.3b. ("Exploded view of Fischer's Fuga 10)

One of the problems with this approach is the connection of the gems to each other. You may need to transpose a gem to another key to make it connect neatly to the preceding or following, and you may need to go back and reconsider which version of the theme is the subject and which is the answer.

BINARY FORM

Baroque dances are almost always in binary form, characterized as having two sections, each of which is repeated: AABB, notated with repeat signs (‖: A :‖: B :‖). The first section often modulates to the dominant (or, if in a minor key, to the relative major). The second section often begins in the dominant (or relative major), explores more distant keys, and returns to the tonic (often with a reprise of some motivic material).

Binary form and imitative texture join forces in inventions and gigues. Bach's Two-Part Invention in F Major corresponds to a binary scheme without the repeat signs. (The A section appears in example 12.27, the B section is shown in example 13.11.) The B section begins with the same motivic material in the dominant, with the added difference that the lower voice begins first. A few fugues in *WTC* can also be likened to binary forms (e.g., fugues in C major and C minor, *WTC I*; for the form of the latter, see below).

Example 20.4a. (Bach, English Suite 5, E minor, gigue, opening of A section)

Example 20.4b. (Bach, English Suite 5, E minor, gigue, beginning of B section)

One kind of dance that is particularly contrapuntal is the gigue. Often, at the beginning of the B section the motivic material is presented in melodic inversion. Above is an example from the gigue of Bach's English Suite No. 5 in E minor. We have already studied the opening in example 15.14. Discuss the splices in examples 20.4a and b.

Example 20.5. (Handel, op. 6, no. 2, fourth movement, mm. 1–39)

Example 20.5. (*Continued*)

Example 20.5. (*Concluded*)

RITORNELLO FORM IN FUGUE

Concerto movements and cantata arias (and some choruses) employ *ritornello form*, in which large blocks of thematic material and episodes alternate. Although this sounds like the form of a fugue, the difference lies in the lack of independence of the lines: in ritornello form in a concerto, the principal melodic material usually stays on top. Fugue and ritornello form can be combined, as in Bach's C major Overture, first movement, in which the fugal episodes are played by the *concertino* (two oboes and bassoon).

Another example of this type of marriage of ritornello form and fugue is to be found in the fourth movement of Handel's op. 6, no. 2 (example 20.5). In this concerto grosso, the thematic sections are mostly presented in successive entries played by the tutti. At the opening, the decisive theme, with its characteristic metric ambiguity, is presented five times. Then in m. 21 a descending circle-of-fifths sequence leads to a cadence in the dominant (mm. 26–27). At this point, a theme in a contrasting affect (X) is sounded by one of the solo violins, accompanied by the tutti strings; the theme is imitated by the other violin. This episode with its own theme ends with a half cadence in m. 39.

Also, some fugues bring back a whole contrapuntal complex, not as a succession of entries but as a block. The C minor fugue from *WTC I* (example 16.18) is such a fugue, where the blocks are three themes rotated in triple counterpoint (see "Competing Analyses of the C Minor Fugue from *WTC I*" below).

EXERCISE 20-C

1. *Analysis:* Obtain a score and continue the analysis of the Handel op. 6, no. 2 fugue. What type of multiple fugue is it? Identify entries, fragmentary entries, cadences, sequences, stretti, invertible counterpoints, and so on.

2. *Analysis:* Make a scheme of a fugue of your or your teacher's choice.

3. *Composing (long):* Fill it in with your own material.

4. *Composing (long):* Compose a fugal gigue in binary form with melodic inversion of the theme, making a fresh exposition at the beginning of the B section.

COMPETING ANALYSES OF THE C MINOR FUGUE FROM *WTC I*

The score of this fugue appears in example 16.18. After the exposition, Bach never brings back the theme in imitation. Rather, the whole box comes back with the subject and its two countermelodies. This fugue has been analyzed many times, and a quick tour of these competing interpretations shows that there is probably no single "right" analysis. The authors cited here use many different criteria and come to different conclusions, partly *because* of their choice of criteria.

Everybody agrees that Bach uses five of six possible rotations of themes A, B, and C to make the ritornelli (where A is the subject and B and C are countermelodies). Authors disagree, however, about what the larger form might be. They also disagree as to whether the music between the second and third entries is part of the exposition or an episode. This goes to the question of whether the first theme group must consist of an entry in each voice. Also, authors disagree about what the function of mm. 13–14 is. The diagram in example 20.6 shows the segmentation made by some of the authors whose views are discussed below.

Frederick Iliffe analyzes the fugue into the standard three-part form that was popular in the late nineteenth century, which he terms "enunciation section," "modulatory section," and "recapitulatory section" (it is unclear to us why the subject in m. 20 is part of the modulatory section and not already part of the recapitulatory section).[6] He calls the music right before the third thematic entry a "codetta" (which he defines as "a connecting link"), a term that, when used by Sabbatini, implies remodulation within the exposition.

Erwin Ratz interprets the fugue as combining both a tripartite and a binary form type.[7] The fugue is tripartite in that the first three entries in mm. 1–8 are in the tonic key of C minor, with the next entry (mm. 11–12) appearing in the relative major key, and the remaining entries (mm. 15–28 with interspersed episodes) being again sounded in the tonic key. (His placement of the "recap" is easier to understand than Iliffe's.) Alternatively, the form of the fugue is binary for Ratz in that the second part (mm. 15–28) recapitulates the motivic material and some of the harmonic progressions of the first part (mm. 1–14). These correspondences are noted by Ludwig Czaczkes as well and appear in example 20.6. For example, the episode in mm. 5–6 corresponds to the episode in mm. 17–19; the episode of mm. 9–10 corresponds to the first two measures of the episode of mm. 22–26.

Czaczkes relies on the same correspondences noted by Ratz in his two-part interpretation to draw a more decisive two-part form.[8] He says the function of mm. 13–14 is to "lead into" the second part. He is the only one of our authors to claim that the opening entry "corresponds to" the subject in the final pedal point.

Joel Lester, like Czaczkes, stresses that all the elements in the second half appear in the same order as in the first, adding that each element in the second half is a "heightened" version of the corresponding element in the first half.[9] Heightening can mean an increase in the number of parts, the use of dissonance, or an increase in the length of a section, as in the correspondence between mm. 9–10 and mm. 22–26. He calls mm. 5–6 an episode and does not discuss mm. 13–14.

Ulrich Siegele suggests that we consider an imaginary process of composition in which Bach composes first the pattern of entries by pitch (I–V–I followed by V–I–I) and by register (middle-high-low followed by middle-high-low), then builds a totally thematic fugue into which he inserts episodes later.[10] His view is based on how Bach worked with Reincken's fugues. Siegele proposes that only at the very end of this process does Bach need to insert the E-flat entrance in mm. 11–12.

Laurence Dreyfus also bases his analysis on the three-part contrapuntal combinations, which he calls "inventions," recalling the precompositional "boxes" that we have deduced from reading Marpurg and Mattheson.[11] These are labeled "FC" (for "fugal complex") in example 20.6. He says, however, that Bach did not necessarily have a plan for which combination came when or which type of episode came when.

These analyses take into account many features of Bach's fugue, yet they still leave out a couple of important ones. For instance, one could argue that the central episode in mm. 13–14 is the "keystone" of an arch form because these two measures contain a sequence of a unique type (ascending circle of fifths) and contain the most extreme spacing as well, leading to the registral climax on the downbeat of m. 15.

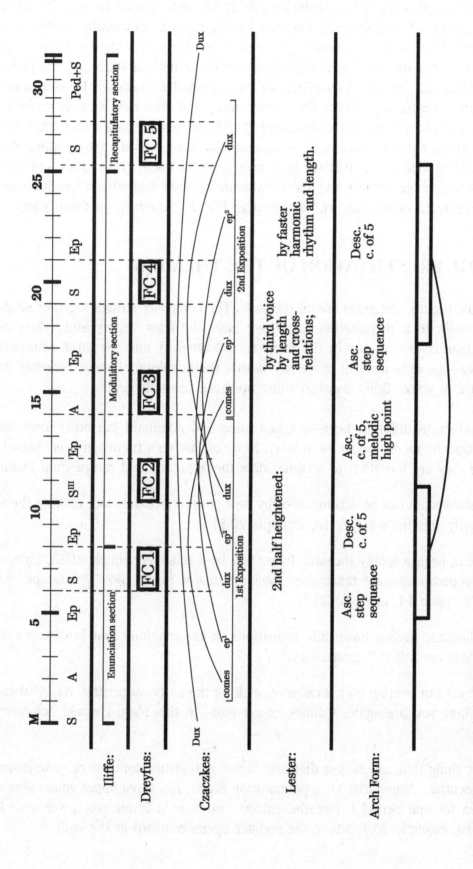

Example 20.6. (Diagrams of Iliffe, Czaczkes, Dreyfus, Lester, and Arch Form)

Likewise, one might wish to look more closely at the fifth episode in mm. 22–26 to see exactly how it is "heightened" (Lester's term). For two measures, it is essentially identical to the second episode transposed down a fifth. (However, you could also argue that the bass-line pattern is identical, untransposed, to that in mm. 9–11, shifted two beats earlier!) If Bach had stopped the sequence here, as he did in m. 10, he would have had an entry in A-flat. However, he adds another measure of the same harmonic pattern and bass line (descending) but with new motivic material in the right hand, leading down another step to the dominant. The next measure and a half (mm. 25–26) may be understood as dominant prolongation with a sequentially rising soprano (the joining of two different sequences, one falling, one rising, that we have seen often in Bach). These four and a half measures (mm. 22–26) constitute the longest and most elaborate episode and surely "produce an even bigger craving for the repetition of the subject," as Marpurg has it ("Marpurg on Fugal Form," [2], above).

VARYING THE PRESENTATION OF THE THEME(S)

In wholly thematic fugues, the gems are all thematic. The composer strings together single statements of subject or answer. In a permutation fugue, we have the least variety since there are only four stones (if the fugue is in four parts): the subject (and answer) and the three countermelodies that all recur regularly—the only element of variety is that the positions of these melodies are constantly rotated from voice to voice. Other ways to shine up these thematic gems:

1. Present them in different keys—not just tonic and dominant but other keys, and even in the opposite mode (major vs. minor). None of Fischer's fugues in this chapter do this because they are too short to accommodate the approach and return from distant keys.

2. Single statements can be accompanied by new countermelodies too, making them appear more spiffy (Fischer's Fugue 18, example 20.8).

3. Stretto can help: a totally thematic fugue will be a relatively simple affair, unless myriad stretto opportunities are taken (see Bach's C major fugue, *WTC I*, example 9.15, and Fischer's Fugue 14, example 20.7).

4. Some thematic fugues have little transitions or retransitions that break up periodicity; often these are called "unnecessary."

5. The subject can overlap with a cadence, making the entry surprising. As Mattheson said: "Look! here you are again; I didn't expect that—in this place I would not have looked for you!"[12]

6. Another thing that can help a thematic fugue is registral contrast or progression (Bach "Sicut locutus," *Magnificat* 11, a permutation fugue, has three upper voices sing countermelodies for one period before the subject enters in a lower voice; see also Fischer's Fugue 14, example 20.7, where the register opens outward at the end).

Example 20.7. (J. K. F. Fischer, Fugue 14 in A-flat major) *Note Lydian key signature.*

Example 20.8. (J. K. F. Fischer, Fugue 18 in B minor) *Note Dorian key signature.*

MELODIC INVERSION

Melodic inversion is rarely used in totally thematic fugues (the countermelody in Fischer's Fugue 18, example 20.8, is one example; Pasquini's "Fuga in basso continuo," example 19.14, is another). However, it can occur after later episodes. Other uses of melodic inversion include:

1. The answer presents the subject in inversion (*The Art of the Fugue*, Contrapunctus 5).

2. The theme/countermelody pair is presented in mirror inversion (*The Art of the Fugue*, compare Contrapunctus 8, mm. 159–162, with Contrapunctus 11, mm. 145–149).

3. The theme is presented in simultaneous inversion with itself (*The Art of the Fugue*, end of Contrapunctus 5).

4. The answer presents the subject in inversion and diminution (*The Art of the Fugue*, Contrapunctus 6). Here the theme provides part of the CA.

5. The answer presents the subject in inversion and augmentation (*The Art of the Fugue*, Contrapunctus 7).

6. The subject appears with its inversion in stretto (*The Art of the Fugue*, Contrapunctus 5).

VARYING THE THEME/COUNTERMELODY PAIR

A fugue that uses a regularly recurring countersubject (or counteranswer) can vary the presentation of the theme/countermelody pair through:

1. Invertible counterpoint at the octave. This permits entries to come above or below preceding ones.

2. IC10 and IC12. This can change harmony or induce thickening of texture (G minor fugue, *WTC II*; Fischer, Fugue 3, mm. 13–14).

3. Time shifting the CM.

4. Making a stretto of the CM.

INTRODUCING EPISODES FOR CONTRAST

A relatively commonplace way to break up thematic entries is to insert sequential episodes. Their melodic material often resembles that of the subject or countermelody but fragments them and repeats them. Try to remember examples you have seen in this book of each of the following. Episodes

1. Can be used to transit between different key areas.

2. Can be used to vary texture (in a concerto, they can involve soloists).

3. Can be of different sequential types.

4. Can use embedded progressions.

5. Can be punctuated by cadences or be cleverly elided with the thematic entry (see C minor fugue, *WTC I*).

6. Can have sequences that are repeated and that can also be varied by means of the usual devices of invertible counterpoint, mirror, and melodic inversion (Handel, example 11.7).

MEANS OF VARYING INTENSITY

There are many kinds of intensity (dynamics are missing from this list because loudness is rarely indicated in scores of Baroque fugues). Try to remember examples you have seen in this book of each of the following:

1. Harmonic rhythm (fast/slow chord changes)

2. Surface rhythm (long/short notes)

3. Distance from tonic (more/less, major/minor)

4. Register (high/low, expanding/contracting)

5. Texture (thick/thin)

6. Contrapuntal intensity (complex/simple)

FINAL PROJECT

Compose a four-voice fugue, satisfying the following demands:

1. The subject must be at least eight steps long (e.g., two measures of 4/4, two and two-thirds of a measure of 3/2, etc.); it must require (and get) a tonal answer; it must be able to be overlapped with a cadence; you may have a transition and/or retransition. Show the structure of the tune (head, sequence, if any, and tail).

2. The countersubject must be used at least throughout the exposition and be invertible at the octave; the countersubject may also have to be invertible at another interval, depending on the menu choices below.

3. You must include at least one gem from each group in the following menu. Each gem must be at least four steps long and must involve the theme and/or the CM.

    *   Invertible double counterpoint in three parts at the octave and tenth *or* at the tenth and twelfth

    *   Invertible double counterpoint in four parts at the octave, tenth, and twelfth *or* stretto of theme or CM at two different time intervals

    *   Canon of theme or CM over a pedal *or* three-voice stretto at the unison at the same time interval

    *   Theme overlapping with cadence at the end of the episode *or* end of the episode turning out to be the head of the theme

    *   Melodic inversion *or* augmentation *or* diminution

    *   Mirror inversion *or* sequence with embedded progression (model four steps long + two repetitions)

4. Your fugue must contain at the minimum:

    Exposition   Ep1   two entries   Ep2   one to three entries   pedal

5. The entries in the exposition must come in an asymmetrical order (not SATB or BTAS); the first episode must modulate to vi or ii if the fugue is in a major key, to III or VII if a minor key; the sequential episodes may only contain the same type of sequence if the second one is varied by a gem from the menu; the second episode may modulate to more distant keys; the last set of entries may contain the stretto or any of the canons; the pedal may be dominant or tonic. You must label all parts of your fugue-theme groups, transitions, episodes, types of sequence, keys, and all gems. Include a Roman numeral analysis of harmonies (in ambiguous situations, write a note explaining your choices).

The gems can occur anywhere. For instance, the canons can occur as part of the sequences; the double counterpoint in three parts can occur in the exposition or be a variation of the first episode; the stretto could occur at different time intervals over the pedal, killing two birds with one stone.

NOTES

1. Tovey, *The Forms of Music*, p. 26.
2. Marpurg, *Abhandlung von der Fuge*, IV, 3, p. 120.
3. Marpurg, 1, §2, pp. 100–1.
4. Marpurg, 3, pp. 121–23.
5. Marpurg, p. 120.
6. Iliffe, *The Forty-Eight Preludes and Fugues of John Sebastian Bach*, p. 6.
7. Ratz, *Einführung in die Musikalische Formenlehre*, pp. 90–92.
8. Czaczkes, *Analyse des Wohltemperierten Klaviers*, pp. 58–61.
9. Lester, "Heightening Levels of Activity and J. S. Bach's Parallel-Section Constructions," pp. 68–70.
10. Siegele, "The Four Conceptual Stages of the Fugue in C minor, WTC I," pp. 197–224.
11. Dreyfus, *Bach and the Patterns of Invention*, pp. 169–88.
12. Mattheson, *Der vollkommene Capellmeister*, III, 20, §100.

APPENDIX

LIST OF SUBJECT TYPES AND ORDERS OF ENTRY IN FUGUE EXPOSITIONS FROM *THE WELL-TEMPERED CLAVIER*

Opening interval[1]	Key of fugue	Book	Embellishment of opening interval	Begins w/rest	Tonal/real	No. of splices	Scales at beg. & end	Order of entry[2]
1–5	C–	I	8–7–8	Y	T	2	T, T	ASB
"	D#–	I		N	T	2	T, T	ASB
"	Bb–	I		N	T	2	T, T	SAT1T2B
"	C#+	II	1–3–1	Y	T	1	T, D	BSA(inv)
"	Eb+	II		N	T	2	T, T	BTAS
"	F+	II	8–7–8	Y	T	2	T, T	SAB
5–1	F#+	I		Y	T	1	D, T	SAB
"	C+	II	5–4–5	Y	T	1	D, T	ASB
"	F–	II		Y(pu)[3]	T	1	D, T	SAB
5–3	Eb+	I		N	T	3	D, T	SAB
"	B–	I		Y	T	2	D, D	ATBS
"	C–	II		Y	T	1	D, T	ASTB
"	F#–	II		Y	T	1	D, T	ASB
"	G+	II		Y	T	2	D, D	SAB
"	G–	II		Y	T	1	D, T	TASB
"	Ab+	II		Y	T	1	D, T	ASTB
"	A–	II		Y	T	1	D, T	BAS
"	B–	II		Y(pu)	T	1	D, T	ASB
8–7	C#–	I		N	R	—	T, T	BT2T1A (tonal)S
"	G#–	I		Y	T	1	T, D	TASB
"	A+	I		N	T	2	T, T	SAB
"	B+	I		Y	T	2	T, T	TASB
"	D#–	II		Y	R	—	T, T	ATBS
5–6	C#+	I		Y	T	1	D, T	SAB
"	F+	I		Y(pu)	T	1	D, T	ASB
"	F–	I		Y	T	1	D, T	TABS
"	G–	I		Y	T	1	D, T	ASBT
"	Bb+	I		Y	T	3	D, T	SAB
1–3	E–	I		N	R	—	T, D	SB
"	A+	II	1–2–3	Y	R	—	T, T	BAS
"	B+	II		N	R	—	T, T	BTAS
1–2	C+	I		Y	R	—	T, T	ASBT
"	D+	I		Y	R	—	T, T	BTAS
"	D–	I		Y	R	—	T, T	SAB
"	E+	I		Y	R	—	T, T	ASB
"	F#–	I		Y	R	—	T, T	TABS
"	G+	I		N	R	—	T, T	SAB
"	A–	I	8–7–8	Y	R	—	T, T	ASBT
"	C#–	II	8–7–8	N	R	—	T, T	BSA
"	E+	II		N	R	—	T, T	BTAS
"	E–	II		Y	R	—	T, T	SAB
"	G#–	II		N	R	—	T, T	SAB
"	Bb–	II		N	R	—	T, T	ASBT
2–1	Bb+	II		Y	T	2	T, T	ASB
7–8	F#+	II	7–6–7	Y(pu)	R	—	T, T	ASB
1–4	D+	II		Y	R	—	T, T	TASB
"	D–	II	1–2–3–4	N	R	—	T, T	ASB

NOTES

1. The two pitches of the opening interval listed are both harmonized. Embellishments of an opening interval are all NHTs.

2. In the "order of entry" column the subjects are in boldface; answers appear in normal type. The designations for the parts do not necessarily correspond to vocal ranges. The parts of the three-part fugues are designated S, A, B, the ones of the two-part fugue S, B, and the ones of the two five-part fugues S, A, T1, T2, B.

3. pu = pick up

BIBLIOGRAPHY

Campion, François. *Traité d'accompagnement et de composition selon la règle des octaves de musique*. Paris: G. Adam, 1716.

Caplin, William. *Classical Form: A Theory of Formal Functions for the Instrumental Music of Haydn, Mozart, and Beethoven*. New York: Oxford University Press, 1998.

Czaczkes, Ludwig. *Analyse des Wohltemperierten Klaviers*. Vienna: Paul Kaltschmid, 1956.

David, Hans T., Arthur Mendel, and Christoph Wolff, eds. *The New Bach Reader: A Life of Johann Sebastian Bach in Letters and Documents*. New York: Norton, 1998.

Dreyfus, Laurence. *Bach and the Patterns of Invention*. Cambridge, MA: Harvard University Press, 1996.

Fenaroli, Fedele. *Partimenti*, books I, II, IV, V, VI. In *Monuments of Partimenti*, edited by Robert Gjerdingen, 1800–. https://web.archive.org/web/20170112164654/http://faculty-web.at.northwestern.edu/music/gjerdingen/partimenti/collections/Fenaroli/index.htm.

———. *Partimenti ossia basso numerato*, book III. In *Monuments of Partimenti*, edited by Robert Gjerdingen, 1775. https://web.archive.org/web/20161114175024/http://faculty-web.at.northwestern.edu/music/gjerdingen/partimenti/collections/Fenaroli/Book3/index.htm.

Gédalge, André. *Traité de la fugue*. Paris: Enoch and Cie, 1901.

———. *Treatise on Fugue*. Translated by A. Levin. Mattapan, MA: Gamut Music, 1964.

Gingras, Bruno. "Partimento Fugue in Eighteenth-Century Germany: A Bridge between Thoroughbass Lessons and Fugal Composition." *Eighteenth-Century Music* 5, no. 1 (2008): 51–74.

Gjerdingen, Robert O. *Music in the Galant Style*. New York: Oxford University Press, 2007.

Glickman, Sylvia, and Martha Furman Schleifer, eds. *Women Composers: Music through the Ages*. Vol. 6. New York: G. K. Hall, 1999.

Heinichen, Johann David. *Thorough-Bass Accompaniment According to Heinichen*. Translated by George J. Buelow. Lincoln: University of Nebraska Press, 1992.

———. *Der General-Bass in der Composition*. Dresden, 1728. Reprint, Hildesheim: G. Olms, 1969.

Holtmeier, Ludwig. "Heinichen, Rameau, and the Italian Thoroughbass Tradition: Concepts of Tonality and Chord in the Rule of the Octave." *Journal of Music Theory* 51, no. 1 (2007): 5–49.

Iliffe, Frederick. *The Forty-Eight Preludes and Fugues of John Sebastian Bach*. London: Novello, [1897?].

Kirnberger, Johann Philipp. *Die Kunst des reinen Satzes in der Musik*. Berlin, 1776–1779. Reprint, Hildesheim: G. Olms, 1968.

———. *The Art of Strict Musical Composition*. Translated by David Beach and Jürgen Thym. New Haven, CT: Yale University Press, 1982.

Kunze, Stefan. "Gattungen der Fuge in Bachs Wohltemperiertem Klavier." In *Bach Interpretationen*, edited by Martin Geck, 74–93. Göttingen: Van den Hoeck and Ruprecht, 1969.

Ledbetter, David. *Bach's Well-Tempered Clavier: The 48 Preludes and Fugues*. New Haven, CT: Yale University Press, 2002.

Lester, Joel. *Compositional Theory in the Eighteenth Century*. Cambridge, MA: Harvard University Press, 1992.

———. "Heightening Levels of Activity and J. S. Bach's Parallel-Section Constructions." *Journal of the American Musicological Society* 54, no. 1 (2001): 49–96.

Mann, Alfred. *The Great Composer as Teacher and Student: Theory and Practice of Composition*. New York: W. W. Norton, 1987. Reprint, Mineola, NY: Dover, 1994.

———. *The Study of Fugue*. New York: W. W. Norton, 1965. Reprint, New York: Dover, 1987.

Marpurg, Friedrich Wilhelm. *Abhandlung von der Fuge*. Vol. 1. Berlin, 1753. Reprint, Hildesheim: G. Olms, 1970.

———. *Abhandlung von der Fuge*. Vol. 2. Berlin, 1754. Reprint, Hildesheim: G. Olms, 1970.

———. *Handbuch bey dem Generalbasse und der Composition*. 3 vols. Berlin, 1755–1760. Reprint, Hildesheim: G. Olms, 1974.

Mattheson, Johann. *Der vollkommene Capellmeister*. Berlin, 1739. Reprint, Kassel: Bärenreiter-Verlag, 1987.

———. *Johann Mattheson's Der vollkommene Capellmeister*. Translated by Ernest Harriss. Ann Arbor, MI: UMI Research Press, 1981.

Nelson, Richard B., and Donald R. Boomgaarden. "Kirnberger's Thoughts on the Different Methods of Teaching Composition as Preparation for Understanding Fugue." *Journal of Music Theory* 30, no. 1 (1986): 84–94.

Neumann, Werner. *J. S. Bachs Chorfuge: Ein Beitrag zur Kompositionstechnik Bachs*. PhD Diss., University of Leipzig, 1938.

Niedt, Friederich Erhardt. *Musicalische Handleitung*. 3 vols. Hamburg: Benjamin Schillern, 1710–1721. Reprint, Buren: Frits Knuf, 1976.

———. *The Musical Guide*. Translated by Pamela L. Poulin and Irmgard C. Taylor. New York: Oxford University Press, 1989.

Pasquini, Bernardo. *Opere per tastiera*. Vol. 7. Edited by Armando Carideo. Latina, Italy: Il Levante Libreria Editrice, 2006.

Rameau, Jean-Philippe. *Traité de l'harmonie réduite à ses principes naturels*. Vol. 1. Paris: Ballard, 1722. Reprint, AIM *Miscellanea*, 1967.

———. *Treatise on Harmony*. Translated by Philip Gossett. New York: Dover, 1971.

Ratz, Erwin. *Einführung in die Musikalische Formenlehre*. 3rd ed. Vienna: Universal Edition, 1973.

Renwick, William. *The Langloz Manuscript: Fugal Improvisation through Figured Bass*. Oxford: Oxford University Press, 2001.

Rotem, Elam, and Sean Curtice. "The Rule of the Octave." *EarlyMusicSources.com* (website). 2021. https://www.earlymusicsources.com/youtube/theruleoftheoctave.

Sabbatini, Luigi. *Trattato sopra le fughe musicali*. Venice: Sebastiano Valle, 1802. Reprint, Bologna: Forni, 1969.

Sánchez-Kisielewska, Olga. "The Rule of the Octave in First-Year Undergraduate Theory: Teaching in the Twenty-First Century with Eighteenth-Century Strategies." *Journal of Music Theory Pedagogy* 31 (2017): 113–34.

Sanguinetti, Giorgio. *The Art of Partimento*. New York: Oxford University Press, 2012.

Schoenberg, Arnold. *Theory of Harmony*. 3rd ed. Translated by Roy E. Carter. Berkeley: University of California Press, 1978.

———. *Preliminary Exercises in Counterpoint*. Edited by Leonard Stein. London: Faber and Faber, 1988.

Schubert, Peter. *Modal Counterpoint: Renaissance Style*. 2nd ed. New York: Oxford University Press, 2008.

Siegele, Ulrich. "The Four Conceptual Stages of the Fugue in C minor, WTC I." In *Bach Studies I*, edited by Don O. Franklin, 197–224. Cambridge, MA: Cambridge University Press, 1989.

Spitta, Phillip. *Johann Sebastian Bach*. Leipzig: Breitkopf and Härtel, 1921.

Tovey, Donald Francis. *The Forms of Music*. Cleveland, OH: World Publishing, 1956.

Walker, Paul. *Theories of Fugue from the Age of Josquin to the Age of Bach*. Rochester, NY: University of Rochester Press, 2000.

INDEX